Sightings

Mirrors in Texts —Texts in Mirrors

Sightings

Mirrors in Texts —Texts in Mirrors

Joyce O. Lowrie

Amsterdam - New York, NY 2008

The paper on which this book is printed meets the requirements of "ISO 9706:1994, Information and documentation - Paper for documents - Requirements for permanence".

ISBN: 978-90-420-2495-3
©Editions Rodopi B.V., Amsterdam - New York, NY 2008
Printed in the Netherlands

For Ernest

Contents

Acknowledgements

For helpful suggestions, *in-sights*, laughter, contestations, serious and concerned help from colleagues and friends, as well as generous subventions from various venues, I have more people and institutions to thank than I am able to remember. From the start, I beg indulgence from those I have unwittingly left out. Since institutions and subventions are at the core of my ability to do research, I will begin there.

Wesleyan University, in Middletown, CT, USA, has a generous sabbatical policy, making it possible for me to concentrate more fully on doing research and writing this book. Other generous grants have also made this publication possible. The Thomas and Catharine McMahon Memorial Fund, located in the Department of Romance Languages & Literatures, and bestowed upon our department by my now deceased friend and colleague, Joseph H. McMahon, in honour of his parents, has been more than munificent with its monetary help; Wesleyan grants in *Supplementary Support of Scholarship* have helped in more ways than the institution knows. I am grateful for a *National Endowment for the Humanities* grant that provided resources as well. A semester's stay at the *Camargo Foundation* in Cassis, France, was inspiring, joyful, and productive. Michael Pretina, Patrick and MaryAnn Henry, Red and Pat Watson, the Walkers, Anne-Marie Franco, all provided stimulation, conversations, help, and encouragement. Patrick and MaryAnn volunteered to read my chapter on *La Princesse de Clèves* and their helpful suggestions are responsible for my re-writing that chapter in its entirety.

Libraries. Jean Marie Goulemot, a friend of long standing, has written a book entitled *L'Amour des bibliothèques* (2006). Indeed. I love libraries. I am what another friend, Hope Glidden, who is herself one, calls a *rat de bibliothèque*. Among the libraries I love are Yale's Stirling Library, the Olin, Science and Art libraries at Wesleyan, the *old* BN (Richelieu), and the *new* BNF (Tolbiac) in Paris. Not only were the staffs of all of these institutions generous with their help (I *sight*, in particular, Alexandre Portelli at the BNF and others whose names I do not even know), but also readers, friends, and scholars in those places provided stimulating ideas on my subject.

My role model in France is Madame Marie-Louise Roger, widow of the historian of science, Jacques Roger. Her knowledge of the French language is unsurpassable. She is my Madame Rosemonde, who plays the role of gathering together manuscripts at the end of *Les Liaisons dangereuses*. Her keen and piercing but ever kind wit made me chortle numerous times throughout the years. Monique Lambert, a close friend in psycholinguistics, made many helpful remarks not only in her own subject, but in mine. Philippe Cusson, my own *Rastignac* from Bordeaux, kept me laughing as he teased me, asking when I was going to finish my book, and would I make a lot of money on it and would they make it into a movie! His elegant and knowledgeable circle of friends in Paris have been invaluable in asking precise questions about mirrors that led me in directions I never would have dreamed I would go.

Friends and colleagues whose thoughts and projects who have stimulated me throughout include, in alphabetical order, Robert Conn, Andrew Curran, Ellen Nerenberg, Seth Fagen, Christian Foy, Susanne Fusso, Jean and Sheila Gaudon, Antonio González, Jon & Karin Gunnemann, Stirling Haig, David and Amy Jaffe, Catherine Lafarge, Paula Paige, Michael Armstrong-Roche, Norman Shapiro, Marcello Simonetta, Joseph Siry, Anthony Valerio. Having read initial stages of my manuscript, Carl Viggiani provided friendly and most prudent advice, restraining himself even as I wished him to have been more draconian in his evaluations.

For extra support and encouragement at the Susan B. and William K. Wasch Center, I am most grateful to Karl Scheibe, William and Sheila Barber, Ann Gertz. Joseph Reed, in particular, provided witty remarks, laughter, and hilarity with his recurrent shouting of the phrase: "It will all work out! You'll see! Everything will be just fine!" in moments in which he felt frustration and discouragement on my part.

I cannot thank my students, too numerous to mention, who suffered through advanced courses and many Senior Seminars, and who wished they could forget the meaning of the word *chiasmus*! Katherine Brown, Daniel Walinsky, Deirdre Stiles Delesalle, Jeanne Lavallee and Malak Nour are just a few among so many.

For technical support at Wesleyan's *Technology Support Services* my deep gratitude extends to Scott Michael, who went so far as to call me from Wesleyan to Paris when I found myself hopelessly entangled in cybernetic pretzels. I also thank Joanne Agostinelli, Ben Jackson, Jerry Maguda, Harriet Epstein – but more importantly, the intelligent and faithful one, Debbie Sierpinski, who, more than anyone else, helped me reformat my original manuscript according to the *Oxford Manual of Style*.

I am grateful to Ms. Rosalind Eastaway, who found ways around administrative strictures and hurdles and made things happen when I thought they were impossible.

My gratitude extends to my editors, Dr. Rob Fisher and Margaret Breen, who helped, both in Great Britain and the US, to make the publication of this book possible. Rob Fisher was always "spot on" withhis help, generosity, and especially, with his particular brand of British wit!

I thank my daughter, Michèle Lowrie, whose delightful and sometimes sardonic remarks and gifts of books and of her own academic articles inspired me onward and upward with her own scholarship, thus keeping me from giving up. Paul Keyser provided guidance with his arguments and cybernetic knowledge.

I am simply incapable of expressing my fathomless gratitude to Ernest B. Lowrie, my husband, the person who not only provided the most support of all, but who sacrificed his own valuable time and energy, manifested undaunting courage, and yes, love, in his constant and unquestioning giving of himself in oh, more ways than I can or ever would be capable of expressing.

Chapter I

Veluti in Speculum (As in a Looking Glass)

We have surprised him
At work, but no, he has surprised us
As he works.

John Ashbery

1.   **To See or Not to See**

Mirrors are mesmerizing. Due to their double nature they evoke fascination as well as fear. They reflect the self, which can be, but is not always a pleasant experience; they reflect others, who can be both like one's self and different; and they reflect the world, an agreeable garden of delight at times, a frightful and hostile forest at others. They are ambiguous in the sense of the word's "admitting of two or more meanings," as *Webster* says. It is no wonder that Alice's adventures occur in "wonder" land. To "wonder": a verb meaning to cause astonishment and admiration or the feeling of being aroused by something strange, unexpected. Looking in mirrors makes one wonder. Narcissus saw his reflection, reacted in wonder, and then fell in love with what he saw. The word *miroir* comes from the popular Latin *mirare*, "mirer," "regarder attentivement," or from the classical Latin *mirari*, "*s'étonner*," as the *Robert* states. Both can occur when one is gazing at a looking glass, a painting, or a text.

The double: to look into a mirror is both a reflective and a reflexive experience. J. Baltrusaitis claims that the mirror is an allegory not only of precise vision, but also of profound thought, of examining a problem attentively. *Reflectere*, he asks, does it not mean "to send back..." and "to reflect," does it not mean "to meditate"?[1] The verb, in Latin, according to D. Colin, means to "curve backwards," or "re-curve." When we see our reflection in a mirror, he says, we are projected "backwards," as it were, into our past; it is an action that has to do with memory. A "reflection," a "reflex," the verb "to reflect," all of these expressions have the same etymology. Hence our ancestors, says Colin, believed that to look into a mirror was equivalent to looking at one's past or to return to one's past.[2] The mental process of retrogression for the sake of reconsideration is designed in terms of optics. Baltrusaitis states that a mirror is an instrument of self-knowledge. It alone reveals persons' images, their doubles, their phantoms, their perfections as well as their physical deformities. Sighting mirrors is a science of the illusions of science.[3] And as K. Scheibe says, in his book on *Mirrors, Masks, Lies and Secrets*, "a reflected visual image looks simple enough, but it presents a considerable interpretive challenge.[4] He also points out that mirrors are key elements of the intelligence community, and that many technical devices used in that profession fall into the category of mirrors.[5]

"To sight" is both a transitive and an intransitive verb. Sightings made in this book have to do with inspecting, with scrutinizing chosen texts for their reflective and reflexive properties, with comparing connective threads in texts for their chiastic and interlocking structures. Archeologists refer to "polythetic types" when they draw a line or delimit a "site," when they establish boundaries around what they intend to study. I intend to "sight," to draw a boundary line around a series of chronologically arranged texts that have structures in common, and note what relationships exist between these structures, between the meanings of texts chosen, the contexts in which they were written, and French prose fiction in general. That such an exercise is not an easy one is expressed, in relation between the delineation of persons and social events by Henry James, in his preface to *The Awkward Age*: "...though the relations of a human figure or a social occurrence are what make such objects interesting, they also make them, to the same tune, difficult to isolate, to surround with the sharp black line, to frame in the square, the circle, the charming oval, that helps any arrangement of objects to become a picture.[6]

There is one trope, in particular, that forms that "sharp black line," the frame that helps define the "arrangements of objects" herein. It is the chiasmus, a figure of speech that comes from the Latin form of a Greek word meaning to organize in the shape of the letter *Chi* (X, = a cross), that is, to cross over. The Greek verb χιασμός begins with the letter *chi* (X). Inversion, or reversal, is graphically inscribed into the visual as well as linguistic make-up of the syntagm. The term denotes, primarily, a two-part sequence, the second part of which repeats the two main elements of the first in inverted order:

$$a\text{-}b\text{---}b\text{-}a, \text{ or}$$
$$\begin{matrix} a & & b \\ & \times & \\ b & & a \end{matrix}$$

Chiasmus goes beyond being a simple figure of speech. It is a rhetorical structure that applies to syntagms, to sentence structure, to prose and poetic phrases, to musical motifs, to images depicted in paintings, to film, semiology, syntactical configurations, political rhetoric and even in advertising. As E. Souriau describes it, "the chiasmus sets off in one direction, and then, even as it continues to move in the same trajectory, that of the phrase's continuity, it turns back, and the same elements march past in reverse.[7] One well-known example of chiasmus is Quintillian's purported phrase "one does not (a) live to (b) eat; one (b) eats to (a) live." (I prefer to say "one does not eat to live, but lives to eat.") Other examples are Mae West's "it's not the men in my life [that matter], it's the life in my men." And then there is President John F. Kennedy's famous phrase, "ask not what your country can do for you; ask what you can do for your country.[8] Modern-day advertising has used the trope with a vengeance, including "[This product]...can't add years to your life, but it might help add life to your years." Chiastic patterns go far beyond what some critics have denigrated by calling them "sheer ornamentation." The scope of the trope's usage is immense. Mirror patterns apply to paragraphs, short poems, Biblical texts, short stories, novels, epics. Many Christian writers exploited the rhetorical device because of its cross symbolism.[9] Milton used it. Alexander Pope used it. Victor Hugo used it with gusto, since it formed part of the way in which he expressed his thoughts. A significant example of Hugo's rhetoric would be: "Un roi chantait en bas, en haut mourait un Dieu."[10] Chiastic patterns are used so frequently that one hardly notices them. Some writers use them more than others. I have chosen well-known as well as not so well-known novels and short stories to demonstrate the diversity and significance of their usage.

The *Dictionnaire des genres et notions littéraires*[11] defines "chiasme" as a figure that repeats a series of syntagms in reversed order. The symmetrical exchange, it says, may apply to identical terms or to syntactical functions that are analogous. Quintillian's phrase, stated above, is one example that is frequently given to exemplify chiasmus. Examples abound throughout poetry and prose. Ronsard's phrase, quoted by Lausberg: "Gourmand de tout, de tout insatiable," is just one of many.[12] A phrase by Racine in *Andromaque* is also frequently cited to show that antithetical rhetorical effects are also reinforced by their mirror disposition: "Immoler Troie [a] aux Grecs [b], au fils d'Hector [a] la Grèce [b]." In this case, the structure is what I call imbricated structure, or a-b—a-b.

P. Bacry makes a clear distinction between two different modalities of the trope. He reminds us that "trope" comes from the Greek word *tropê*, meaning "that which turns," "that which changes meaning," that which changes direction as well as meaning."[13] The two modalities he points to and illustrates are the grammatical chiasmus, which concerns the grammatical nature of words (verb, noun, adjective) and the second is one that addresses words' syntactical meanings. He illustrates the first of these (which he calls the grammatical chiasmus) with the dictum that appears in Racine's *Plaideurs*:

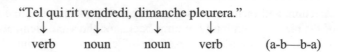

"Tel qui rit vendredi, dimanche pleurera."

verb   noun   noun   verb   (a-b—b-a)

But when Vigny writes "le roulis aérien des nuages de mer," his phrase illustrates "semantic fields" that are crossed:

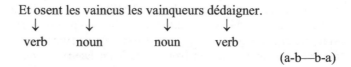

Sea   air   air   sea   (a-b—b-a)

Nothing, says Bacry, keeps a grammatical chiasmus from being, also, a semantic one. The example he gives of chiasmus that is both "grammatical" and "semantic" comes from Du Bellay:

Et osent les vaincus les vainqueurs dédaigner.

verb   noun   noun   verb

(a-b—b-a)

One notices that the central part of the chiasmus (b—b) is taken from the verb *vaincre*. This central node, however, underscores an opposition in meaning, an antithesis between losers and winners. A second antithesis is found in the opposition of the verbs *oser* and *dédaigner*, "to dare" versus "to scorn." These verbs belong to contrasting fields of meaning.[14]

    P. Schofer and D. Rice call attention to the fact that "we have...created an artificial situation in which tropes are analyzed in isolation...." They argue that perceptive studies are needed in order to "lay the groundwork for extending our four basic tropes beyond the single word and on to the process of the entire text."[15]

    If chiasmus means a crossing-over, a doubling back, what I call imbricated structures are a variation of chiasmus in that they also involve repetition (a-b—a-b): "Do *cats* eat *bats*" (a-b), "do *cats* eat *bats*" (a-b), asks Alice on her way to Wonderland, thereby using imbricated structure (a-b—a-b). Bacry chooses to call this "parallel construction" or symmetry.[16] Two examples of parallel disposition (or imbricated structure) given by Bacry are found in *Andromaque*. Hermione uses not only chiasmus to decry Pyrrhus, but parallel or overlapping construction when she reproaches the man she loves. She reproaches him for turning, ceaselessly,

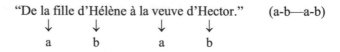

"De la fille d'Hélène à la veuve d'Hector."   (a-b—a-b)

a   b   a   b

In the previous act, Andromaque describes to her lady-in-waiting the sack of Troy by the Greeks, in which the Trojans were:

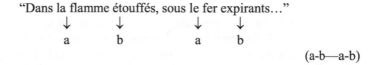

"Dans la flamme étouffés, sous le fer expirants..."
↓   ↓   ↓   ↓
a   b   a   b

(a-b—a-b)

These examples of parallelism (a-b—a-b) result from the inversion of the two formulas, "étouffés dans la flamme," and "expirants sous le fer."[17] Bacry also notes that both chiasmus and "parallelism" can be combined in the same linguistic formula that he quotes from Racine. When Racine states that at the beginning of the battle of Troy that the aim is to:

"Immoler Troie aux Grecs, au fils d'Hector la Grèce,"

the strength of that verse lies not only in its syntactical chiasmus, but in the appearance of the crossed words that seem to appear in the construction of the phrase. The verse contains complements that are contracted to their attribution. The first grouping contains what Bacry calls a "complement d'objet" (a), which is followed by a "complement d'attribution" (b), and the second grouping contains a "complement d'attribution" (b) that is followed by a "complement d'objet" (a). Thus:

"Immoler Troie   aux Grecs,   au fils d'Hector   la Grèce"
(a—complément   (b—complément   (b-complément   (a—complément
    d'objet)   d'attribution)   d'attribution)   d'objet)

The strength of the phrase lies not only in the syntactic chiasmus that is created, but also in the combination of the syntactic chiasmus with the parallel attribution existing in its semantic plan:

Troy (a)   Grèce (b)   Troie (a)   Grèce (b)

"This doubling," says Bacry, which is chiastic in its syntactical armature, and parallel in its semantic field, renders this a perfect example of classical equilibrium, with both parts of its structure weighing equally on either side of the cesura."[18]

Chiastic and imbricating structures are both mirror, or repetitive structures. P. Brooks says that "repetition is so basic to our experience of literary texts that one is simultaneously tempted to say all or nothing on the subject."[19] Even though one might be tempted to say nothing, *especially* because one cannot say "all," readers of texts make connections, "sight" relationships between micro- and macro-structures, and find pleasure, in Roland Barthes's terminology, in so doing. A great part of the pleasure of reading is the pleasure of sighting, of finding mirrors in texts and texts in mirrors.

P. Brooks also reminds us that "rhyme, alliteration, assonance, meter, refrain, all the mnemonic elements of fictions and indeed most of its tropes are in some manner repetitions which take us back in the text, which allow the ear, the eye, the mind to make connections between different textual moments, to see past and present as related and as establishing a future which will be noticeable as some variation in the pattern."[20] Few could do better when it comes to experiencing "le plaisir du texte."

Because "sightings" are, tautologically, the act of those who sight, they reflect the eyes of those who read and see mirrors in texts, of those who take aim in order to see what they can see. As M. Nüridsany reports in *Effets de miroir*, "if the mirror is a round eye, the eye itself is a mirror in which others see themselves."[21] In his book on *Mirrors and Masks: The Search for Identity,* the sociologist A. L. Strauss quotes a rhyme that expresses the dialogical aspects of one's looking to others who will, in turn, respond to one's acts, either with approval or disapproval:

> Each to each a looking-glass
> Reflects the other that doth pass.[22]

To look through a sight is to test for straightness or trueness by looking along the length of an instrument. It is through reading and rereading that literary critics become aware of patterns, test for consistence and variations in structures of language. Sightings do not always come up with completely accurate notations: mirrors, and the reading of mirrors, can deceive. Notions relating to reflections that I examine in this book are not bound by any "trope-ical" straight-jacket. They are sights, instruments to be used for reflection. To sight-see is to profit from similarities, correspondences, linkages, as well as differences. While many may have been missed, looking and finding intertexts in texts and realizing that the "seer" in the text reflects the text in the seer is to see and read – to read and see. To wring the changes on Stendhal's famous phrase in *Le Rouge et le noir* in which he describes the novel as "a mirror along the road,"[23] it is clear that the mirror-text is "empty" if the spectator is not there to see it. So critics who reflect upon mirrors have a triple task in making sightings: they must see the "mirror" itself, the object of their sightings (the text, in which there are "literal" mirrors, mirror-characters and scenes as well as texts that reflect other texts), their own reflections (the real and implied readers of and in the text), and the road often travelled (the contexts and receptions of those texts and the ideologies reflected in them).

Aristotle said that masters of metaphors have an eye for resemblances. Treatments of "the same and the different" in the making of metaphors and in narratology have stressed the tension that exists between resemblances, or the differences that exist in the very project of detecting resemblances and repetitions (see Walter Benjamin, Derrida, Miecke Bahl). These tensions are found in each of the texts sighted in this book.

In a book on *Horace's Narrative Odes*, M. Lowrie says: "Art's declaration of its own eclipse makes it no less art. We as readers have an obligation to consider what art does, above what it says. If Horace makes a statement that politics wins over aesthetics in this book, this hardly means his poetry qua artefact has itself any less aesthetic value."[24] A study of the mechanisms of symmetry as well as of asymmetry deals not only with what art does, but also with what it says. Asymmetry may cancel out a seemingly symmetrical structure, but as it does so, it says something about what it is doing as well as about what it is saying.

2.   Mirrors in Texts

Repetition is present not only in "reality," calling the thorny question of mimesis in literature to mind, but it is also present in all art forms, painting, dance, architecture, music, cinema. Self-portraits, across the ages, are particularly revealing. Mirrors in French fiction and their repetitive modalities across a broad chronological spectrum are the unifying focus of this book. They appear in a variety of ways, and in a chosen number of works that, despite their chronological, cultural, and contextual diversity, starting with the seventeenth and ending with twentieth-century texts, have numerous elements in common.

Mirrors in literature may be "real," that is, they are referential: the signifier may point to a physical object, a signified that is, of course, another signifier, but which, nevertheless, is described as a material object or an object of material culture that may be large or small, elaborate or plain, framed or unframed. The observation may be a pleasing experience (Zola's Nana admires herself, narcissistically, in a full-length mirror) or terrifying (in the fantastic genre, images reflected in mirrors are more fearsome than fanciful, creating a sense of what Freud calls the *unheimlich*). There are "mirrors on the wall" that tell the truth: thus did the Witch in Snow White find out that she was not "the fairest of them all." There are mirrors that de-form. In that way G. Rodenbach's protagonist in *L'Ami des miroirs* "follows" images he sees in his labyrinth of mirrors. He ends up rushing headlong into one (so as to enter that "fabulous" world), and crushes his skull on the hard surface, doing himself, literarily, and literally, in. In Rodenbach's *Bruges-la-morte*, water and mirrors create multiple *mises en abyme* of the novel: Bruges, with its labyrinthine canals, bridges, and quays, with houses that have mirrors attached to windows or doors so that the inhabitants may "spy"

---

on passers-by without being observed, is ideal for a Symbolist novel's setting. The protagonist (or antagonist) of Rodenbach's novel carefully wipes the surface of a mirror in which he believes he sees the *imago* of his wife, who has died. It is no accident that modern mirrors (i.e., glass mirrors with silvered backings) were "born" in Venice, the city of reflections, or that a Symbolist novel that accentuates doubles, reflections, and *mises en abyme* should be located in Bruges, the "Venice of the North." The narrator of Barbey d'Aurevilly's *Une Page d'histoire* "sees" the dead lovers of the Tourlaville chateau in a mirror. It is in Tourlaville, in fact, that a mirror-manufacturing company existed that was brought to Paris by Louis XIV. Its owner's last name, Néhou, figures as "Néel de Néhou" in another of Barbey's works. The narrator of J. Lorrain's *Les Trous du masque*, who wears a hood to a strange party in a sexually equivocal setting, tears off the hood, looks in a mirror, and sees nothing. In Mandiargues's *La Motocyclette*, Rebecca sees herself as a figure drawn by Vitruvius, outstretched, reflected in an "X" form in a mirror of a bath-house in Strasbourg.

Mirrors in literature require that one be aware not only of the literalness of their presence, but also of the contexts of their presence. Works that use history in a deliberate manner, such as *La Princesse de Clèves* or Barbey's *Une Page d'histoire*, require that the reader inquire into sources and influences, and analyze the integrations of those historical and ideological references within the text. Synchronic and diachronic imbrications of chronicle and fiction become a necessary target for sightings.

While trying to avoid the simplistic contrast between "the world" and "the text," the "sighter" must combine textual awareness with an involvement in the politics of reading. Texts are in and of this world. It is for this reason that a novel such as *Les Liaisons dangereuses* weaves into its creation strategies that insist on narrative veracity. That the eighteenth-century epistolary novel specialized in trying to achieve verisimilitude, in trying to convince the reader of what was later Balzac's dictum, "all is true," is applicable even to the fantastic genre. That the *Liaisons* reflect the clockwork mentality of its age, only to be done in, de-constructed, as was the century, by a Revolution in its conclusion, cannot be ignored in sightings of meanings of texts and their contexts.

Sighting mirrors in literature also involves what some readers call the biographical fallacy. While this approach frequently presents pitfalls, some texts "ask for" biographical elucidations. Jean Lorrain's short story, *Le Crapaud*, for example, invites the reader to look into the relationship that J. Lorrain had with his mother. The conclusions derived therefrom illumine the text's reading. An application of Freudian concepts to the biographical data deepens the significance of mirror imagery in the work.

Formal questions resulting from rhetorical strategies, primarily from the use of chiastic and imbricated structures, are directions towards which I have aimed my sights, especially since such differing texts as *La Princesse de Clèves* (1678), *Les Liaisons dangereuses* (1782), Balzac's *Facino Cane* (1836), Barbey's *Une Page d'histoire* (1882), G. Rodenbach's *L'Ami des miroirs* (1901) and *Bruges-la-morte* (1892), J. Lorrain's *Le Crapaud* (1895), and P. de Mandiargues's *La Motocyclette* (1959) share structural and iconic characteristics. These texts mirror each other both formally and in-formally.

The presence of "the mirror in the middle" in the uses of repetition and in the creation of imbricated structures makes visible the entire frame, form, or armature that is inseparable from the meaning of a text. Questions of *mises en abyme* are related to the task of mirror sightings, and many of the texts I have chosen to analyze contain "a mirror in the mirror." "Mirrors in mirrors" include those that apply to the novel that M. A. Caws calls "everybody's favourite *mise en abyme*,"[25] Gide's *Les Faux-monnayeurs*. Mirrors in paintings, as Gide, once again, would have it, such as the well-known Arnolfini portrait, or Quentin Metzys's representations, pose questions involved in mirrors in literature. The deeply intriguing painting of *Las Meninas* by Velásquez, in which the King and Queen, who are outside the painting, are nevertheless supposedly reflected in the mirror depicted on the back wall, contain problematics of "the mirror in the text," the title given, in the English translation, to Lucien Dällenbach's *Le Récit spéculaire*,[26] the book in which he creates a typology of the question. Favorite examples of *mises en abyme* are the 1940's can of "Dutch Cleanser" on which was depicted a Dutch lady holding a can of "Dutch Cleanser," on which was depicted a lady holding a can of "Dutch Cleanser," *ad infinitum*, or the French cow represented on the box of "La Vache qui rit" that wears earrings made out of boxes on which are represented the smiling faces of "vaches qui rient." And the usual example is the Russian doll, one replica of which is found inside the other, in seemingly infinite regression....

In a 1974 novel by G. Charpy, *Volubilis des miroirs*,[27] the author equates the delirium of one of his characters with narratological *mises en abymes*: "In the story that loses itself in itself, and whose episodes burst as they are retold thousands of times, these recits are like prisms that engender themselves as under an electric light that resend broken mirrors endlessly, under the sunlights [sic] and the showers of morning-glories."[28]

Ekphrasis, the description of a work of art in a work of literature, be it "real" or fictional, is also a "figure in the carpet" of sightings. These descriptions are frequently *mises en abyme* that reflect the main body of the text, supporting it or undermining it. They may consist, in themselves, of mirror imagery. In *La Princesse de Clèves* Nemours steals Mme de Clèves's portrait that had been copied from M. de Clèves's painted miniature, and later, it is she who contemplates, with adulation, Nemours's portrait that had been copied from Mme de Valentinois's painting of Nemours and of others at the siege of Metz. These are mirror-*scenes* rather than examples of ekphrasis, but they do involve depictions of the characters in paintings that not only mirror the mirror-scenes in the novel, but reflect the complexities of historical and affective representation. Other ekphrastic depictions contain proleptic properties, such as the description of Marguerite de Ravalet in Barbey's *Une Page d'histoire*. The Cupid in the painting with blood on his wings predicts Marguerite's death by the guillotine. Even though the narrator believes it was painted on her portrait after her death, it reflects, or inscribes, verbally and "visually," her death. How do chiastic or imbricated structures, a-b—b-a, or a-b—a-b, that on the surface seem closed, locked up tight, acquire significance that succeeds in undermining their being "locked up"? This, too, is a narratological question posed by mirrors in texts. Mme de Clèves undermines expectations. The conclusion of the novel was widely protested in the seventeenth century, and has prompted a great deal of critical, primarily feminist, writing in our own time. Passion throws sand into the gears of the carefully crafted machinery of *Les Liaisons dangereuses*. In Balzac's frame narrative, *Facino Cane*, the frame and the framed reflect each other but are in tension at the same time. In Barbey's creation of a poetics of incest (sighted in *Une Page d'histoire*), the tale de-constructs. Is it vengeance of protagonists who get out of hand and take over, undermining not only the conventions of their times, but their very creators' efforts to shape their destinies? These are questions addressed in *Sightings*.

What stories, what myths, embedded in shrouds of time, contain, in essence, many of the questions I address in this book? When it comes to micro-syntagms that reflect a tale's themes, Alice, coming to us from England, both in *Wonderland* and *Beyond the Looking-Glass*, provides mesmerizing paradigms. When it comes to macro-structures of a text's entire armature, Narcissus, coming to us from ancient literature, and from Ovid in particular, is our "paradigmatic man." I will move from "micro" to "macro" models, or touchstones. From Alice to Narcissus and back – as in a looking glass.

In a chapter of *Logique du sens,* G. Deleuze addresses the question of Alice's vertical fall or descent into the rabbit hole, which is followed by lateral moves. He says: "… it is by dint of sliding sideways that one passes to the other side, since the other side is nothing other than the other way around."[29] The act of writing is both horizontal and vertical. In Western script, one moves from left to right (unless one is Leonardo, who wrote in mirror script), and one's hand moves back from the right to the left, to repeat the initial gestures. The vertical descent is a movement that is not an "effet de surface." It is initiatory in character, it represents a "descent into the self" that entails a return to the surface.

When L. Marin describes arrivals in places and spaces, he analyzes the passage itself from one space to another. He calls the act a crossing, or a passage from one domain or dwelling-place to another, "with all the dangers that are there implied, since passengers put themselves outside of the laws of the place in which they abide without yet having found those of the place they are going." One result of this that one could call a space that is "an in-between borders" location, is finding oneself in a "lawless" place in which there is neither authority nor legitimacy."[30] Both Deleuze and Marin can be applied to Alice's moves from her "normal" world into another one.

3.   A Micro-Paradigm, or Crossing the Borders

Leave it to a brilliant mathematician and logician to cross (X) the borders from reality to fantasy, from this side of the mirror to the other, from a land of consciousness to a land of dreams and then back. Lewis Carroll did so going and coming. In Alice's *Adventures in Wonderland* (1869), chiastic phrases provide micro-models that are paradigmatic. When Alice begins to get sleepy and crosses the border into "Wonderland," she thinks she is falling down a rabbit hole in search of the White Rabbit. As she falls (it is not unlikely that the expression "to fall asleep" may have inspired Alice's descent), she imagines coming out on the other side, where everyone would be head downwards. "The Antipathies, I think," she amusedly names the topsy-turvy creatures she would supposedly encounter. One might also think of a "descent into the self," as Freud would analyze dreams, or as Lacan would analyze a child's self-discovery by bobbing up and down in front of a mirror. Whereas Deleuze points to the horizontal "sliding" that takes place in Alice's adventures, after she takes a vertical plunge by "falling" down the rabbit-hole, the central location of both directions is accentuated by L. Carroll himself. Speculation about what would happen if one were to fall through a hole that went straight through the middle of the earth was an ancient one, raised by thinkers that included Plutarch, Francis Bacon, Voltaire, Galileo and others. The latter gave the following answer to the question: "..the object would fall with increasing speed but decreasing acceleration until it reached the centre of the earth, at which spot the acceleration would be zero. Thereafter it would slow down in speed, with increasing acceleration, until it reached the opening at the other end. Then it would fall back again. By ignoring air resistance and the coriolis form resulting from the earth's rotation…the object would oscillate back and forth forever. Air resistance of course would eventually bring it to rest at the earth's centre."[31] And just so for the "Antipathies," one might conclude. As for Deleuze's horizontal "sliding" in *The Looking Glass*, one could point to chapter 7 of Carroll's *Sylvie and Bruno Concluded*, where Carroll alludes to the Moebius strip on the one hand, and to running trains by the sheer force of gravity on the other: the train would run on a straight track from one town to the other, and since, at the centre, the train would be closer to the centre of the earth, the train would acquire enough momentum to carry it to the other half of the tunnel. One cannot ignore that both vertical "fall" and horizontal "sliding" would take place in exactly the same time (were one to forget air resistance and the wheels' friction). Both would occur in forty-two minutes.[32] Alice's fall and her "sliding" over draw attention to the bipolar structure of each of these "movements."

When Alice asks whether cats eat bats, or the other way around, the narrator disparages her questions and addresses the reader: "for, you see, as she couldn't answer the question, it didn't much matter which way she put it."[33] It is because she was too sleepy that "she couldn't answer the question." But it cannot be denied that it would matter very much to the cat or the bat in question were Alice to answer the questions positively – at least on *this* side of the border.

Since chiastic states are mirror states, it is fitting that language be spoken that is appropriate to the "state" (or "land") one is in when speaking it. When Alice crosses the border, the language she uses on her way is chiastic, and she frequently hears chiastic "dialect" and sees chiastic states of affairs when she reaches the land of the White Rabbit, the Cheshire Cat, the Mad Hatter, the March Hare, the Dormouse, the Gryphon, the Mock Turtle, and others.

L. Carroll's narrator has twentieth-century readers become aware that "the mirror stage" was raised before Freud, Lacan and others raised it, especially when it comes to questions of sameness and difference in language, literature, and life. The child that Freud describes in *Beyond the Pleasure Principle* (the same one who threw his toys saying 'o-o-o' for '*fort*' ["gone"] and then hailed their reappearance with a joyful '*da*' ["there"], thus compensating for his mother's departures and returns), found a way of making himself "disappear."[34] Having discovered his own reflection in a full-length mirror that did not reach the ground, he would crouch down, making his mirror-image vanish.[35] Instead of playing at disappearing, Alice knowingly "pretends" to be two people. Not only is she psychologically clever, but she is so, literarily, as well. In textual reception, readers are themselves, as well as an Other. Dialogue is a pedagogical enterprise. Identity and difference are of the essence, even as pretense means participating, Narcissus-like, in the image in the mirror.

But Wonderland gives Alice pause. Take the Cheshire Cat. One cannot *take* the Cheshire Cat, the Mad Hatter might say, but let us take micro- examples of imbricated structure and of chiasmus evident in what the Cheshire Cat says and does. When he explains to Alice: "You see, a dog *growls* when it's angry, and *wags its tail* when it's pleased. Now I *growl* when I'm pleased, and *wag my tail* when I'm angry. Therefore I'm mad,"[36] there is interlocking structure: a-b—a-b. Three pages later, when he disappears but leaves his grin behind, Alice thinks: "Well, I've often seen a *cat without a grin*...but a *grin without a cat*! It's the most curious thing I ever saw in all my life!",[37] one sees there an example of chiasmus (a-b—b-a).

In his book *Philosophy Through the Looking-Glass*, J.-J. Lecercle studies what he classifies as *délire* texts. The word, he explains convincingly, cannot be translated into English. The distinction between *délire* (characterized by the writings of Artaud, Roussel, Leiris, Wolfson), and *nonsense* is an important one. In "nonsense" there is still "sense" (or perhaps what Deleuze calls "la logique du sens") that may be divined or interpreted, since a mirror-image can usually be understood, even in reverse. A poem such as "Jabberwocky" has enough portmanteau words for the sense of the "manteaux" to be guessed by their "hangers." *Délire* texts need explanatory devices to pierce through the veil of their secrets. Roussel's *délire* texts necessitated his posthumous *Comment j'ai écrit certains de mes livres* in order to be fully understood. I raise this distinction in order to say that *délire* texts are not analyzed here.[38]

But we are still in Wonderland, and Alice is attending the Tea Party where a significant discussion in which chiastic phrases are used (even if they don't *call* it that). The question of "why is a raven like a writing desk?," the famous riddle the Mad Hatter poses, returns the reader to Deleuze. Carroll himself gave an answer to "why is a raven like a writing desk?" in the preface to his 1896 edition of *Alice*: "Because it can produce a few notes, though they are *very* flat; and it is never put with the wrong end in front!" An even better answer is given by S. Loyd, the American puzzle master in his *Cyclopedia of Puzzles.*[39] Here is his solution, which is in keeping with Carroll's alliterative style: "... because the notes for which they are noted are not noted for being musical notes."[40] During the discussion of this weighty riddle, when Alice stumbles around, looking for an answer, she is immediately criticized by the March Hare:

–"Then you should *say* what you *mean*," the March Hare went on.

–"I do," Alice hastily replied; "at least–at least I *mean* what I *say* – that's the same thing you know."

–"Not the same thing a bit!" said the Hatter.

–"Why, you might just as well say that 'I *see* what I *eat*' is the same thing as 'I *eat* what I *see*!'"

–"You might just as well say," added the March Hare, "that '*I like what I get*' is the same thing as '*I get what I like*'!"

–"You might just as well say," added the Dormouse, who seemed to be talking in his sleep, "that '*I breathe when I sleep*' is the same thing as '*I sleep when I breathe*'!"

–"It *is* the same thing with you," said the Hatter, and here the conversation dropped, and the party sat silent for a minute, while Alice thought over all she could remember about ravens and writing-desks, which wasn't much.[41]

The Hatter is perfectly right in his statement about the Dormouse. When he, the Hatter, begins to sing a parody of Jane Taylor's well-known poem, "The Star," the Dormouse begins to sing in his sleep: "Twinkle, twinkle, twinkle, twinkle—." He goes on so long that the participants at the party have to pinch him to make him stop.[42] Even though the Dormouse goes on and on, mumbling the same word over and over in his sleep, he only *says* it, in print, four times, thus creating a completely repetitive "chiasmus," which is not one at all, as the Hatter might say. It is actually closer to J. L. Borges's short story about Pierre Ménard, who spends his life rewriting *Don Quixote*, in Spanish, repeating, word for word, what Cervantes wrote in his eponymous epic.

I have used Alice as a paradigm for chiastic and interlocking micro-structures because crossing textual borders into a looking glass necessarily entails crossings and turnings about in a Wonderland of repetitive linguistic patterns. They stop us short – or long – when we reflect upon them.

Every chiastic micro-syntagm must be examined not only for its structure but for its meaning. The March Hare is right. The phrases "to say what you mean and to mean what you say" are different, even though the repetition of the same words may delude the spectator/auditor/reader into thinking they are the same. G. Deleuze does not quite understand that, in his analysis of meanings in Carroll's word-games. Deleuze believes that "I say what I think and I think what I say," "I like what I get" and "I get what I like," "I breathe when I sleep" and "I sleep when I breathe" all have the same meaning. He states that both parts of a chiastic equation do not mean the same thing. He states that "Le sens est toujours double sens, et exclut qu'il y ait un bon sens de la relation." He also says that "Les événements ne sont jamais causes les uns des autres, mais entrent dans des rapports de quasi-causalité, causalité irréelle et fantomatique qui ne cesse de se retourner dans les deux sens:[43] "To see what I eat" is extremely different from "I eat what I see" – and wouldn't it be nice if "I like what I get" were the same as "I get what I like." It is only in the case of the Dormouse that both syntactical elements of the chiasmus are true, even if they are not stated in the same manner: he breathes when he sleeps, and because he sleeps so much he sleeps when he breathes.

4.   Metaphor, Metaphor, All Is Metaphor or: Seeing is Believing

The myth of Narcissus provides one of the principal metaphors for the seer and the seen in the texts I analyze in this book. The myth provides motifs of the double, of water as reflective of the Other and the Same, of questions relating to appearance and reality, of the representation of a representation, of blindness and in-sight, of "amorous reciprocity."[44] The myth provides questions of pathologies within "amorous reciprocity," since Narcissus, in post-classical literature, has frequently been interpreted as being a pathological rather than a metamorphic case. The myth contains elements that elucidate the detection, description, and iteration of chiastic and interlocking structures. The metaphoric functioning of the myth provides analogues with structural devices not always detected – and private eyes, looking at the myth, render them more visible. The reader becomes an Other – or, as Narcissus, Alice, and Rimbaud would have it, in the act of reading, "Je" is "Un Autre."

The Narcissus myth may well have its origin in ancient beliefs in the existence of persons' having doubles. Plato's own "creation myth" has the androgyne at its core. His androgynous creature could turn in circles before having been split. Homer postulated a double nature to human beings, a corporeal one and an invisible image that would be liberated by death. Even today, members of certain Indian tribes refuse to be photographed, since a "copy" would steal their identity: the "reproducer" as vampire is a motif that has manifested itself in different ways throughout the centuries.

Ovid is perhaps the earliest of classical writers to tell the tale of Narcissus. I will mention other sources named and described by L. Vinge[45] when relevant, most especially Philostratus and Pausanias. The Narcissus narrative appears in Book III of the *Metamorphoses*,[46] following close upon the tales of Cadmus, Acteon, and Semele. Multiple mirrors and dualities are present in the myth. The narrative of Bacchus's being twice-born, from Semele (female) and from Jove (male), precedes Jove and Juno's argument over who enjoys the most pleasure in love-making, male or female. Jove bets that women do, while Juno holds the opposite view. They turn to Tiresias, who had had the experience of being both. When he had seen two huge serpents mating he had struck them with his staff, and had been changed into a woman. During the eighth year Tiresias saw the *same* serpents, struck them once *again*, and was changed back into a man. Being asked to arbitrate the gods' dispute, he took Jove's side. Furious, Juno made him blind, and since "no god may undo what another god has done,"[47] Jove gave him the power to know the future to compensate for his loss of sight.

The first to experience Tiresias's prophetic powers was the nymph Liriope, who had been ravished, in a stream, by the river-god Cephisus. When her child was born, Narcissus was so beautiful that "already at that time he was able to be loved."[48] When asked whether he would live to a well-ripened age, Tiresias replied: "If he ne'er know himself."[49] When he was sixteen years old, and when he "might seem boy or man," both young men and women sought Narcissus's love.

Ovid has his narrator then tell the Echo episode. Echo had chattered on and on, occupying Juno while Jove dallied with the nymphs, who were Echo's friends, thereby emphasizing the power of language to betray. When Juno discovered Echo's trick, she took revenge by allowing Echo only the power of vocal repetition of the latter parts of phrases others had said.

Having fallen in love with Narcissus, Echo follows him. When he is separated from his friends, Narcissus calls out: "Is anyone here?" and Echo calls back "Here." He cries out "Come!", and she repeats "Come!".[50] When he says "Let us meet," she replies "Let us meet," and comes out of the woods to embrace him. He flees and fleeing, says: "'Hands off! embrace me not! May I die before I give you power over me!' 'I give you power over me!' she says, and nothing more."[51]. Spurned, she flees, and slowly withers up from grief. Only her voice and bones remain, and then nothing remains but a voice, echoing others' half-phrases. Echo is a paradigm of literal repetition. But when she repeats only half-phrases, she subverts meanings, making many of them have sexual connotations, thus becoming a symbolic challenge to hermeneutics.

Young men fall in love with Narcissus too. One scorned youth prayed: "So may he himself love, and not gain the thing he loves!"[52] ("*Sic amet* ipse licet, *sic* non potiatur *amato*!") The repetitive syntax in Latin is imbricated, a-b—a-b. Nemesis hears and answers the youth's prayer: Narcissus finds a cool clear pool with a smooth surface in the woods, and when he sees his own reflection, he is mesmerized by its beautiful form. "He looks in speechless wonder at himself," the reader is told, "and hangs there motionless in the expression, like a statue carved from Parian marble."[53] Lying prone, he admires the image he sees in the water. His eyes are like "*twin* stars"; his locks are worthy of *both* "Bacchus and Apollo,"[54] and on his face, neck, and cheeks, the colour pink (or "blush") is *mingled* with white. Phrasal repetition and the double again come to play in the description of his reflexive admiration: "All things, in short, he admires for which he is himself admired."[55] He praises, and is himself what he praises; and while he seeks, is sought; equally he kindles love and burns with love.[56] Plunging his hands into the water, he tries to clasp himself. He tries to kiss the pool. The narrator, at this point, intervenes, in an apostrophe: "O fondly foolish boy, why vainly seek to clasp a fleeting image? What you seek is nowhere; That which you behold is but the shade of a reflected form and has no substance of its own."[57] He continues to look, enchanted, and the narrator has him resort to speech, in the first person. Reflective, reflexive, and repetitive "dialogue" foregrounds both active and passive voices – and then, that sudden and devastating revelation takes place: "Oh, I am he! I have felt it, I know now my own image. I burn with love of my own self. I both kindle the flames and suffer them".[58] Tiresias's prophecy has come true. Narcissus has come to know himself, and for that reason, he will die. Grief at not being able to part from his own body overcomes him; with white hands he beats his bare breast, which turns pink, and slowly his strength is sapped. He concludes: "We two shall die together in one breath."[59] Two are one. The ruddy colour mixed with white slowly disappears. Echo empathizes with Narcissus's grief, and as often as he says "Alas!" she echoes "Alas!" When Narcissus finally says to himself "Farewell!," Echo echoes the word, "farewell!"

The epilogue reveals that even as Narcissus is received in the infernal regions, "he kept on gazing on his image in the Stygian pool."[60] When the naiads, the dryads, and Echo looked for Narcissus's body in order to prepare the funeral pyre, they found only "a flower, its yellow centre girt with white petals."[61] Tiresias's fame grows abroad, and the narration of Pentheus, whose death Tiresias will also predict, is told next, a myth once again involving twice-born Bacchus.

5.   Bacchus to Bacchus

Ovid structures his myth back to back, or, since repetition, opposition, and reversals play such an important role throughout Book III of *The Metamorphoses*, one could also say "front to front." While L. Vinge regards the Narcissus myth as being formed of two principal parts, the Echo and Narcissus episodes, the structure, seen in the entire context of Book III of the *Metamorphoses*, is chiastically quadri-partite.[62] The narratives of Cadmus, Acteon, and Semele form a Prologue, with the tale of Semele being crucial to the "performative" aspect of the myth, Bacchus's birth. The four-part chiastic armature of the core includes (a) Tiresias, (b) Echo ("vocal" specularity), (b) Narcissus ("specular" vocality,) and (a) Tiresias again; this narratological "node" is followed by the Epilogue, in which Bacchus causes Pentheus's death. The Epilogue includes the parenthetical tale of Acoetes and the Lydian sailors who become metamorphosed into dolphins, a reflection of the water motif that permeates all of Book III.

The structure of Book III may be schematized as chiastic:

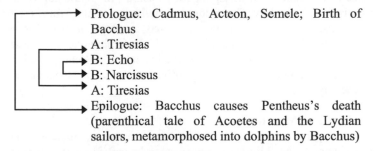

Prologue: Cadmus, Acteon, Semele; Birth of Bacchus

A: Tiresias

B: Echo

B: Narcissus

A: Tiresias

Epilogue: Bacchus causes Pentheus's death (parenthical tale of Acoetes and the Lydian sailors, metamorphosed into dolphins by Bacchus)

The Echo/Narcissus myth, with Prologue and Epilogue, is framed by Bacchus's double birth in the beginning and by Bacchus's causing Pentheus's death in the end. Life and death, the Alpha and the Omega, form the mirror's frame, with youth echoing youth being placed, symbolically, at the centre of the structure. Youth will vanish, leaving behind a voice and a beautiful flower, objective correlatives of the implied poet and his work that demonstrate the accomplishment of Tiresias's prophecies. Death will occur in the end, even as the work of art (voice and flower) remains.

In a sketch for a twentieth-century text (that was never written out), we are told that Boris Vian left, in his papers, this plan for a short story:

> Une nouvelle: Narcisse. Il aime à recevoir des lettres. Plein.
> Il n'en reçoit jamais. Un jour, il a l'idée de s'en envoyer. Il
> s'en envoie. L'idylle se noue. Le ton monte. Et il se donne
> rendez-vous sous l'horloge à trois heures. Il y va, bien
> habillé. Et à trois heures, il se suicide.[63]

That Narcissus might be seen as an epistolary novel unto himself is an ingenius idea. We see him talking, no, writing to himself across the ages, and then, in true twentieth-century fashion, the death of the "novelist" takes place, leaving behind a double, or, rather, a void not only of the narrator but of the narratee. That this short story was never written by Boris Vian, but only sketched, makes a case for an "unfinished chiasmus," a term that is not so oxymoronic as it seems, given the virtual "endings" that can only be sensed in the virtuality of many 20th-century writings. In G. Molinié's view, "on ne s'écrit pas de lettre à soi-même."[64] Vian, however, envisages that possibility as a variation of the Narcissus myth.

Molinié sees the art of persuasion, or the role of rhetoric, as a social act. He states that "there is no such thing as solitary rhetoric, there is no desert rhetoric, nor one of retreat…In general, it is the other that one tries to persuade. Persuasion is an act of communication."[65] That Narcissus sees his reflection as an *other* means that he tries to persuade that other to communicate with him. As a metaphor for chiasmus, his binocular vision is repeated: his two "seeing eyes" are doubled, making a total of four. He first believes that the reflected eyes, though reversed, are different from his own. It is only later that he will take an "I" for an "I," becoming one and the same person, and recognizing the univocity of the/his self. The Echo paradigm is carefully structured into the visual repetitiveness of vocal specularity, or specular vocality.

6.   Micro and Macro-Motifs

In all parts of Book III of *The Metamorphoses*, micro-motifs of duality, self-knowledge, blindness, vocality, sight and in-sight, vengeance, error, love, illusion, artistic production, and hermeneutics are foregrounded. They reflect the macro-structure of the whole. The myth contains a double reflexive core, and reflective motifs precede this core: Tiresias's serpents are prefigured by the serpent that Cadmus kills; when Diana bathes (the water motif will be repeated throughout), Acteon sees her; in punishment he is metamorphosed into a stag and observes his features and horns in a clear pool. He says: "Oh, woe is me!," prefiguring Narcissus's "Alas!," but Acteon cannot be "heard," since he has no Echo other than the narrator's that is "heard" by the reader. And Bacchus being twice born follows from the Jove/Juno discussion of male/female pleasure in love-making, a question that leads to the exposition of Tiresias's double nature and to Narcissus's being loved by both males and females.

Contrast, repetition, and ambiguity are constantly emphasized in the myth, as mathematical figures play a role in Ovid's paradigms. Tiresias strikes the same serpents twice, once when he is changed into a woman, and again during his eighth year as a woman. Narcissus is sixteen years old when he falls in love with his own image, twice Tiresias's years of transformation. Tiresias's gift of prophecy (in-sight) is opposite to blindness, both of which can be envisaged as a reflection of Narcissus's initial blindness regarding his own image, and his eventual recognition of himself. Narrative has forever had as one of its aims the reader/listener's coming to self-knowledge. "Know thyself," prescribed the delphic oracle. Narcissus's mother, Liriope, was ravished by a river-god in the river. Narcissus was thus conceived by and in the water. He is loved by both males and females, and in his sixteenth year Ovid presents him as ambiguously divided between being boy and man. Echo's echo echoes Narcissus's narcissism: both repeat, one vocally, one visually. Echo repeats, and is a model of imbricated structure, while Narcissus, looking at himself in the pool, sights an image of himself, which is perforce reversed, and is thus a model of chiasmus.

The power of vision, of reading and seeing (or "sighting"), is underscored in the cases of Tiresias, of Echo, and is intensified in the Narcissus narrative. The following quotations illumine this aspect of the text: "he *gazes* at his *eyes*, twin stars"; "that which he *sees* he burns for, and the same delusion mocks and allures his *eyes*"; he "*gazes* on that false image with *eyes* that cannot look their fill and through his own *eyes* perishes"; "I am *charmed*, and I *see*, but what I *see* and what *charms* me I cannot find."[66] This last phrase is a clear chiasmus in Latin: "et *placet* et *video*; sed quod *video*que *placet*que, non tamen invenio."[67] The active and the passive modes are emphasized in all of the semantic structures of the myth, making it a paradigm of the give and take that characterizes mirror imagery and structure, as well as reading – and mis-reading.

Intertwining motifs are poetically mingled and enhanced by Ovid in the Narcissus myth by his use of two colours, pink and white. At first, Narcissus admires the "glorious beauty of his face, the blush mingled with snowy white."[68] Later, when he grieves, he beats his breast, which turns "the colour of a delicate glow."[69] The narrator creates a simile to describe that colour. Narcissus's breast is "just as apples sometimes, though white in part, flush red in other part, or as grapes hanging in clusters take on a purple hue when not yet ripe."[70] Near the end, the colour is gone: "No longer has he that ruddy colour mingling with the white."[71]

Ekphrasis is not absent from the Narcissus myth. One of the motifs that surfaces in ekphrasis is the question of timelessness and time. Works of art outlive their creators. M. Krieger's analysis of Keats's "Ode On a Grecian Urn" emphasizes the Alpha and the Omega of the text, since an urn is both round like a womb and is used to contain the ashes of the dead, like a tomb. Time and motion are depicted on Keats's urn – the young men and women dancing on the urn are forever static, forever in place, even as they depict movement, progress. When Narcissus sees himself, "he looks in *speechless* wonder at himself and hangs there *motionless* in the *same* expression, *like a statue carved from Parian marble.*"[72] While this actively prefigures death, it is also a metaphor for "wonder," or "amazement," in its depiction of Narcissus as a sculpture. We viewers, like Narcissus, are mesmerized, stopped "dead in our tracks" by the power of the work of art – which he is. His "speechless wonder" implies a voice, a poet's voice, to give him life, to make of him a deathless myth – so long as there are Echos who will repeat that voice. Voicelessness and voice – timelessness and time: the reader is both sightless and seer, like Tiresias. Those who have eyes to see will sight ekphrastic statues throughout literature, carved, perhaps, "from Parian marble."

Another source of ekphrasis in the Narcissus myth is that of Philostratus, a prose writer who lived during the first part of the second century. His *Eikónes* contain descriptions of paintings, as the title suggests.[73] In his verbal representation, Philostratus says: "The pool paints Narcissus and the painting represents both the pool and the whole story of Narcissus."[74] In the cave of Achelous, with its statues that are old and in ruins – youth and old age are represented ekphrastically. By the pool, which is associated with Dionysus because it is wound round with ivy and vines, white flowers grow there as well, thanks to Narcissus.

Philostratus's statement calls to mind a story told much later about Giotto, and the painting of a fly. The story raises the issue of reality and illusion in painting and literature. In his second edition of Giotto's *Life*, Vasari says that when Giotto was still young, he found himself alone in Cimabue's atelier. He painted a fly on the nose of a figure that had been painted by the Master. The fly was so true to life that when the old artist returned and sat down to work on his painting, he tried several times to chase away the fly.[75] Describing the flowers growing at the edge of Narcissus's pool, Philostratus's narrator states that a bee had settled on one of them: "whether a real bee has been deceived by the painted flowers or whether we are to be deceived into thinking that a painted bee is real, I do not know. But let that pass. As for you, however, Narcissus, it is no painting that has deceived you, nor are you engrossed in a thing of pigments or wax; but you do not realize that the water represents you exactly as you are when you gaze upon it, nor do you see through the artifice of the pool."[76] The fact that the image of Narcissus depicted in the pool is reversed, that left is right and right is left is not raised by Ovid's or Philostratus's narrators, but it is certainly so viewed in literary and iconographic renditions of Narcissus throughout the history of literature and art. It is up to the reader/viewer to see that as a reflective medium, water forms part of the structure of this myth as a macro-model of chiasmus.

Works of art depicted ekphrastically presuppose the object sighted, the "voice" sighting it, and the reader or the "seer" of the work in question reading it. Ekphrastic depictions of Narcissus bring to light other issues related to deciphering texts, such as those regarding illusion and beauty. As do the spectators in Plato's allegory of the cave,[77] Narcissus makes mistakes in interpretation. He does not realize, at first, that he is looking at a reflection, at a *trompe l'oeil*. He believes the body he sees to be "the real thing." He does not believe that his "text" is an image, an *imago* that gives back a copy, a likeness, in reverse, of what he sees. He is simply "misreading" (to use Harold Bloom's expression for my own purposes). Secondly, Narcissus thinks, initially, that the body he believes to be "real" is that of an Other. In his apostrophe to Narcissus, the narrator tries to warn the boy/man: "O fondly foolish boy, why vainly seek to clasp a fleeting image.... That which you behold is but the shadow of a reflected form and has no substance of its own."[78]

One of the points Vinge makes about Ovid's representation of Narcissus is that the idea of beauty never comes up as a subject until the boy/man is minutely described in the image that he sees in the pool: "It is what Narcissus sees in the water that is described."[79] While this last statement is true, his beauty had not only been implied by the use of the hyperbolic "pulcherrima,"[80] "the most beauteous nymph," to describe his mother, but by the narrator's phrase "already at that time he was capable of being loved" to describe the baby at the time of birth. Reality (in beauty) and artifice (in reflection) are conjoined. The baby was a reversed "photocopy" of his mother.

Another account of Narcissus's paradigmatic significance in terms of motifs that relate to chiasmus has to do with Pausanias's account of the myth. It is found in his book on Boetia.[81] Ezio Pellizer states that Pausanias found it intolerable that a young man should be so stupid as to fall in love with his own reflection without realizing that he is doing so. For this reason, Pausanias invented a different version, "aimed at attenuating an absurdity."[82] In other words, Pausanias has Narcissus's demise be the result of Narcissus's incestuous love for his twin sister. He says: "They were *exactly alike* in appearance, their hair was *the same*, they wore *similar clothes*, and went hunting *together*."[83] Because his twin sister dies, Narcissus goes to the pool of water to be consoled by the reflection he sees there. He is never deceived into thinking it is himself he sees, but he *imagines* that what he saw was his sister. Deception versus imagination. We are returned, almost, to the tale of Cimabue and the fly. In Pausanias's account, however, Narcissus's "reading" is the result of a willing suspension of disbelief and of incestuous love. A poetics of incest, so elaborated in French decadent writings of the nineteenth century, goes back in intertexts to the depths of Greek and Roman myths.

Transformation: Ovid's narrator tells us that in the place where Narcissus's body had lain, a beautiful circular bloom was found. Its yellow centre was "girt with white petals."[84] The circular blossom's circular centre is a *mise en abyme*, a "mirror in the middle" that reflects the chiastic structure of the narrative. Ovid never has his narrator describe Narcissus's metamorphosis explicitly. His body simply disappears, and in its place the flower is found. The narrator describes a slow transformation in Acteon's case as well as in the case of the Lydian sailors, where Acteon slowly grows horns, and the sailors develop fins in the place of arms. But Narcissus the flower simply *takes the place of* Narcissus the boy/man. Narcissus is a paradigm for metaphor, metonymy, and for mirror-structure and motifs.

The homosexual motif, as well as thematics of incest, reinforce the myth's make-up. Ovid emphasizes it, and other writers state the name of the outraged boy/man whose love is rejected by Narcissus, Ameinias. The stress in the homosexual narrative is placed on Sameness, not only of sex but of fate. Echo, a young woman, is rejected by Narcissus first of all. Then Narcissus meets Ameinias, whom he rejects, bringing upon himself the *same* rejection that Ameinias had suffered. The incest motif is similar (Ovid and Pausanias have a number of elements in common), and a poetics of incest will be developed in this book, as it appears in the work of such writers as B. d'Aurevilly and J. Lorrain. In Barbey's short story brother loves sister (or mother), sister loves brother, but societal taboos, the Other, or delusion, as in J. Lorrain's tale, interfere and put an end to the vicious circle. Similarity and difference: homosexuality and incest stress both, just as chiastic and interlocking structures do.

7.   Narcissism

In most classical literature, Narcissus is depicted as a victim of illusion. His initial error in judgment is one of the principal ideas stressed by Ovid. *Vanitas*, or the notion of self-love as arrogance, was attributed primarily to Narcissus by later writers. That he was part of a "vengeance of the gods" cycle, especially in Ovid's and Conon's versions of the myth, is true, but he is not treated with scorn or disdain by those who best and first expressed his misfortune.

The word "Narcissism," with all of the psychological connotations attached to it, is primarily a twentieth-century idea. It has, not surprisingly, a dual paternity, H. Ellis and S. Freud. A few others who stressed the arrogance motif were such writers as the German psychiatrist P. Naïke, who used the word "Narcissism" in the report he made in 1899 on his translation of Ellis's essay, "Auto-Eroticism." He translated the expression "Narcissus-like tendency" as "Narcissism." Ellis also describes his own conversations with Freud by stating that Freud listened carefully, then took over his ideas and used them himself. Freud's essay, "Zur Einführung der Narzisissmus," came out in 1914, and a fourth party who could have contributed to the origin of the word was O. Rank. As Vinge says, "as early as 1911 Rank had published 'Ein Beitrag zur Narzissismus,' and in the essay, 'Der Doppelgänger' (1914), he seems to have been the first to use the word 'narcissism' in connection with literary criticism when carrying out an extensive study of the phenomenon with the help of literary material."[85] Rank shows that in literature the idea of the double is commonly related to negatively interpreted narcissism and death. Freud links his interpretation of the word to paranoia and suicide.

Other twentieth-century interpretations of "Narcissism" (many of which impute that present meanings of the word were intentionally contained in Ovid's representation of the myth) include those of A. Wesnelski (1935), J.G. Frazer (1911), H. Mitlacher (1933), L. Pfandl (1935), H. Bunker (1947), E. Erikson (1950), H. Spotnitz and P. Resnikoff (1954), J. van Lumey (1955), J. Frappier (1959), E. Köhler (1963), R. Wisniewski (1966), R. Derche (1962), J. Bowlby (1980), R. Stotler (1985), S. Freud (1988), Gide, Valéry, Gasquet, and so many others....

In the introduction to his book on literary Narcissism, "Narcissism Revisited: From Myth to Case Study," J. Berman describes O. Kernberg's and H. Kohut's post-Freudian theories of Narcissism.[86] Kernberg, a professor of psychiatry, has been considered as one of the leading authorities on the subject since the 1960s.[87] Kohut, an Austrian-born neurologist, came to the United States after World War II, where he began his training. Both should be consulted in psychological analyses of Narcissism in texts.

Berman makes use of criteria published in 1980 of the third edition of the *Diagnostic and Statistical Manual of Mental Disorders* (*DSM-III*), noting that *DSM-III* had not even mentioned the term "narcissism" in its 1968 edition. The definition given in the *Manual* to what it called "Narcissistic Personality Disorder" deserves attention:

> a grandiose sense of self-importance or uniqueness; preoccupation with fantasies of unlimited success; exhibitionistic need for constant attention and admiration; characteristic responses to threats of self-esteem; and characteristic disturbances in interpersonal relationships, such as feelings of entitlement, interpersonal

exploitativeness, relationships that alternate between the extremes of overidealization and devaluation, and lack of empathy.[88]

Because the positions expressed by the authors listed above are laid out by Vinge[89] and Berman,[90] I do not intend to analyze them here. Suffice it to say that the psychological implications of the word "Narcissism" are of interest when pathologies are created and expressed. The "sight" to keep in mind is the relationship between the micro- and the macro-texts, and the links between structures, iconography, and historical interpretations. There is no question that the words "a grandiose sense of self-importance or uniqueness," or "fantasies of unlimited success," or "exhibitionistic need for constant attention and admiration," or "interpersonal exploitativeness" apply to Mme de Merteuil and Valmont, not to mention many other "heroes" in the history of the Narcissistic literature that I examine in this book.

Of particular interest to a twentieth-century interpretation of the word "Narcissism" is that of L Barkan.[91] Barkan contrasts Narcissus with Pygmalion by stating that while Narcissus has "illusory self-love" and was "literally reduced to an image of himself," Pygmalion is a true artist who creates "artistic and amorous outward creation[s]." Narcissus's solipsism, Barkan says, "involves a primary refusal to make...connections [between individuals and the world.]"[92] This is one of the primary offenses that many twentieth-century scholars impute to Narcissus. "Narcissism," to them, equals solipsism. In their view the Narcissus myth could not possibly be a paradigm for anything but self-love, vanity, and a rejection of others. Be that as it may, any reflective motif is rich in interpretative possibilities, and the fact that an echoing voice and a flower remain emblematic of the Narcissus narrative, despite or perhaps because pain and death are involved, means that the metamorphic aspects of the myth translate into an appreciation of the act of creation, of the pain that goes into any act of writing (and birthing) in which meaning and structure hold up a mirror of the creative act to the reader.[93]

C. Nouvet interprets the myth as being one that does not emphasize egoism but narrates the importance of responsibility (or lack thereof). By this she means the duty of responding (she underlines the Latin word *respondere*) to another one's call. "Narcissus," she says, "is indeed punished because he failed to respond to the other."[94] And yet, if one considers the other to be the reader, as can be the case of certain twentieth-century epistolary novels, one might ask, as does B. Bray when he quotes M. Butor on Diderot: "Le triomphe du romancier par lettres, a écrit un jour Michel Butor à propos de Diderot, n'est-il pas de réussir à faire écrire certaines de ses lettres par le lecteur?"[95] If the other is the reader, the story of Narcissus is one of triple, if not quadruple voyeurism, since the reader "sees" Narcissus and his reflection, as well as Narcissus's viewing himself in the pool.

8.   Lacan: Staging the "Mirror Stage"

Lacan's "mirror stage" is cited frequently, in literary critical works, by both proponents and opponents of his ideas. The fact that he has brought together psychoanalytic thought and linguistics makes him singularly visible in areas of reflective, reflexive, and linguistic analysis. Lacan's studies of the relationship of the self to the self, of self to Other, and of the way the unconscious is primarily expressed in linguistic forms provide nodes of thought that relate both to the structure and to the deep structures of texts.

Infants discover themselves early in life, says Lacan, between the ages of six and eighteen months, by seeing themselves reflected in a mirror. The difference, he states, between children and chimpanzees, placed in a similar situation, is that the latter, faced with a mirror reflection, soon become bored by the inanity of the image, whereas children become enchanted by what they see, and find the experience a playful one. They come to know the correlations between the gestural aspects of the imagery and the reflected environment, and make correlations between this virtual complex and the reality that it doubles, be it in terms of their own bodies, those of others, or of objects they see beside them.[96] The "mirror stage" is a visual *Gestalt*. It is more than the discovery of the body; it is the discovery of the self, of the reflected world, of persons and things surrounding the child.

The above description is that of a salutary discovery of a self's *imago*.[97] "The mirror stage" is a playful, joyful, and integrative experience. But in his *Seminaire* I, as well as in his *Ecrits*, Lacan moves from an analysis of the mirror stage to the problematics of Narcissism. Because authors such as B. d'Aurevilly, J. Lorrain, G. Rodenbach, and P. de Mandiargues represent what could be described as pathologies in their works (incest, sadism, suicide, the castration complex, belief in imaginary duplications and multiplications of personages caused by rejection, etc.), the relationship that Lacan establishes between Narcissism and certain pathological situations is important to the relationships that exist between the unconscious, means of expression, and meaning.

While Lacan posits that the mirror stage manifests a *transitif normal*[98] the breach in the unity of "seer" and "seen" can lead to an alienated identity. When a breach is created between the "inner life" and "the world around us" – both of which are perceived in the image in the mirror – this results in paranoia.[99] Active and passive become confused. Children who hit say they have been hit, those who see others fall, cry. It is in this process of identification that the child experiences the whole gamut of reactions and counter-reactions, and the conduct resulting from those experiences reveals structural ambivalence: the slave identifies with the master, the actor with the spectator, the seduced with the seducer. The erotic rapport in which the individual identifies with an image that is alienating thus becomes what will be called the self.[100]

In "L'Agressivité en Psychanalyse," Lacan sets aside such areas as culpability, hypocondriac fixation, primordial masochism.[101] He is interested in aggression – and the cause of human aggression is clearly laid at the feet of Narcissism: "There is no doubt that it [aggression] comes from 'narcissistic passion.'"[102]

Even as he interfaces Freudian theories with his own arguments, Lacan posits as an origin of aggression (and of other pathologies not expressed) the subject who becomes a rival to himself.[103] Lacan returns to Freud, even while criticizing him.[104] Because the *imago* of the father (*le nom du père*), or *Père*, becomes a rival to the self, this results in the murder of the father and in the guilt consequent to this act. Guilt leads to further aggression, and finally to the endless complications of master and slave relations.

Freud acknowledges the power of the "external" associations that exist for a subject and views that power in light of the "internal" associations they replace, in disguise. In Freud the signified deserves pursuit in its relationship to the signifier that expresses it. Lacan, however, posits the *S*ignifier over the *s*ignified by using the Saussurian algorithm: "signifiant sur signifié."[105] There is clear supremacy of signifier over signified, in his view.

Lacan's interest in linguistics is heightened by his interests in textual creation, in rhetoric, stylistics, and explications of texts. His analyses of Poe's *Purloined Letter* have caused many a scholar to rethink the role of the floating or "flying" signifier in a text. He bases some of his thought on Freud's theories that dreams are like language – if not hieroglyphic script that can and should be deciphered.[106]

The equation of a mirror with hieroglyphs makes one think of a quotation by R. Mirami, written in 1582, and cited by Baltrusaitis in *Le Miroir*:

> I say that for certain people mirrors are a hieroglyph of truth in that they discover everything that is presented to them as being the truth that cannot be hidden. Others, on the contrary, take mirrors to be symbols of falsehood because they reveal, frequently, things that seem different from what they are.[107]

That mirrors mirror both truth and falsehood is a notion that permeates the history of the interpretation of "the looking-glass." Baltrusaitis calls looking at mirrors the science of illusion, even as he goes on to use a chiasmus to depict both the history and the science of mirrors. He calls it "science and illusion, and the illusion of science."[108]

Freud's, and, after him, Lacan's interest in rhetoric is most explicitly stated in the list of tropes Lacan enumerates in his "Fonction et champ de la Parole et du Langage":

> Ellipse, et pléonasme, hyperbate ou syllepse, régression, *répétition*, *apposition*, tels sont les déplacements syntaxiques, *métaphore*, *catachrèse*, *augonomase*, *allégorie*, *métonymie* et *synecdoche*, les condensations sémantiques où Freud nous apprend à lire les intentions ostentatoires ou démonstratives, dissimulatrices ou persuasives, rétorsives ou séductrices, dont le sujet module son discours onirique.[109]

Although Lacan does not, to my knowledge, say anything about chiastic structures, his interest in tropes per se, as the above quotation reveals, would naturally include chiasmus due to his interest in repetition and apposition as they relate self to Other, self to Other-within-Self, and self to "le nom [or 'le Non'] du Père."

One may note a certain similarity between J. Brenman and Lacan. Brenman relates the text to the position of Narcissus, whether Narcissus is cited or not: "As long as a narrative relies on the position of characters, as long as it puts into play a certain conception of the self, it is bound to cite Narcissus, willingly or not. It necessarily repeats the erasure which the Ovidian narrative exemplifies."[110]

9.   The "Real" Thing: A Micro-History of Mirrors as Material Production

Narcissus used his pool as a place for reflection. This means that water itself, as a reflective surface, may be the first mirror in existence, a dangerous one at that. As G. Genette says, "Water is the locus of all betrayals and of all inconstancies: in the reflection it proposes, Narcissus is neither able to recognize himself without disquietude, nor to love without danger."[111] Other people's faces, in that they reflect our own actions, words, and expressions, may also be cited, along with water, as reflective surfaces.

Mirrors as objects, as material production or crafts, were created "to perpetuate [the] miraculous phenomenon...of Man's reflection in water,"[112] since calm water, as Narcissus discovered, is a natural reflective surface. The mirror itself may be as ancient as its myth. The discovery of glass, without which later mirrors could not be made, goes back to the Phoenicians and the Egyptians. The Phoenicians were supposedly the first accidental "makers" of glass itself. It is ironic that it was Pliny the Elder who describes, in one of his thirty-seven tomes of *Natural History*, the discovery of glass, especially since he himself perished when Vesuvius erupted in 79 B.C.E. He describes sailors of a ship laden with nitrum (sod and potash) who were preparing a meal on a beach. Since they could not find stones to prop up their cooking vessels, they used nitrum from their ship, which fused with the shore's sand, and thereby witnessed a metamorphosis: a new translucent liquid flowed from under their pots, and this was the origin, says Pliny, of glass.

It is known that the Phoenicians used glass as a glaze for pottery as early as 3000 B.C.E. In Mesopotamia, seals and glass beads date from 2500 B.C.E, according to archeological evidence. The earliest known beads of glass from Egypt date from around 1500 B.C.E. By the fifth century B.C.E., glass was made in Greece, and through their conquests and trade, the Romans spread the use of glass technology and the use of glass objects as far as China, Scandinavia, and the British Isles. When the Roman Empire fell, Constantine moved to Byzantium, where glass continued to be made. It went into decline, however, and did not become popular again until the seventh century A.D. when objects were found in Torcello, an island near Venice. The coincidence between this and Venice's later predominance in becoming the very centre of mirror-making, as we now know them (the use of glass with a metallic backing), is significant.

We must remember that when Saint Paul says, in I Corinthians 13, that "now we see in a glass darkly," he does not mean metallic-backed glass mirrors, as we now think of them. Those only came into existence in the twelfth and thirteenth centuries. Mirrors were first made of polished metals, or reflective surfaces such as obsidian.

The round mirror retrieved in archeological digs at Susa, ancient capital of Elam, situated southwest of what is today Iran, may very well be the original prototype of mirrors later found in Egypt, Greece, Etruria, in Scythian regions, Persia, China. The Cairo Museum owns a beautiful hand-held polished metal mirror with a handle made of ivory that dates from the twentieth century B.C.E., and it is displayed along with Tutankhamen's treasures. This pharaoh reigned from 1354 to 1346 B.C.E.

Bronze Scythian mirrors have been found in the Caucasus. Not only is it stated in the Hebrew Bible's Genesis myth that God created persons "in His own image," but in Exodus 38.8, we learn that for the altar of the holocaust, Moses made "the bronze basin and its bronze support from the mirrors of the women who served at the entrance of the tent of Meeting."[113] The Chinese bequeathed to the world mirrors made of bronze that were platinized or silvered. Bronze, silver, gold, tin, steel, iron pyrite, volcanic glass (obsidian), and rock-crystal were all used throughout the centuries for productions of reflecting surfaces.[114] Decorative designs were frequently imprinted on the backs of polished metallic surfaces, making of them objects of beauty, just as their reflective side implied the reflection of beauty – or of "reality."

Slightly convex disks of metal were used in ancient and classical times. Hand mirrors were adopted from the Etruscans and the Romans by the Celts, and by the end of the early Middle Ages they were common throughout Europe. In one Etruscan tomb that I have seen, a woman is depicted as admiring herself in her mirror. It is said that the Athenian Demosthenes, 384 B.C.E, practiced his speeches and gestures facing a reflective surface.[115] He had elocutionary problems at the beginning of his career, and he practiced so as to correct them. He went on to become, as we know, a magnificent orator and political figure. Language is foregrounded in Demosthenes's case, as is beauty, life, "reality," and death in the Etruscan woman's depiction. All of these elements appear in the Narcissus myth – and in the texts "sighted" in this book.

The scientific importance of mirrors became apparent when Euclid (third century B.C.E.) laid the foundation of optics, particularly of catoptrics, defined by *Webster* as "relating to a mirror or reflected light: produced by or based on reflection." Ptolemy and Hero of Alexandria went on to develop Euclid's principles. The work of Arab and Italian mathematicians, in the Middle Ages, made all kinds of mirrors possible – flat, curved (concave and convex), "burning" and magic mirrors in various shapes, ellipses, columns, pyramids, etc.[116]

Women hung small elaborately decorated mirrors from their belts during the Middle Ages and later. The use of glass with a metallic backing began to be fabricated in the twelfth and thirteenth centuries, and by the time of the Italian Renaissance, Venice (or Murano), and then Nurenberg, became the centres of mirror production, with their new techniques for blowing glass.

Venetian mirrors were highly prized, especially those with bevelled edges. By the seventeenth century, the secrets of Venetian mirror-making had been divulged, and they were extensively made known and reproduced in Paris and London. They were expensive, and large ones caused wonder, admiration, and envy.

In a collection that came from the house of Leonardo da Vinci, mottoes were inscribed on the back of mirrors. One in particular may have Narcissus as an intertext. It says: "To be together or to die," a motto that would be entirely applicable to B. d'Aurevilly's heroes in *Une Page d'histoire*. Leonardo, among other painters, thought that looking at one's painting in a mirror was an instructive exercise. His interest was in the exact duplication of reality: "When you wish to see if your picture is exactly like the real thing," he said, "take a mirror, reflect the living model in it, and compare this reflection with your work – and see how near the original is to the copy."[117] Mirrors in texts – texts in mirrors: this chiasmus is meaningful when one remembers that Leonardo's own texts were frequently written in mirror-writing, that is, in reverse.

By the eighteenth century, large mirrors for public consumption began to be produced in France. They were sometimes surrounded by frames that held candlesticks, thereby increasing the lighting properties of their reflections. The tradition became established to incorporate mirrors over mantlepieces and doors. The architectural uses of mirrors grew, and became more elaborate. Full-length ones supported by tall frames with feet became popular in the nineteenth century, and soon they were built into wardrobes and other pieces of furniture. Zola's Nana was thereby able to adore her own image in a full-length mirror.

"Burning glass," *Webster* says, was "a positive lens for producing intense heat by converging the sun's rays approximately to the principal focus of the lens the point of convergence being a very small image of the sun". It was used in antiquity. Like language, it could focus on a given target to the point of "firing it up." Curved mirrors could be spherical, cylindrical, parabolic, ellipsoidal, or hyperboloidal. They, too, resembled language: they could be elliptical or hyperbolic. They could diminish or exaggerate, make what was reflected small or large. Fun-house mirrors can be fun, making the observer with a sense of humour look fat or thin, tall or short, crooked or straight. But like language, once again, they can amuse or terrify, create identity or bring to mind alienation, the void. Mirrors are metaphors for both life and death.

It was in the middle of the seventeenth century that mirrors began to be used to double the size of rooms. Until then they were made, mostly, in Venice/Murano, and were fairly small, only about twenty-eight inches high. Toward the end of the century, however, new technology in Italy caused envy in Colbert, and he started to bring Murano specialists to France so as to create mirrors that were about nine feet tall. Mirror plate was placed in panelling, in decorative frames, and even on ceilings for decoration or the enlargement of spaces. Colbert's machinations in using diplomats, allies, spies and in kidnapping Venitians for their knowledge, the most famous example of mirror galleries in the world became the Hall of Mirrors at Versailles. The centre of the industry, which was initially called *La Manufacture des Glaces de Miroir* was in the faubourg Saint-Antoine. It then became known, outside of Paris, as the Manufacture Royale de Saint-Gobain, and it exists still today. I only learned, recently, when I visited Saint-Gobain, that the glass panels that I. M. Pei designed to be used to create the world-famous glass Pyramid that is now the entrance to the Louvre were created in Saint-Gobain. This is ironic, since Louis XIV hated the Louvre as a residence, and constructed Versailles, instead, as a magnificent monument to his reign as the Sun King. Mirrors were used throughout to add brilliance and light to the Sun King's abode.

Let us return to the Galerie des Glaces at Versailles. It possesses seventeen arched doors adorned with bevelled mirrors in bronze gilt mouldings. They stretch rhythmically along the 225 feet of the Hall and duplicate the windows on the opposite side. In *Le Mercure gallant*, Donneau de Visé called the mirrors "pseudo-windows placed opposite the real ones," and he said that they "multiplied a million times over the gallery's size, so that it seems to have no end." [118] They are 73 meters long, 10,50 wide, and 12,30 high. Mansart built the Galerie in 1678 (the same year *La Princesse de Clèves* was published). The marble was added on to the walls in 1679, and the sculptures were put in place in 1680. Le Brun painted the arches, or vaulting, between 1681 to 1684. The Gallery incorporated the terrace built by Le Vau, a gigantic balcony from which the King and his Court could watch the sunlight playing on the fountains, amid a setting of trees and flowers. The Sun King wished to reflect and magnify his power and his glory into infinity, and the lavish use of mirrors helped him do just that. As J. Baudrillard says, "it is no accident that the century of Louis XIV can be summed up by the Galerie des glaces..."[119]

Roche, Baltrusaitis, Eymard, Goldberg, Nüridsany, Melchior-Bonnet, in *L'Histoire du miroir* (1994), and more recently, DeJean, in *The Essence of Style* (2005), tell the tale of how mirrors came into being, and then analyze the sociological, historical, and ideological implications of their production throughout the centuries. Melchior-Bonnet, in particular, shows the importance of the mirror in antiquity and how it related to medieval spirituality. In describing its importance to humanism, she depicts how mirrors were considered to be a self-portrait of God. She signals the relationship between the Renaissance and the way humankind came to focus upon itself, a point made, as well, by Baltrusaitis. Due to the importance of its fabrication during the seventeenth century, Melchior-Bonnet and DeJean show the cloak-and-dagger means utilized by French officials (mostly Colbert) to entice and kidnap Murano mirror-makers to France to ply their trade and their secrets. Many of these workers lost their lives in the social, political, and economic intrigues that dominated a State that saw mirrors as a necessary reflection of its social, political, and material grandeur. Its narcissistic need to reflect itself became greater and greater, as technical improvements and skills made the size as well as the demand for mirrors increase. By using Italian mirror-makers, the manufacturing company of Saint-Gobain made that expansion possible.

J. DeJean (her book is subtitled "How the French Invented High Fashion, Fine Food, Chic Cafés, Style, Sophistication, and Glamour") traces the prime elements of what we call "style" today, to the reign of Louis XIV and to Versailles.[120] She devotes chapters to hairdressing, haute couture, shoes, cooking, cafés, champagne, diamonds, the illumination of Paris, the invention of the umbrella, shopping, perfumes, cosmetics, and "la toilette." Chapter 9 is devoted almost entirely to the political schemes, plots and intrigues of Colbert as well as the extent to which he went to bring mirrors to

Versailles. Mirrors, diamonds, and the use of thousands of candles, whose lights were reflected in those mirrors made Versailles the palace of light, a suitable metaphor for a Sun King. They helped create the means of the Sun King's making his magnificent chateau the most luminous and "glitzy" (DeJean's word) palace on earth. J. DeJean's chapter 9 is entitled "Power Mirrors." She begins her chapter by saying that "mirrored ceilings, dressing rooms with floor-to-ceiling mirrors, mirror-lined elevators – mirrors are now so ubiquitous that very few people realize that they were once both fabulously expensive and immensely rare, the ultimate luxe commodity and power toy."[121] No one visiting Paris and France today can fail to notice how many mirrors exist everywhere, both inside and outside of buildings.

In 1666, Louis XIV visited the new mirror factory in the Faubourg Saint Antoine, where various workers had either been poisoned, or had committed suicide so as not to reveal their secrets. In despair, they had lost hope of ever returning to their home country. They longed for Venice, or Murano, and their families, from whom they had been kidnapped. Colbert's mastery in seducing Murano experts in mirror-making is called, by DeJean, "a long-running soap opera," given all the diplomatic as well as undiplomatic means that were used to extricate the secrets of mirror-making, of bringing the specialized workers to Saint-Gobain, and of showing how the new fashion for mirrors expanded, in a feverish fashion. One can "sight" them in the Maisons-Lafitte (Galerie des Glaces, 1650), in Versailles (1679-1694), in the Salon de la Guerre (1680), in Bavarian rococco castles such as the "Galleria degli spechi" in Mantua. At Versailles, Louis XIV even constructed outdoor grottoes that were covered with mirrors. Throughout Europe mirrors became more and more popular, and by the eighteenth-century they were placed on the walls of cafés, bars, above fire-places. They were used extensively in public places.[122] In the nineteenth century one cannot but think of Manet's famous painting of the woman standing before a mirror at the bar, in the circus. The ubiquity of mirrors, in the twentieth and twenty-first centuries, not only in Paris, but in all of France, cannot fail to be noticed by visitors to France.

Those acquainted with Louis XIV's court knew what mirrors could do: they multiplied "cette galerie qui paraist n'avoir point de fin," as the Sun King hoped to do with his own realm.[123] But an incident that is narrated about Louis XIV reveals "the other side" of his own discovery of mirrors. In the *Journal des Sçavants* (1679), it was related that the first time a full-sized mirror was placed before Louis XIV in order for him to appreciate its size and effect. He was holding a sword in his hand, and when the king looked up he saw a man, holding a sword, facing him. He was asked to advance, and as he did the figure he saw holding a sword "advanced" toward him. He believed that he was under attack. He manifested so much fear and was so ashamed of having shown fear that he asked that the mirror be removed.[124]

Later he came to appreciate the value, the glamour, and the shining glitter that huge mirrors could provide. The "magnificence" of his realm, his desire for grandeur and for making Versailles the most shining place in all the earth belied the nefarious side of what the mirrors could also reveal: the fear of Louis the Fourteenth.

*   *   *   *

It is not surprising that the context for a novel such as *La Princesse de Clèves* (1578), even though based on sixteenth-century historical facts, would reflect the magnificence of its own seventeenth-century times. That its mirror-scenes and personages would reveal what lay beneath the surface is also true. The structure of the novel mirrors its meanings, and its meanings mirror its structure. Mirrors are mesmerizing. Madame de Lafayette would magically enthral generations of readers with the mirror-scenes and structures in and of her texts, with the texts in her mirrors.

Notes

[1] J. Baltrusaitis, *Le Miroir: Essai sur une légende scientifique – révélations, science-fiction et fallacies*, Elmayan, Le Seuil, 1975, pp. 9-13. In this book citations will first be acknowledged in the notes. Further references will be included in the body of the text. All emphases have been added and all translations are my own, unless otherwise stated.

[2] D. Colin, *Dictionnaire des symboles, des mythes et des légendes*, Hachette, Paris, 2000, p. 369.

[3] Baltrusaitis, pp. 9-13.

[4] K. Scheibe. *Mirrors, Masks, Lies and Secrets*, Praeger, New York, 1979, p. 59.

[5] ibid., p. 56.

[6] H. James, *The Art of the Novel: Critical Prefaces,* ed. R. P. Blackmur, Scribner's, New York, 1950.

[7] In *Vocabulaire d'esthétique*, Paris, PUF, 1990, p. 362. In diplomatic language, the term also means "signe en marge d'un manuscrit pour indiquer un endroit critique (t. diplom.)," in Walter v. Wartburg, *Französisches Etymologisches Wörterbuch*, Tüningen: J. C. B. Mohr [Paul Siebeck], 1949. Translations, in this book, are my own, and they are used especially in short phrases in order not to interrupt the flow of the prose. The original French passages have been maintained when deemed appropriate.

[8] Cited by T. Mermall, "The Chiasmus: Unamuno's Master Trope," *PMLA*, 105, 1990, pp. 245-255.

[9]For example, H. Horvei, *Der Chiasmus, ein Beitrag zur Figurenlehre*, Selbstverlag, Bergen, 1981; M. Weiss, *The Bible from Within: The Method of Total Interpretation*, The Magnes Press, Jerusalem, 1984; M. Burrell "Theme and Variation in the *Chanson de Roland*: The Use of Chiasmus," *Parergon*, 32, 1982, pp. 13-18; W. H. Shea, "Chiasmus and the Structure of David's Lament", *Journal of Biblical Literature*, 105, 1, 1986, pp. 13-25; *Biblical Quarterly*, 46, 1, 1984, pp. 31-33; J. Starobinski, "Sur l'emploi du chiasme dans *Le Neveu de Rameau*," *Revue de Métaphysique et de Morale*, 89, 2, 1984, pp. 182-196; Michael *Biblical Quarterly*, 46, 1, 1984, pp. 31-33; J. Starobinski, "Sur l'emploi du chiasme dans W. G. E. Watson," "Further Examples of Semantic-Sonant Chiasmus," *Catholic Biblical Quarterly*, 46, 1, 1984, pp. 31-33; M. Fishbane, *Text and Texture: Close Readings of Selected Biblical Texts*, Schocken Books, New York, 1979.

[10] Cited in the *Grand Larousse universel*, Paris, 1995, p. iii.

[11] Albin Michel, Paris, 1997, pp. 107-108.

[12] ibid.

[13] P. Bacry, *Les Figures du style*, Berlin, Paris, 1992, pp. 9-10. In Chapter I, "Des Figures," Bacry reminds his reader that the roots of many words in French are grounded in Greek vocabulary. *Le tropique*, for instance, is the parallel line located on the Equator where the inclination of the sun is reversed at the moment of the solstice; the "heliotrope" is a flower that, as we all know, "turns itself towards the sun." That is why tropes have been used, since Antiquity, to designate figures of speech that seem to make words change their meaning (p. 9).

[14] Bacry, pp. 120-124.

[15] D. Rice, "Metaphor, Metonymy, and Synecdoche Revis(it)ed," *Semiotica*, The Hague, Mouton 21, 1-2, 1977 p. 145. In his introduction to Dumarsais-Fontanier's *Les Tropes*, 1, Slatkine Reprints, Génève, 1967, Gérard Genette reminds us that "aujourd'hui où les développements des études inspiréees par...Saussure met au premier plan les problèmes de la signification dans tous les ordres du langage, il est presque inutile d'insister sur l'intérêt que présente un retour sur les oeuvres maîtresses de la tradition rhétorique"(vi).

[16] Bacry, p. 123.

[17] ibid., p. 123.

[18] ibid., p. 124.

[19] In "Freud's Masterplot," *Yale French Studies*, ed. "Questions of Reading: Otherwise" New Haven: Yale University Press, pp. 279-300.

[20] ibid., pp. 287-288.

[21] M. Nüridsany, *Effets de miroir: textes choisis par Michel Nüridsany*, IAPIF, Paris, 1989, p. 114.

[22] A. L. Strauss, *Mirrors and Masks: The Search for Identity*, London, New Brunswick Transaction Publishers, 1997, p. 36.

[23] "Un roman est un miroir qui se promène sur une grande route. Tantôt il reflète à nos yeux l'azur des cieux, tantôt la fange des bourbiers de la route." Stendhal initially attributes the epigraph to Saint-Réal, in chapter XIII, but in a simpler form: "Un roman c'est un miroir qu'on promène le long d'un chemin." Stendhal, *Le Rouge et le noir*, éd. La Pléiade, II, Gallimard, Paris, 1952, chap 19, p. 557.

[24] M. Lowrie, *Horace's Narrative Odes*, UP, Oxford, 1997, p. 351.

[25] M. A. Caws, *The Art of Interference: Stressed Readings in Verbal and Visual Texts*, Princeton University Press, Princeton, 1989, p. 239.

[26] L. Dällenbach, *The Mirror in the Text*, transl. J. Whiteley with E. Hughes, Chicago UP, Chicago, 1989. Originally published as *Le Récit spéculaire: essai sur la mise en abyme*, Ed. du Seuil, Paris, 1977.

[27] G. Charpy, *Volubilis des miroirs*, J. Dullis, Paris, 1974.

[28] ibid., p. 26.

[29] G. Deleuze, *Logique du sens*, Editions de minuit, Paris, 1969, p. 19. Deleuze says this in his "1ère série de paradoxes – effets de surface."

[30] L. Marin, *Le Portrait du roi*, Editions de minuit, Paris, 1981, p. 226.

[31] Cited by M. Gardner in *The Annotated Alice*, Penguin Books, London, 1970, n.4, pp. 27-28.

[32] ibid., p. 28.

[33] L. Carroll, *Alice's Adventures in Wonderland*, Macmillan & Co., London, 1859, p.6. Emphases are added, unless otherwise noted.

[34] S. Freud, *Beyond the Pleasure Principle*, trans. J. Strachey, Liveright Publishing Co., New York, 1950, pp. 13-14.

[35] ibid., p. 14.

[36] Carroll, p. 91.

[37] ibid., p. 94.

[38] I am grateful to Richard A. Watson, a fellow at the Camargo Foundation, spring 1995, for pointing out Lecercle's text to me. I am also grateful to Pat Watson for learned and humane exchanges on an astounding variety of subjects, as well as to Patrick Henry and Mary Ann Henry for their helpful suggestions on the chapter on *La Princesse de Clèves*.

[39] S. Loyd. *Cyclopedia of Puzzles*, Lamb Publishing Co., New York, 1914, p. 114.

[40] In Gardner's *The Annotated Alice*, p. 95, n. 3.

[41] ibid., pp. 97-98. Emphases added except in "it *is* the same thing with you".

[42] See Gardner, pp. 58-98, n. 6, for a complete rendition of Jane Taylor's poem.

[43] Deleuze, pp. 46-47.

[44] See E. Pellizer's article on "Reflections, Echoes and Amorous Reciprocity: On Reading the Narcissus Story," in *Interpretations of Greek Mythology*, ed. J. Bremmer, C. Helm, London, 1987, pp. 107-120. The expression I later use to refer to Echo's verbal reflexivity as being "specular vocality" is used by Pellizer, p. 113.

[45] In *The Narcissus Theme in Western European Literature Up to the Early Nineteenth Century*, trans. R. Dewsnap in coll. with L. Grönlund, and N. Reeves, in coll. with I. Söderberg-Reeves, Gleerups, Lund, 1967.

[46] Ovid. *Metamorphoses*. Loeb Classical Literary ed., Harvard University Press, Cambridge, 1984.

[47] ibid., p. 149.

[48] The Loeb translation is too gender-restrictive: p. 148, lines 345. Translation mine, since the Loeb Classical Library translates "iam tunc qui posset amari" as "whom a nymph might love even as a child" (p. 149).

[49] Ovid, p. 149.

[50] ibid., p. 152.

[51] ibid., p. 151, p. 153.

[52] ibid., p. 153.

[53] ibid., pp. 154-55.

[54] ibid., p. 155.

[55] ibid., .p. 155.

[56] ibid., p. 155.

[57] ibid., p. 155.

[58] ibid., p. 157.

[59] ibid., p. 157.

[60] ibid., p. 159.

[61] ibid., p. 161.

[62] Brooks Otis sees Narcissus as part of a series of vengeance episodes, but "amatory pathos" also connects the text to its context, he says. (See Vinge, p. 3).

[63] Note 18, p. 31 of B. Bray's "Transformation du roman épistolaire au vingtième siècle," in *Romantishe Zeitschrift für Litteraturgeschichte*, Heidelberg, 1977, pp. 23-39.

[64] The quotation from Molinié's *Dictionnaire de rhétorique* is found in M.-C. Grassi's *Lire l'épistolaire*, Dunod, Paris, 1958, p. 32.

[65] Grassi, p. 32.

[66] Ovid, p. 155.

[67] ibid., p. 154, lines 446-7.

[68] ibid., p. 155.

[69] ibid., p. 159.

[70] ibid., p. 159.

[71] ibid., p. 159.

[72] ibid., p. 155.

[73] See Vinge's representation of Philostratus in her chapter on "Descriptions in Prose of Works of Art Representing Narcissus", p. 29.

[74] Cited by Vinge, p. 29.

[75] Vasari, *Lives of Seventy of the Most Eminent Painters, Sculptors, and Architects*, ed. E. H. and E. W. Blankfield and A. A. Hopkins, I, Scribner's, New York, 1926, p. 78.

[76] Cited by Vinge, pp. 29-30.

[77] Plato, *The Republic*, X.

[78] Ovid, p. 434, line 432.

[79] Vinge, p. 13.

[80] Ovid, p. 154, line 344.

[81] Pausanias, *Description of Greece*, trans. W. H. S. Jones, Loeb Classical Library, Cambridge, 1935. ("On Boetia" IX:31:7-9).

[82] Pellizer, p. 112.

[83] Pausanias. See Books VIII-X, 4, p. 311. Reference in p. 81.

[84] Ovid, p. 161.

[85] Vinge, p. 51.

[86] See J. Berman, *Narcissism and the Novel*, N.Y.U. University Press, New York, 1990.

[87] Kernberg's book, *Borderline Conditions and Pathological Narcissism*, Jason Aronson, New York, 1975, is a classic in the field. Kohut's book on Narcissism is entitled *The Analysis of the Self*, International University Press, New York, 1971.

[88] American Psychiatric Association, *Diagnostic and Statistical Manual of Mental Disorders*, 3rd ed., American Psychiatric Association, Washington, D.C., 1980, p. 315.

[89] Vinge, pp. 50-54.

[90] Berman, pp. 1-55.

[91] L. Barkan In *The Gods made Flesh: Metamorphosis and the Pursuit of Paganism*, Yale University Press, New Haven, 1986, pp. 89-90.

[92] Barkan, p. 49.

[93] See P. Henry's article on "Pygmalion in the *Essais*: 'De l'affection des pères aux enfans'", *The French Review* 68, 2, 1994, pp. 229-238.

[94] In "An Impossible Response: The Disaster of Narcissus," 104, *Yale French Studies*, n. 79, *Literature and the Ethical Question*, Yale University Press, New Haven, 1991, pp. 103-134.

[95] M. Butor, N. 36 in «Transformation... » p. 38.

[96] J. Lacan, *Ecrits*, Seuil, Paris, 1966, p. 93. See also pp. 112-113.

[97] ibid., p. 113.

[98] Ibid.

[99] *Séminaire I*, cf. "Sur le Narcissisme," and "Les deux narcissismes", Seuil, Paris, 1975, pp. 125-147.

[100] Lacan, *Ecrits*, p. 113.

[101] *Séminaire I*, p. 115.

[102] ibid., p. 116.

[103] ibid., p. 117.

[104] Ibid.

[105] See « L'Instance de la lettre dans l'inconscient ou la raison depuis Freud, » *Ecrits*, p. 497.

[106] Lacan states: "Qu'on reprenne donc l'oeuvre de Freud à la *Traumdeutung* pour s'y rappeler que le rêve a la structure d'une phrase, ou plutôt, à nous en tenir à la lettre, d'un rébus, c'est-à-dire d'une écriture, dont le rêve de l'enfant représenterait l'idéographie primordiale, et qui chez l'adulte reproduit l'emploi phonétique et symbolique à la fois des éléments signifiants, que l'on retrouve aussi bien dans les hiéroglyphes de l'ancienne Egypte que dans les caractères dont la Chine conserve l'image," *Ecrits*, p. 267.

[107] Cited in *Le Miroir*, p. 9.

[108] Baltrusaitis, p. 13.

[109] J. Lacan. "Fonction et champ de la Parole et du Langage", *Ecrits*, p. 268. Emphases added.

[110] n. 2 in Claire Nouvet's chapter in *Yale French Studies*, no. 79, p. 104.

[111] G. Genette, *Figures I*, Seuil, Paris, 1966, p. 21.

[112] S. Roche, *Mirrors*, Gerald Duckworth & Co., London, 1967, p. 5. Information concerning this aspect of the book was gathered from many sources, including the *Grand Larousse du dix-neuvième siècle*, various editions of the *Encyclopedia Brittanica*; J. Baudrillard's *Le Système des objets*, 1968; J. Rosset's *L'Intérieur et l'extérieur: Essais sur la poésie et sur le théâtre au XVIIe siècle*, José Corti, Paris, 1968; J. Eymard's *Le thème du*

miroir dans la poésie française, 1540-1815, Service de reproduction des thèses, Lille, 1975; J. Grenier's *Miroirs,* Fata Morgana, Paris, 1980; J. Baltrusaitis's, *Le Miroir,* 1975; B. Goldberg's *The Mirror and Man,* University Press of Virginia, Charlottesville, 1985; M. Nüridsany's selection of texts in *Effets de miroir,* IAPIF, Ivry-sur-Seine, 1989; S. Melchior-Bonnet's *Histoire du miroir,* Editeurs Imago, Paris, 1994; J. DeJean's *The Essence of Style,* Free Press, New York, 2005, and a number of other texts. I have listed these chronologically.

[113] (Jerusalem Bible)

[114] Roche, p. 5.

[115] Readers of Stendhal will recognize an example of this in the bishop of Agde's practicing the delivery of his benedictions in front of a large mirror, as Julien Sorel looks on, in *Le Rouge et le noir* [chap. XVIII].

[116] Roche, p. 6.

[117] Cited by Roche, p. 10.

[118] Quoted by Roche, p. 23.

[119] J. Baudrillard, *Le Système des objets,* Gallimard, Paris, 1968.

[120] J. DeJean, *The Essence of Style,* Free Press, New York, 2005, p. 188.

[121] DeJean, p. 177.

[122] Baltrusaitis, p. 24.

[123] Melchior-Bonnet states that although in December 1682 the back of the Galeries had not yet been finished, the décors that had been ordered in 1678 for the royal fêtes were put in place. The description published in the *Mercure* (an apposite name for the newspaper, since mercury and silver coated the backs of glass mirrors) is worthy of citation: "'Les glaces font de fausses fenêtres vis-à-vis des véritables et multiplient un million de fois cette galerie qui paraist n'avoir point de fin, quoy qu'il n'y ait qu'un bout qu'on voye...' Des brancarts d'argent supportant des girandoles alternent avec des caisses d'orangers d'argent; torchères, chandeliers, lustres, girandoles posées sur des guéridons devant les glaces étincellent de mille feux et renvoient leurs reflets" (p. 57).

[124] This anecdote was related by E. G. Robertson in his *Mémoires récréatifs, scientifiques, et anecdotiques,* Paris, 1831, p. 344, n. 22. He refers to the *Journal des Sçavans,* 1679, pp. 284-288.

Chapter II

The Mirror in the Middle: Mme de Thémines's Letter in Lafayette's *La Princesse de Clèves*

"La fameuse *mise en abyme* se retrouve un
peu partout depuis des siècles."
Claude Ollier

"What we call 'our' time is always made up of
fragments of 'the past.'"
Charles Martindale

1.   History, Fiction, Structure and Meaning

In what has been called the first modern French novel, *La Princesse de Clèves* (1678)[1]Marie-Madeleine Pioche de la Vergne, Comtesse de Lafayette (1634-1693), used her carefully researched historical references to the sixteenth-century's world of courtly manners, especially to the last year of Henri II's reign, to reflect the seventeenth-century world in which she lived. She also used those references to undermine many of the conventions of her own day. In fact and in fiction she chose to situate her novel within the context of a year's time (1558-59), as references to Elizabeth's ascension to the throne of England, the marriage of Elisabeth de France, and Henri II's death attest.[2] Also, the very custom of creating miniature portraits, used so adroitly in *La Princesse de Clèves*, had its origin in the 16th century, but continued into the 17th and 18th centuries. The expression "faire faire son portrait" is replete with meaning, if we consider the various meanings the expression can acquire when one thinks of author, narrator, narratee, the personnages being depicted, and their social surroundings in a novel, not to mention the mythic and ekphrastic reverberations the use of the phrase elicits.

"*Histoire*": history and story. Both are enmeshed in Lafayette's novel. Her work may be compared to Louis XIV's using his *Galerie des Glaces* to reflect the grandeurs of his kingdom, on the one hand, and to model a world that, due to those very mirrors, revealed not only the luxuries, but also the excesses and infamies of his reign.[3]

After her marriage, Lafayette surrounded herself in her *hôtel particulier* in Paris on the Rue de Vaugirard with literary and political notables of her day. Her circle of intimate friends included La

Rochefoucauld, Mme de Sévigné, the future Mme de Maintenon, Pierre Corneille, La Fontaine. Lafayette was also close to Daniel Huet, Ménage, and Ségrais. Ménage, in particular, took her under his wing, and had her read Vergil, the novels of Scudéry, and "the interminable history books that the century adored reading."[4]

Françoise Bertaut de Motteville (1621-1689), an older friend of Lafayette's, who had been *femme de chambre* and confidante of Anne d'Autriche, Infanta of Spain and Queen of France by marriage to Louis XIII, and Queen Regent during Louis XIV's childhood, told Lafayette tales of the life she had lived, tales that were later published as *Mémoires* of Anne d'Autriche's court. They resemble, in tone and tenor, Lafayette's own carefully crafted tales about the reign of Henri II.

While the narratives of Motteville influenced Lafayette, other sources of *La Princesse de Clèves* include works by Pierre Mathieu (1631), Mézéray (1643-1651), Jean Le Laboureur (1659), and by others who wrote about the intricate ceremonies of the sixteenth-century's French royal court. Lafayette read Brantôme's *Hommes illustres, Dames illustres*, and *Dames galantes*. She read André Du Chesne on Anne de Boulen (Anne Boleyn), and the *Annals* of Francis Godwin that were translated into French in 1647. She found a description of the historical "Nemours" in Brantôme, and she knew that he had had a passionate love affair with Anne d'Este, whom he married after the death of her husband, François de Guise.

In his introduction to the Pléiade edition of *Romanciers français du XVIIe siècle*, A. Adam states a partial truth: "*La Princesse de Clèves*," he says, "is first and foremost a historical novel."[5] It would perhaps be more appropriate to call it a novel in which historical elements figure, most intricately, in the framework of its fictive textual production. F. Beasley said it well when she remarked that Lafayette deliberately rescripted history so as to promote a transformation, not merely a transcription of the past. Lafayette's aim, says Beasley, was to provide plausible conduct for women in her own day.[6]

Lafayette had initially considered giving the title *Mémoires*, a genre in its own right, to her novel.[7] It became, however, *La Princesse de Clèves*. This is, in itself, significant. It points to the fact that her works were not "romans à clef,"[8] something many of her contemporaries believed to be the case due to the careful manner in which she constructed, to rephrase Stendhal, her "mirror along a courtly road." Positively, it points to the creative method she used to rescript the past and weave those carefully researched historical threads into and throughout the tapestry of her fiction. In speaking of *Zaïde*, Lafayette's second novella, Niderst describes her work as containing precise historical information that alters or provides nuances to the author's creative intentions (xix-xx). The way in which Lafayette constructed her text, logically, clearly, coherently, tells us that it is a seventeenth-century classical *oeuvre* that was part of a society in which *galeries des glaces* were used to compose and expand the beauties of its reflected universe. But there are, as always, other sides to mirrors: "classical" and "baroque" frequently go hand in hand. Chiastic and imbricated structures, which might be considered as "classical," are inscribed in Lafayette's usage of hyperbole, which could be called "baroque."

In her introduction to Marie-Catherine, Comtesse d'Aulnoy's *Contes de Fées,* E. Lemirre sees two perspectives depicted. Fairy-tales, she says, were filled with "pierreries," with jewel-like reflections of matter. But there are also reflected images that are other than dream-like: "It's their own reality that worldly men and women who love to tell tales place "en abyme.'"[9] Hyperboles of desire form part of d'Aulnoy's *Oiseau bleu* (1697). She describes 60,000 women admiring themselves with pleasure in a large valley that contained nothing but mirrors. Each woman saw herself as she would like to be: redheads were blond, brunettes had black hair, the old saw themselves as young.[10]. D'Aulnoy also relates how Queen Florine, who had gone looking for her prince charming, arrives at the foot of a steep mountain that is prodigiously high. One side of it is made of ivory, the other of glass.

These narratives take us back to the tradition of Marie de France, one of France's first women poets. The world she reflected in her *Lais* was a courtly one, as is the one reflected in *La Princesse de Clèves.* Like D'Aulnoy's it was something of a fairy tale, on the one hand, filled with the hyperbolic beauty of a supremely elegant and majestic court that was decorated with "fine gold and surrounded with pearls." But the reality of the "magnificence" mirrored in *La Princesse de Clèves* there displays, chiastically, a constantly corroding and corrupting universe that was filled with passion, jealousies, envy, and lies. Reflections, imbrications, counterpoints: all of these words apply not only to the novel's micro- and macro-dispositions, to rhetorically chiastic phrases and structures that are singularly contained within a universe that is classically ordered, structured, and closed, but also to a world that is excessive, ambiguous, multivalent, and open. As G. Slethaug says in his preface to *Beautiful Chaos,* "randomness and order are self-referential iterations, each reflecting and reversing the other, simultaneously held together and pulled apart" (x).[11]

Chiasmus represents similarity as well as contrast. In *La Princesse de Clèves* it relates to the unity of passion shared by Mme de Clèves and Nemours, to the similarity between Mme de Clèves's and Mme de Thémines's passion, to mirror-scenes with which the novel is filled, as well as to the other side of passion, to the nefarious influence of jealousy, misinterpretation, confusion, and lies. These pervade the court and slowly make their way into Mme de Clèves's own discoveries of what is found inside the looking glass: herself. She too will discover passion and the nefarious consequences of jealousy in a text that Lafayette deliberately and strategically places at the centre of her work: Mme de Thémines's letter. The letter, this "mirror in the middle," shapes, more than any other "narrative," Mme de Clèves's perceptions of herself, and reveals to her a sorority that she will join, embrace, and emulate. L. Horowitz describes the infinitely complicated trajectory of Mme de Thémines's letter. Horowitz says Lafayette repeats historical names, such as "Amboise," or the "anciens ducs d'Aquitaine," and she states that Lafayette's goal was to evoke "an entire civilization and culture, from its moments of origin to the time of its demise in the religious warfare about to erupt as the events of Lafayette's novel unfold." She links historical names to their precedents, thereby showing the admixture of present to past, of passion to death.[12].

Most critics who have written about the imbricated narratives in *La Princesse de Clèves* (1678) agree that the passions and intrigues depicted in them occupy an integral place in the novel.[13] And yet, the mirror function of Mme de Thémines's letter in relation to the heroes' final interchange, and the way interlocking order operates in the novel's structure have not been sufficiently sighted for what in-sights they bring.[14]

While it has been said that the division of *La Princesse de Clèves* into four parts has, primarily, to do with the way in which the novel was first published, that is, in four different "volumes," the geographically symbolic disposition of Books I and II, a-b--b-a (Paris-Coulommiers--Coulommiers-Paris), and the interlocking structure of Books III and IV, a-b-a--a-b-a (Paris-Coulommiers-Paris--Paris-Coulommiers-Paris), are basic to the meaning of the text. Each book has approximately the same number of pages, Book III being slightly longer than the others. There are four imbricated narratives in the text, and the one revolving around Mme de Thémines's letter, which, by being the fourth account, is the most important incident in Mme de Clèves's affective development, is told at the end of Book II and is continued in the beginning of Book III. It is the novel's most significant *mise en abyme*, and it is privileged by its central location in the text.[15]

The novel's structural patterns reveal the evolution of the discovery of jealousy and love by Mme de Clèves, and show how repetition and resemblance are proleptic of Mme de Clèves's unfolding insights into her self and her world. As these patterns develop, she finally becomes who she is and what the novel becomes when she decides to exile herself from Nemours. While the novel has been called, by some, a *Bildungsroman*, the term applies only up to a point because it denies the synchronic aspects that enhance the text, and settles for diachronicity alone.[16]

The order in which the imbricated narratives are recounted is fundamental to the text's rhetorical strategy. They concern, in the main, Mme de Valentinois, Mme de Tournon, Anne de Boulen, and Mme de Thémines. The arrangement of rescripted historical vs. fictive accounts is disposed in imbricated order, that is: Valentinois (hist.)-Tournon (fict.)-Boulen (hist.)-

Thémines (hist./fict.) Not only does the juxtaposition of history to fiction cause the historical to valorize the fictive, as many critics have noted, but it also causes the fictive to valorize the historical: one becomes a reflection of the other. [17] The last imbrication, Mme de Thémines's letter, is an admixture of both. The letter that both "pre-flects" and reflects, both prefaces and perfects Mme de Clèves's actions, is most likely based upon Lafayette's hearing a similar incident narrated to her by her older friend, Mme de Motteville. Although Motteville's records of events, entitled *Mémoires de Mme de Moteville sur Anne d'Autriche et sa Cour*[18] were published well after her death, there is little doubt that the latter influenced her younger friend's perceptions of history, of oral narratives, and of her writing style.

Chapter VII (vol.I) of Motteville's *Mémoires* begins with the narration of an episode that took place in 1643 involving a lost and found letter, as well as the intricate set of circumstances that had to do with finding out who was its scriptor. By using this intertext, the language of which sounds very similar to that of *La Princesse de Clèves's* narrator, Lafayette creates a reflexive alchemy of history and imaginative prose.[19]

There is imbricated order in the juxtaposition of the narrators' sex. The first narrator is Mme de Chartres, the second M. de Clèves, the third the Reine Dauphine, and the fourth the Vidame de Chartres. Lafayette makes sure that the contrapuntal juxtaposition of female to male narrators emphasizes the role of woman in narrating and in the creation of discourse. An admixture of readers of Mme de Thémines's letter also reveals sexual imbrications. The letter, written by Mme de Thémines, is read by Chastelart, who gives it to the reine dauphine, who gives it to Mme de Clèves, who gives it to Nemours, who returns it to the vidame de Chartres, to whom it was originally destined. The written note by Mme d'Amboise, Mme de Clèves's friend, is what it takes to convince the latter that the missive had not been addressed to Nemours. And finally, both men and women have read it many times since, and even written about it, as I am so doing.

That each of the narrators of the imbricated narratives comes to a bad end (the first two will die, the third will eventually be decapitated, and the Vidame de Chartres will be exiled) does not bode well for the fate of those who tell tales. This is one way of saying that narrators face mortality while narratives live on. It says that the use of narrative, historical *and* fictive, is a powerful tool. Mme de Clèves could, herself, be considered the fifth imbricated narrator in her own right in the novel, since, in the end, she will tell the story of her love to Nemours, thus professing her love's intensity as well as presaging its demise. She will eventually, like the narrators who precede her, choose exile away from both court and Coulommiers.

If one considers the role of the narratees, there is a progressive development in the complexities of their situations. Mme de Clèves is the sole recipient of the first account. In the second, M. de Clèves first hears the story from Sancerre, then renarrates it, in its entirety, to his wife. In the third, Mme de Clèves is one among other ladies of the court when the Reine Dauphine tells the tale of Queen Elizabeth's mother, Anne de Boulen. The fourth narrative is the most complex: because he has lost his letter, the Vidame de Chartres narrates his series of adventures to M. de Nemours, who must relate the importance of the event to M. de Clèves in order to gain admittance to the bedroom of Mme de Clèves, to whom he retells the story. The increasing complexity of the metadiegetic narratives coincides with the increasing complexity of Mme de Clèves's own psychological development and with her growing awareness of her love for Nemours. [20]

2.   Jealousy, Mistaken Identities and Lies in the Imbricated Narratives

Lafayette builds up the narratives, reflexively, toward "the mirror in the middle," Mme de Thémines's letter. In the first episode, the Duchesse de Valentinois's liaison with Henri II is narrated by Mme de Chartres to a young and innocent Mme de Clèves shortly after her marriage, and not long after her first encounter with M. de Nemours. The events' relationship to the present is clear, since the King and Mme de Valentinois are still very much at the centre of courtly activities.

Mme de Chartres begins by revealing how Mme de Valentinois, who is the present king's mistress, and was the mistress of the king's father before him, François Ier, had managed to rid herself of her former rival, the Duchesse d'Etampes, with whom François Ier had also had a liaison. She then became the mistress of François Ier's second son, Henri II. The father was sufficiently jealous to take away his affection from Henri II and devote himself to his third son, the Duc d'Orléans. After François Ier's death, Mme de Valentinois banishes Mme d'Etampes and continues to have affairs nonetheless. One in particular, with the Comte de Brissac, brings out the king's jealousy. Not only is jealousy at the core of this narrative, but Mme d'Etampes loses all, and, eventually, so will Mme de Valentinois, after the death of Henri II. The reigning Queen will have her exiled just as Mme de Valentinois had had Mme d'Etampes exiled.

This narrative reveals a morally corrupt world that exists beneath a brilliant surface. Lafayette's friend, Motteville, uses a tone similar to that of the narrator *of La Princesse de Clèves* when she describes the court of Anne d'Autriche: "Quelle est sa corruption, et combien doit s'estimer heureux celui qui n'est point destiné à l'habiter. L'air n'y est jamais doux ni serein pour personne.... [Les courtisans] ignorent le prix de l'équité, de la justice et de la bonté... Ils sont incapables de connaître la vertu et de suivre ses maximes..." (I, pp. 99-100). In her narrative, Mme de Chartres chose the same tone as that of Mme de Motteville to emphasize the lack of virtue that existed in the court, and the distinction that exists between what is and what seems to be.

Her frequently cited phrase, "things are not what they seem," relates to mistaken identity, to the taking of one thing for another, to a quid pro quo. Mme de Clèves's reading of Mme de Thémines's letter will be just that: a quid pro quo. Mme de Chartres's account emphasizes jealousy, and jealousy leads to pain and grief. The word "jealousy" appears six times in her telling of the past. She concludes that only absence leads to wisdom, as Motteville would say in her own *Mémoires*.

Soon after Mme de Chartres concludes her narrative, Mme de Clèves will almost immediately discover that passion and jealousy are closely related. When Mme de Chartres tells her daughter that Nemours is suspected of having a secret passion for the Reine Dauphine, Mme de Clèves is so surprised by this statement, which is false, that she turns pale, returns home, and "exiles" herself in her room.

The realization that she loves occurs to Mme de Clèves because she has come to know jealousy in two ways: intellectually, through her mother's "oral history," and through an internalization of this knowledge in her own life, which is a direct result of her mother's "fiction," or "lie," to put it simply. The first imbricated narrative, the principal motifs of which are jealousy, pain, and exile, is immediately mirrored in Mme de Clèves's own experience of jealousy, pain, and temporary "exile." It prepares the use of the same motifs that will appear in Mme de Thémines's letter.

The second narrative is told to Mme de Clèves by her husband, when he goes to Coulommiers and tells his wife the story of Sancerre and of Mme de Tournon's death. Not only had Sancerre lost his mistress, but he had discovered, after her death, that she had betrayed him with his best friend, Estouteville. The experience resulting from the narration of Sancerre's jealousy is more intense for Mme de Clèves than that revealed in the first episode because it is "closer to home." It is M. de Clèves, her very own husband, who narrates the story to his wife. Both he and Mme de Clèves knew, or thought they had known, these persons well. After hearing this tale, Mme de Clèves says to her husband that she believed Mme de Tournon incapable of "either love or deception."[21] It is significant for "the mirror in the middle" that "love" and "deception," are pronounced in the same breath. This knowledge comes about as a result of ultimate "exile," or death. Mistaken judgments had been made by both M. and Mme de Clèves, and mistaken judgments will appear in Mme de Thémines's letter, as well.

Immediately after hearing this narrative, Mme de Clèves returns to Paris, where the Reine Dauphine reveals to her that Nemours had given up the possibility of a glorious marriage with Elizabeth, Queen of England, and that it is rumoured that he must have some great passion in France. For a second time Mme de Clèves goes through an acutely jealous moment when she thinks it is the Reine Dauphine who was the cause of Nemours's actions. Only when this is denied does Mme de Clèves regain peace. The internalization of her experience of jealousy follows, once again, the conclusion of the second narration. Her feelings reflect the jealousy experienced by Sancerre in the second *récit*, and are the result of mistaken identity. This taking of one thing for another, or what one might call a non-deliberate metaphor, will feature prominently in the reading of Mme de Thémines's letter.

Mme de Clèves manages, some time later, to get her friend, the Reine Dauphine, to talk about Elizabeth. The Dauphine narrates the story of Anne de Boleyn, Elizabeth's mother, who was said to have been put to death because of Henri VIII's jealousy of the Vicomte de Rochefort, an intimate friend of his wife, and because of the king's budding love for Jane Seymour. Love, jealousy, friendship, untruths, infidelity, and death are also "admixed" in this third imbricated narrative.

3.   Mme de Thémines's Letter: Losing and Finding Identity

The lost and found letter is, in its own right, not only the encoding of what J.DeJean calls an elliptical text[22] in its own right, but it is the objective correlative of the previous imbricated tales. It is a reflection of the narrations told before, where passion, jealousy, infidelity, and untruths figure prominently, and it attains even greater importance by becoming, in itself, the cause of the fourth narration, that of the Vidame de Chartres. Divided into two parts, the strategically located tale inspired by the losing and finding of a text that will be "reproduced," through inscribing reminiscences of its initial reading, poorly remembered as they are, will thus attain doubled significance. The narrator describes the purloined portrait scene and the tournament in which M. de Nemours was hurt after the third tale had been told. At the end of the tournament, Mme de Clèves was handed the letter said to have dropped out of Nemours's pocket, and was asked to read it to see whether she could recognize its author's handwriting.

No matter how sophisticated or narratologically wise the real reader is during a first reading, she is in the same situation as is Mme de Clèves in not knowing the identity of the author of the letter. Both readers share in the reading act. The novel's reader most likely takes the same amount of time to peruse this epistle as it took Mme de Clèves. Time is not telescoped. The words in the first sentence, the words on the page, are the same as are those that Mme de Clèves reads: real and fictive readers are complicitous in trying to divine the identity of the letter's writer. They suspect, if not believe, that the addressee is Nemours. By taking one thing for another, as did Narcissus when he first saw his reflection in the pool of water, the novel's heroine reflects previous examples of mistaken identity, and involves the reader more intimately in participating in "misreading."

The anonymous missive begins: "Je vous ai trop aimé pour vous laisser croire que le changement qui vous paraît en moi soit un effet de ma légèreté; je veux vous apprendre que votre infidélité en est la cause".[23] It would take eighteenth-century narrators to exploit epistolarity to the fullest, but one already sees, in this instance, a letter clearly encoding the thematics of reading, of "double" reading or of irony, into the interior of its own narrative.[24] The first part of the sentence ("je vous ai trop aimé...") reflects Mme de Clèves's situation in regard to Nemours. The second part, ("je veux vous apprendre..."), creates the image of another woman who exists, now, in Mme de Clèves's mind, and whom, she believes, is jealous of Nemours because he loves another, or more than one woman besides herself.

4.   Specular Orality – Oral Specularity

The writer of the missive, Mme de Thémines, had been the letter's first "reader" (as author), and the Vidame its second. He had bragged about its contents in front of others, who had teased him, and to defend himself he was even prepared to read passages of it aloud to his audience, who would be virtual "third readers," or oral history narratees. He cannot do so because he had haplessly lost the letter. While the real reader of the novel is told, by the narrator, immediately after perusing the letter "with" Mme de Clèves, to whom the missive belonged, Mme de Clèves herself will not know immediately who had written it. She still believes that it had been addressed to Nemours. The novel's narrator allows Mme de Clèves to remain in a situation in which she continues to take one thing for another, while the real reader is allowed illumination. This split creates double knowledge, or irony: the real reader knows the "truth," while Mme de Clèves, like Narcissus, goes through illusion before arriving at the truth. The reader is made to become a spectator, a voyeur of this sad spectacle, thus presaging the two principal voyeuristic scenes at Coulommiers.

The previous imbricated narratives had been told to Mme de Clèves. The experience of *reading* the letter, and becoming aware of the unfolding of her own feelings, line by line, as she reads the letter and then reflects upon her own reactions to that reading, comes "closer to her" than did *hearing* the previous tales. She becomes a female Narcissus, looking at her own reflection in the mirror/letter. Unlike Narcissus, however, she is horrified by what she sees. She finally and fully understands the sorority of women who suffer from the faithlessness of men.

Mme de Clèves's misreading will make it much harder for Nemours to convince her that she is wrong when he tries to narrate the story of the Vidame's plight. Words written on a page create greater authority than words that are heard. It will take, in fact, an *other* authorial act, also *written* by a woman, the note composed by Mme d'Amboise, Mme de Thémines's friend, to convince Mme de Clèves of her own "misreading."

One could argue that Mme de Clèves's is not a misreading because she reads her own story into it. Hers is, perhaps, the "closest" reading of all, as I intend to show by juxtaposing excerpts of the letter's content, grammar, syntax and vocabulary, to the vocabulary, syntax, grammar, and content that Mme de Clèves uses in her final conversation with Nemours. The letter tells her story as it has developed so far. It also tells it as it will unfold in the future. *That* fact Mme de Clèves cannot know, and neither can the real reader upon a first reading. One can only suspect it, and see how specularity, reflexivity, chiastic and imbricated rhetoric develop, narratologically.

In the sense that Gide gives to the reflexive *récit*,[25] the letter is a *mise en abyme* of the first order, of "simple reflection," as Dällenbach puts it, of the novel itself.[26] It is the novel writ small. The same motifs that are woven throughout *La Princesse de Clèves* appear in Mme de Thémines's letter to the Vidame. In the second sentence we observe the hiddenness motif:

> Vous êtes bien surpris que je vous parle de votre infidélité; vous me l'aviez *cachée* avec tant d'adresse, et j'ai pris tant de soin de vous *cacher* que je la savais, que vous avez raison d'être étonné qu'elle me soit *connue*. Je suis surprise moi-même que j'aie pu ne vous en rien faire *paraître* (98).[27]

Upon reading this, Mme de Clèves, who had tried to hide her feelings from the man she loves, Nemours, presupposes that because of someone else (that is, herself), Nemours had deeply wounded an honourable woman. The words are narrating her own experience, she believes. She had known jealousy before, and structurally, what she is reading about had occurred to her after hearing each of the imbricated narratives. The difference, now, is that she has *textual* proof, written proof, she believes, that make her previous and present reactions legitimate.

Hiddenness vs. revelation: this juxtaposition is constantly present in the letter. As is true of the Narcissus myth, the verbs *cacher, connaître*, and *paraître* are used throughout, and reflect Mme de Clèves's own drama. She had tried to hide her passion from herself, her mother, Nemours, her husband, the world. Because she would be incapable of doing so, because she would reveal her love in order to seek protection from it, her own husband would die of jealousy. Mme de Thémines's letter is replete with hermeneutical codes that have to do with feigning, pretending, dissimulating, and they echo the "appearance vs. reality" element present in the first intercalated narrative that is so well summarized in Mme de Chartres's famous phrase, "[ce] qui paraît n'est presque jamais la vérité."

The author of the letter is *sustained* by her very pretense: she says she was sustained by the pleasure of dissimulating with the Vidame.[28] Mme de Clèves will also be sustained by concealing her feelings in her various retreats from Nemours. Mme de Thémines says: "Je *feignis d'être malade pour cacher le désordre de mon esprit*; mais je le devins en effet et mon corps ne put supporter une si violente agitation." Mme de Clèves will, herself, pretend illness as escape several times in the novel, especially when she comes to realize that Nemours had revealed to her husband what he had overheard at Coulommiers. And she does, in fact, pretend illness immediately after reading the letter. She is so disturbed, her thoughts are so dis-ordered, that she simply forgets that she had been told to be present at the Reine Dauphine's apartments, and, instead, she goes to bed and feigns sickness. When her husband returns from court, he is told that she is asleep. But she is anything but tranquil. She spends the night in distress, reading and rereading the fateful missive.[29] One might even read an encoding of Mme de Clèves's final illness in the statement made by Mme de Thémines: "je le devins [malade] en effet." Chaos has overtaken her thoughts and body.

Two sentences, in particular, show how the woman writing the letter has suffered: "Je suis surprise moi-même que j'aie pu ne vous en rien faire paraître. Jamais douleur n'a été pareille à la mienne".[30] The claim of being *sui generis* is one that has been applied, numerous times, to Mme de Clèves.[31] When she finishes reading the letter, however, her reactions are as extreme as, and as similar to those expressed by Mme de Thémines. The narrator describes them in this manner: "Jamais affliction n'a été si piquante et si vive".[32]

The statement made by Mme de Thémines that "*jamais* douleur n'a été pareille à la mienne" will be repeated in the mirror phrase the narrator uses to relate Mme de Clèves's reaction to the letter: "*Jamais* affliction n'a été si piquante et si vive".[33]

The uniqueness of Mme de Clèves's consequent "writing" of her life, over which so much has been made,[34] may be interpreted differently from what it has been in recent criticism. Mme de Clèves will certainly "write" her own life (and death), but within chiastic and imbricated rhetoric, which is a rhetoric of "different and same." Contrary to what James McGuire says about Mme de Clèves's being "irréprésentable en ce qu'elle n'est la répétition de rien," she will repeat Mme de Thémines's experience in various ways: (1) as did Mme de Thémines, Mme de Clèves will tell the man she loves that she had and always would love him; (2) that her experience of jealousy was the worst thing she had ever known; (3) that she had and would always remain virtuous, (4) that she would never see the man she loved again.

The subject under discussion is passion and suffering expressed and denied, rather than the experiencing of a "galanterie," a word that, in the seventeenth-century, meant sexual involvement.[35] This is also true in the case of Mme de Thémines. Although she uses the word "passion" in her letter,[36] this does not mean that she had had "une galanterie" or sexual involvement with the Vidame. In explaining his intricate situation to Nemours, the

Vidame, in fact, confirms this: "J'étais amoureux de Mme de Thémines; mais quoiqu'elle m'aimât, je n'étais pas assez heureux pour avoir des lieux particuliers à la voir et pour craindre d'y être surpris".[37] There is proof, however, in his own words, that he was betraying Mme de Thémines's love for him by having a liaison ("un commerce de galanterie" p. 104) with another woman (with *four* women, *in toto*, as it turns out), and he calls that, in a Don Juanesque ironic litotes, "une *espèce d'infidélité* pour cette autre femme dont je vous ai parlé".[38]

Mme de Thémines states that even though it was not true, she finally convinced the Vidame that she did not love him any more. When she succeeded in doing this, she says, he returned to her. But because she had known such pain, because he had betrayed her by loving someone else as well as herself, she concludes the letter with a resolve: "[Votre infidélité suffit] pour me laisser dans *cette résolution que j'ai prise de ne vous voir jamais"*.[39] In the final dialogue between Nemours and Mme de Clèves, this very phrase, almost, is repeated. Mme de Clèves will say to Nemours: "il faut que je demeure dans l'état où je suis et dans *les résolutions que j'ai prises de n'en sortir jamais"*.[40] That final and irrevocable *jamais* is stated by both Mme de Thémines and Mme de Clèves. Mme de Clèves reflects, or repeats, Mme de Thémines's experience as well as her diction.

Reading and rereading this letter is the most violent experience of jealousy Mme de Clèves has ever had. It is not vicarious, it is not mediated by an oral narrator. It is a direct confrontation with textual production, and reflects the larger text of which it is the central part. So "real" is it, in fact, that Mme de Clèves will refuse to suffer through this type of "descent into hell" again. It is not only a narrative, like the other imbricated narratives, *after* which she comes to know jealousy. It is an experience that is intensified by instant repetition, by her reading the letter over and over again. Further imbricated narratives will no longer be needed when this one is completed. Lafayette has created the ultimate mirror, the most intense experience of complete identification with another text on the part of her heroine.

5.   **Living Out Mme de Thémines's Letter**
       The reading of the letter brings about the second part of the fourth narration, which will be told to Mme de Clèves by the man she loves. Following Nemours's telling of the Vidame's tale, which need not be repeated to the novel's readers because they have already "heard" it from the scoundrel himself when he narrated it to Nemours, and following the incident of Mme de Clèves's joint authorship with Nemours of the poor substitute "mirror" that will not fool the Queen, resulting in the Vidame's disgrace, Mme de Clèves will, once again, relive her moments of jealousy, and the results will be guilt and despair. She will then begin to "live out" Mme de Thémines's letter.

As the letter is an avowal of passion and jealousy, so does Mme de Clèves confess her own passion and jealousy to Nemours in the end, in narrative form. When that occurs, she even asks him not to interrupt her narration. She becomes a narrator in her own right. The words *cacher* and *paraître* will occur frequently in her discourse. Just as Mme de Thémines concluded by saying that she could not tolerate her lover's sharing his love with anyone else, so will Mme de Clèves say the following to Nemours at the conclusion of their last conversation: "La certitude de n'être plus aimée de vous, comme je le suis, me paraît un si horrible malheur que, quand je n'aurais point des raisons de devoir insurmontables, je doute si je pourrais me résoudre à m'exposer à ce malheur".[41]

Mme de Clèves also believes that it is the obstacles themselves that kept Nemours faithful to her, just as the letter-writer recalled that her lover had come back to her only when he thought that she had stopped loving him and that he could, therefore, win her back.[42] In the end, Mme de Clèves recalls Mme de Thémines's letter deliberately. She confronts, head-on, the question of jealousy when she says to Nemours that he had made her suffer such ultimate pangs of jealousy, especially when she had read Mme de Thémines's letter, thinking that it had been addressed to him, that she had come to believe that jealousy was the greatest of all evils.[43] J. Campbell says that in *La Princesse de Clèves* "jealousy is not just a plotting-device added to the novelistic sauce to whet some new public appetite. In the school of love the experience of jealousy is above all the realization that love and jealousy are inseparable."[44] In the end, Mme de Clèves resolves the hermeneutic code.

6. Denial as Affirmation

As in a mirror, it is through *negation* that Mme de Clèves *affirms* – and confirms – her passion for Nemours in the most significant interchange she has with him. One of the striking components of the grammar and syntax of her final conversation with Nemours, as well as that of Mme de Thémines's letter *is* negation. Are we not invited to read "Nemours" onomastically as "Ne[a]mours"?[45]

Mme de Thémines had said: "Je suis surprise moi-même que j'aie pu *ne vous en rien faire* paraître"; "Jamais douleur *n'a été* pareille à la mienne"; "*je ne vous cachais plus* celle que j'avais pour vous"; "c'est ce qui fit que *je n'y allai point*"; "mon corps *ne put supporter* une si violente agitation"; "je feignis...d'avoir fort mal, afin d'avoir un prétexte de *ne vous point voir* et de *ne vous point écrire*"; "je résolus de *ne vous la point* faire paraître"; "je *ne voulais pas* que vous eussiez le plaisir d'apprendre que je savais qu'elle triomphait de moi, ni augmenter son triomphe par mon désespoir"; "Je pensai que *je ne vous punirais pas*...et que *je ne vous donnerais qu'une* légère douleur si *je cessais* de vous aimer lorsque vous *ne m'aimiez plus*"; "il fallait que vous m'aimassiez pour sentir le mal de *n'être point aimé"*; "comme si *je n'eusse pas eu* la force de vous l'avouer"; "je *n'avais eu dessein* de vous laisser voir que mes sentiments étaient changés"; "vous en étiez même persuadé que *je ne vous aimais plus*"; "il m'a paru que vous m'aîmiez mieux que vous n'aviez jamais fait et je vous ai fait voir que *je ne vous aimais plus"*; "votre retour et votre discrétion *n'ont pu réparer* votre légèreté"; and then there is the famous final phrase, "cette résolution que j'ai prise de *ne vous voir jamais*,"[46] that will be repeated by Mme de Clèves in her last interchange with Nemours.

In a novel in which the word *peut-être* appears only 32 times, the words *jamais, ne...jamais, ne...pas, ne...point,* and *ne...plus* appear hundreds of times. Negative sentences abound in the novel, and, as in mirror-imagery, they exhibit frequently sentiments opposite to those they state. One of the striking syntactical examples of this occurs early on. M. de Nemours had "invited" Mme de Clèves *not* to go to the Maréchal de St. André's ball by letting his opinion be known that a loved one should absent herself from a given place if she knew that the person she loved would *not* be there: "Mme de Clèves consentit volontiers à passer quelques jours chez elle pour *ne point aller* dans un lieu où M. de Nemours *ne devrait pas être*; et il partit *sans avoir* le plaisir de savoir *qu'elle n'irait pas*".[47] As Narcissus loved an image that was a reflection, absence, in this case, becomes an image of love. The situation involving the St. André ball turned out to be ironic because Nemours did not have the pleasure of knowing that Mme de Clèves had absented herself for his sake.

Mme de Clèves's final confession to Nemours reflects the previous situation: proof of love will be expressed by stating the intention to be henceforth physically absent.[48] Just as Mme de Clèves came to know that she loved Nemours through her experiences of jealousy and consequent "exiles" from court to country, from Paris to Coulommiers, so does she, in the end, opt *for* negation, and consequent exile, after confessing her love.[49]

7.   The Middle in the Mirror of the Novel's Overall Structure

When Fontenelle wrote to a "fellow geometer" about *La Princesse de Clèves* in May 1678, he stated that it would be natural for his friend to assume that a geometer such as himself, whose mind was completely taken up with measures and proportions would not put down his Euclid in order to read, for the fourth time, a gallant novella unless [that work] were so spellbinding as to entice even mathematicians into reading it.[50] The chiastic and imbricated structure of Lafayette's novel was surely such as to tempt even a mathematician to put down his Euclid and write to another geometer about it.

As J. W. Scott says (echoing J. Rousset and others), "there is no such thing as an unstructured work of art."[51] Scott compares *La Princesse de Clèves* to a classical play. In his discussion of the novel's structure, he says that it is the result of an interest in psychological causality that is shared by many seventeenth-century writers. In the traditional five "acts," he places the incident of the lost and found letter at the end of "Act III," at the climax of the "play," before it begins its dénouement.

J. Garapon stresses the contrapuntal musical nature of the text. He calls the first counterpoint "le contrepoint historique," and the second "les quatre épisodes secondaires."[52] Neither play nor music, as metaphors, quite captures the significance of the rhetorical construction of the text, and despite the fact that Virginia Woolf claimed *La Princesse de Clèves's* form to be invisible,[53] the novel's macro-structure reflects its micro-structure, and vice-versa. The following schemata (I and II are found at the end of the text before the endnotes), reveal the chiastic (a-b—b-a) and imbricated (a-b—a-b) structures, or a variation thereof (a-b-a—a-b-a) of *La Princesse de Clèves* and situate the recurrences of jealousy within the framework of the imbricated narratives.

8.   A Chiastic Micro-Text and an Imbricated Intertext

The "mirror in the middle" is followed by a significant chiastic intertext. Reflecting an imbricated statement that St. Paul makes in his letter to the Romans, it provides further insight into the novel's structure, history, and meaning.

After Mme de Clèves comes to realize "the truth" about Mme de Thémines's letter, that is, that it had, indeed, been addressed to the Vidame and not to Nemours, she and Nemours spend the afternoon composing, in spasms of delight, a chaotic copy or faulty "mirror," a counterfeit replica of Mme de Thémines's letter. With the best of intentions they imitate the original, but create, instead, a parody of textual production. The second letter will encode the "real" letter, but it will be a subversive text within a text that we do not see but are allowed to imagine (much as M. de Clèves's envoy imagines a scene that he does not see at Coulommiers). Then, after having had courriers ask for the letter *twice* during the course of the afternoon – while Mme de Clèves and Nemours had not even re-"composed" *half* of it[54]– the "epistle" is sent to the Reine Dauphine, and Nemours leaves, at *four* o'clock,[55] as does M. de Clèves. The half, double, and doubled figures are significant, since they provide links to the chiastic and imbricated structure of the whole. They also reveal the dyadic nature of organized versus chaotic textual production, that is, Mme de Thémines's "real" letter over against an imitation of it. The numbers above are a deixis pointing to the duplicate letter, to the paired principles operating in the Thémines/Clèves sorority, to the text/intertext that will soon be incorporated into our own reading, and the relationship between micro and macro-texts within the novel.

When Mme de Clèves is left alone, we are told that she examines herself in an intro-speculative manner. Her mirror image causes her to look at herself in a different light. She reviews the events of the previous day and of her delightful afternoon. She becomes not only the reviewer and critic of her own text, but she encodes, as well, the real reader and the literary critic who perceive and become involved in all aspects of the text's appropriation.

Remembering that she had revealed signs of jealousy to Nemours, Mme de Clèves becomes completely distraught. She is so startled by her own reactions that *elle ne se reconnaissait plus elle- même*.[56] She will have the same reaction *after* her final discourse with Nemours:[57] "ce lui était une chose si nouvelle...d'avoir dit elle-même qu'elle aimait, *qu'elle ne se connaissait plus*".[58] The lack of cohesion that she discovers, the absence of "vues claires et distinctes" that she will come to know in herself (she will use this Cartesian intertext too in her final declarations to Nemours)[59] so startles her that she asks herself a series of questions, indicating, thereby, further chaos and self-doubt.

A shift from the third to the first person occurs as the narrator has Mme de Clèves use anaphora to ask herself a series of questions:

> Elle trouva qu'il était presque impossible qu'elle put être contente de sa passion. Mais quand je le pourrais être, disait-elle, qu'en *veux*-je faire? *Veux*-je la souffrir? *Veux*-je y répondre? *Veux*-je m'engager dans une galanterie? *Veux*-je manquer à M. de Clèves? *Veux*-je me manquer à moi-même? Et *veux*-je enfin m'exposer aux cruels repentirs et aux mortelles douleurs que donne l'amour?[60]

Mme de Clèves will then come to certain conclusions about her situation, and her narrator will have her use a striking chiasmus to reveal what she thinks: "[Je suis] vaincue et surmontée par une inclination qui m'entraîne malgré moi. Toutes mes résolutions sont inutiles; *je pensai hier* tout ce que *je pense aujourd'hui* et *je fais aujourd'hui* tout *le contraire* de ce que *je résolus hier*"[61]. Readers familiar with the New Testament hear Pauline echoes in this phrase. It would be difficult to believe that someone as well read and as well educated as Lafayette was unacquainted with this well-known biblical passage, especially since its context is so relevant to the question addressed in the novel.[62]

In his epistle to the Romans, St. Paul devotes a substantive passage to an examination of the role of the law in Christian life. He begins chapter 7 by stating that the law binds only the living and not the dead: "la loi n'a autorité sur l'homme qu'aussi longtemps qu'il vit."[63] At the beginning of the chapter, the question is posed about whether a woman may remarry after her husband's death. This larger context is undeniably relevant to *La Princesse de Clèves*. The Pauline answer is that she may. But Lafayette will have Mme de Clèves act, in the end, in a way contrary to that proscribed, or rather, allowed, by the biblical text. She will, however, make good use of the rhetoric of the biblical intertext that will appear in verses 15, 18, and 19, even as she subverts or undercuts the biblical chapter's initial statement.

Because St. Paul says, in the seventh chapter to the Romans, that he came to know what sin is thanks to the law ("je n'aurais pas connu la convoitise si la loi n'avait dit: *Tu ne convoiteras pas*" (v.7), he concludes that the law is just and good (v.12). But even though we know that the law is good, he is, he says, himself incapable of living up to it. (The biblical passage shifts from "nous" to "je," as Lafayette's will shift from the third to the first person). In verse 15, St. Paul says: "je ne comprends rien à ce que je fais: ce que *je veux, je ne le fais pas*, mais ce que *je hais, je le fais.*"[64] One recalls Mme de Clèves's series of "*veux-je?*" as well as her "*je fais.*" When the narrator has Mme de Clèves think, in third person discourse, that "elle ne se reconnaissait plus elle-même",[65] this is equivalent to St. Paul's saying: "je ne comprends rien à ce que je fais" (v.15).

In verses 18 and 19, the biblical letter-writer will go on to repeat, rhetorically, what he had stated before: "vouloir le bien est à ma portée, mais non pas l'accomplir, puisque le bien que *je veux*, je *ne le fais pas* et le mal que *je ne veux pas, je le fais.*" Willing and doing, according to St. Paul, and according to many other writers of moralistic literature throughout the ages, are in tension, if not at odds with one other, as Mme de Clèves knows so well.

The analytical mind of the apostle leads him on. In verse 20 he says: "Or, si ce que je ne veux pas, je le fais, ce n'est pas moi qui agis, mais le péché qui habite en moi." He will arrive at the conclusion, in chapter 8, that it is the grace of God that will liberate human beings from the trap described in chapter 7. While the notion of sin raised in the Pauline text is not explicit in Lafayette, questions of societal and personal implications of moral behavior are. Lafayette's chiastic text, which reveals uncertainty and indecision (pensais hier-fais aujourd'hui–fais aujourd'hui-résolus hier), and the biblical interlocking text (je ne fais pas le bien-je veux—je fais le mal-je ne veux pas) are micro-structures that repeat the macro-structures of moral dilemmas in *La Princesse de Clèves*.

It seems almost ironic that M. Boixareu calls Mme de Clèves a "fille du siècle de Descartes." He quotes Descartes, in fact, as he applies the following Cartesian notion to Mme de Clèves's beliefs: "Il n'y a point d'âme si faible qui ne puisse, étant bien conduite, acquérir un pouvoir absolu sur les passions." [66] Mme de Clèves's (as well as her mother's) Cartesian beliefs, says Boixareu, express a well-defined conflict that is typical of Corneilles's plays. She believes she can be whom she wishes to be, and, above all, she thinks she can become that which she should be. Boixareu states that all the imbricated narratives are models that Mme de Clèves *could* have followed: "that is why they could be considered as elements of a *mise en abyme* of the novel at a moment when the novel is not yet finished, but which *could* conclude in the manner that Mme de Clèves hears. They function as an eventual mirror: it's up to her to repeat what she has heard, and to suffer the disastrous consequences thereof ".[67]

The tension between what we might call Mme de Clèves's "Cartesian" versus "Biblical" approach to her moral conflict shows her opting for the Cartesian solution. She will not follow any of the narratives' conclusions that she has heard. She does not follow the Pauline message whereby she would give in to a will higher (or other) than her own. She follows Mme de Thémines's "example," which is a narrative she has *read*, has suffered through by incorporating it into her own life, and by which she has come to realize that absence does not make the heart grow fonder. It is, however, the only ("non")-solution she will embrace.

9.   The Macro-Structures of the Novel

The chiastic macro-dispositions of Books I and II oppose court to country, urbane civility to pastoral sincerity.[68] Paris represents a disruptive, destabilizing, and ultimately destructive ambiance for Mme de Clèves. While the city represents a world of discovery of passion, of masks and of make-believe, Coulommiers is an *hortus conclusus* representing peace, authenticity, and self-possession – until Nemours invades it.[69] This was clearly a century of moralist literature if one thinks of La Fontaine, La Rochefoucauld, Pascal, to say nothing of the classical plays of Corneille, Molière and Racine.

J. P. Hugot says that in 1678, the date of publication of *La Princesse de* Clèves, discourses that had a moral aim were as much myth as science. Hugot uses *La Carte de Tendre* to exhibit Scudéry's presenting an image of the heart. It is a "topography of tenderness," according to Hugot, just as certain pages of *La Princesse de Clèves* are a type of "speleology of the moral life." He goes on to say that moral space becomes that of a suffering personal conscience, and that the progression of Mme de Clèves's lucidity, which is amplified by her discourse, follows an implacable destiny that is as rigorous as the verbal structure used to express it. "Certes," he says, "il ne s'agit que de construire cet édifice verbal; la visée morale y est aussi claire que dans les "fables" de La Fontaine ou les "maximes" de La Rochefoucauld; l'on édifie, donc, dans les deux acceptions du terme."[70]

It is no surprise that La Fontaine should create his own version of "the city mouse" and "the country mouse" in the seventeenth century. Thematics of "the city house" as well as "a country house" were a phenomenon that could be increasingly afforded, not only then, but in the centuries to come, by people of means.

The initial juxtaposition of the chiastic "Paris-Coulommiers--Coulommiers-Paris" in Books I and II is further complicated by the imbricated structures of Books III and IV. After the representation of "the mirror in the middle," the specular aspects of Mme de Clèves's life become more complex. The middle of Book III (a-*b*-a) contains the confession scene at Coulommiers, where Nemours observes Mme de Clèves as she tells her husband she loves someone else, which is a reversal of what occurs in Mme de Thémines's letter, where Mme de Thémines reveals to the Vidame that she knows that the Vidame loves someone else. In the middle of Book IV (a-*b*-a) there is repetition and intensification of the middle part of the first "a-*b*-a" formula. The reader observes the voyeuristic portrait scene, also at Coulommiers, in which the real and implied readers observe M. de Clèves's envoy (who represents M. de Clèves's "eyes" or "I") observe Nemours who observes Mme de Clèves as she looks, lovingly, at the representation of Nemours in the painting of the siege of Metz. That this painting had been *copied* from one that belonged to Mme de Valentinois makes of it one more element in the repetitive structure of representation and mimesis. This *emboîtement* of spectacles, this *Galerie des Glaces* is, of course, reflexive of the scene in which Mme de Clèves had observed Nemours furtively purloin her own portrait, which was being *copied* from one that belonged to M. de Clèves. That that scene precedes the "mirror in the middle" by a few pages is neither insignificant nor was it placed there by chance.

M. Paulson cites S. Haig who, in his fine Twayne series book on *La Princesse de Clèves*, points to the place in the novel in which the King, "breaking a last lance with Montgomery, is injured by a splinter in the eye." This is interpreted as a sign of the breaking up of the court's brittle stability.[71] The disintegration of the life and kingdom occurs just before Mme de Thémines's letter goes astray and ends up with Mme de Clèves, who is asked to interpret it. The coincidence of the king's having been struck in the eye and Mme de Clèves's misinterpretation of the reading matter before her eyes, leads the reader to find another deliberate coincidence in the exempla having to do with the act of using eyes to read – or to "mis-read."

We know the results of both "sightings" noted above, Nemours's witnessing the confession scene, and M. de Clèves's envoy's witnessing Nemours's entry into the gardens of Coulommiers. We know the results of both "visions." Nemours sees and will then repeat what he saw, and the envoy "sees" but will lead his master to misinterpret what he had "seen." The confession, as well as the envoy's fallacious report to M. de Clèves, create nefarious consequences in the husband's affective development and in *his* discovery of jealousy that will eventually lead to his death. It is as if country and court were reversed. Coulommiers, a beautiful country retreat that husband and wife had built together, is no longer a peaceful haven of escape from passion and from history for Mme or M. de Clèves. The structural cards have been turned around, "as in a glass," darkly.

The History/story thematics concerning the existence of Coulommiers are well described by L. Horowitz (see *"Truly Inimitable?"*), where Horowitz refers to previous texts that study the historically anachronistic aspects of that "somptueuse demeure." (M. Cuénin, C. Morlet-Chantalat, and F. Beasley [Revising Memory]). "The château," says Horowitz, "did not yet exist in 1558-59, when most of *La Princesse de Clèves* takes place. This makes Lafayette's choice that much richer, as the name was bound to generate for the seventeenth-century audience powerfully reverberating echoes of more recent French history".[72]

10.   Hyperbolic Rhetoric: More is More

As mirrors turn tales, there is another way of looking at the text's conclusion. It involves reading the other side of elliptical rhetoric. Ever since DeJean's "Lafayette's Ellipses..." was published, critics have set their gaze upon the minimalistic aspects of the novel. But the other side of ellipsis is hyperbole. Less turns out to be a great deal more. *Hyperbole*: from the Greek "overshooting" or "excess." Quintilian says it is "an elegant straining of the truth, and may be employed indifferently for exaggeration or attenuation" (*Institutes of Oratory* 8.6.67). It is a statement not intended to be understood literally. Lanham calls it "a use of terms used for emphasis...[It is] self-conscious exaggeration" (86).

Many readers, especially first-time readers of the novel, are struck by the hyperbolic manner in which the text begins: "la magnificence et la galanterie *n'ont jamais paru* en France avec tant d'éclat que dans les dernières années du règne de Henri second".[73] There is more: "*Jamais* cour n'a eu *tant* de belles personnes et d'hommes *admirablement_bien faits*".[74] On the same page we read: "ce qui rendait cette cour belle et majestueuse était le nombre *infini* de princes et de grands seigneurs d'un *mérite extraordinaire*. Ceux que je vais nommer étaient, en des manières différentes l'ornement et *l'admiration de leur siècle*".[75] The narrator then begins to name those who have such extraordinary merit: "le roi de Navarre attirait le respect *de tout le monde* par *la grandeur de son rang* et par celle qui paraissait en sa personne".[76] The duc de Guise "avait donné des marques *d'une valeur si admirable* et avait eu de si heureux succès *qu'il n'y avait point de grand capitaine qui ne dût le regarder avec envie*".[77]

On the next page we learn that "[le duc de Nevers]...avait trois fils *parfaitement bien faits*".[78] We read that:

> [le duc de Nemours]...était *un chef d'oeuvre de la nature*;
> ce qu'il avait de moins admirable, c'était d'être l'homme *le mieux fait et le plus beau*. Ce qui le mettait au-dessus des autres était *une valeur incomparable*, et un agrément dans son esprit, dans son visage et dans ses actions que *l'on n'a jamais vu qu'à lui seul*...[et] une manière de s'habiller qui

était *toujours* suivie de tout le monde, *sans pouvoir être imitée.*[79]

In a novel that has always been defined as the essence of measure, of litotes, and certainly of ellipsis, which is defined by Fontanier as "retrenchement, suppression...lack, to be lesser," it is important to remember that hyperbole is the opposite of litotes.[80] In explaining hyperbole ("exaggerated or extravagant terms used for emphasis and not intended to be understood literally; self-conscious exaggeration" [Lanham]), the *Robert* gives these examples: "nous avons perdu le sens de la mesure. On dit à propos du moindre événement que *les conséquences en seront immenses, qu'il y a une portée incalculable.* On vend dans mon quartier du macaroni *extra sublime...*" (1966, emphases added). These days, *extra* would be translated as *hyper*.

To accuse Lafayette of hyperbole may seem like heresy. But this is not a court of ecclesiastical law. It is a simple case of sighting. That Lafayette uses hyperbole *and* litotes throughout the novel is the case. A case in point: the description of Nemours, at the very start, points to the fact that "ce qu'il avait de moins admirable" (a litotes), was that he was "l'homme le mieux fait et le plus beau" (a hyperbole). The Omega of the text enters the Alpha of the ourobouros' mouth: "Ce qui le mettait au-dessus des autres était *une valeur incomparable*, et un agrément...que l'on n'a jamais vu *qu'à lui seul*".[81] Many critics have made a great deal over the way in which the narrator describes the end of Mme de Clèves's life: "et sa vie, qui fut assez courte, laissa des exemples de *vertu inimitables*".[82] That so much has been said about this final phrase means, perhaps, that readers have let the chance go by to see (1) the hyperbolic rhetoric of the text, (2) the *inimitable* value of repetition of sounds (Nemours's "*v*aleur *in*comparable,"[83] prepares the reader for Mme de Clèves's "*v*ertu *in*imitable" with which the novel concludes), (3) the fact that Nemours dresses "sans pouvoir être *imité*"[84] leads to the notion of being "inimitable" that is said of Mme de Clèves herself, and (4) the understatements followed by hyperboles at both beginning and ending of the novel in the cases of both principal characters: Nemours:–"ce qu'il avait *de moins admirable*> l'homme *le mieux fait du monde.*" Mme de Clèves:–"sa vie, *qui fut assez courte*> laissa des exemples de *vertu inimitables.*"

The word *jamais* also appears, hyperbolically, in the first sentence of the text – and in the last short paragraph of the novel. First: "La magnificence et la galanterie n'ont *jamais* paru en France avec tant d'éclat." Last: "Il fallut enfin que ce prince repartît...aussi accablé de douleur que le pouvait être un homme qui perdit toutes sortes d'espérances de revoir *jamais* une personne qu'il aimait d'une passion *la plus violente, la plus naturelle* et *la mieux fondée* qu'il ait *jamais* été."

"Classical," Jean Rousset reminds us, means reason. It means following appropriate rules of conduct. It is *bienséance*. It means dominating one's passions. "Baroque" is a delight in paradoxes, agitation, and disorder. One might even include chaos in this list. It is a love of *chiaroscuro* and contrasts, night and shade versus brilliance and *éclat*. *La Princesse de Clèves* is both "classical" and "baroque." Its style is both elliptical and hyperbolic. The tension between the two is grounded in the novel's rhetorical micro-texts as well as in its macro-design.

The text's hyperbolic function relates to the "mirror in the middle" by foregrounding Lafayette's genius for creating mirror personages, motifs, and scenes. Her rhetoric is undeniably a mirror rhetoric. Mme de Clèves is a double of Mme de Thémines, and vice versa. They are both passionate and jealous. Their passion is hyperbolic, the opposite of measure, the opposite of knowing what one is doing, the opposite of "clear and distinct ideas," as Mme de Clèves herself says. The first imbricated narrative as well as the Vidames's excesses with women are hyperbolic. Although he is not involved with *"mille e tre"* women, he is nevertheless involved with *four* at the same time: the Queen, Mme de Thémines, Mme X, and Mme de Martigues. Nemours himself thinks this is excessive.

Because she learns the violent and excessive nature of passion, through jealousy, in the various mirrors of the text, and in the particular mirror of Mme de Thémines's text, which is her OTHER, as well as her SELF, and because she becomes excessive to the point of not being able to know herself clearly, Mme de Clèves reacts. She will opt for the opposite of what she really desires. The mirror serves both a passionate and pedagogical function in Lafayette. Nemours, who is also excessive, will have to settle for less and less, until his passionate love disappears, like Narcissus, and becomes metamorphosed into the beauty of Mme de Clèves's own hyperbolic virtue. She will go to extremes to remain virtuous, just as Mme de Thémines had done.

G. Genette states that metadiegetic narratives are connected to the diegesis by means of a "relation of another type, by analogy, by contrast, etc.". Mme de Clèves's final decision is related to Mme de Thémines's letter, and the narratives surrounding it, by means of (1) analogy (they mirror the jealousy and the cases of mistaken identities and facts observed in each), (2) comparison (jealousy appears in all of the metadiegetic narratives, but Thémines and Clèves will differ from the others by opting for what jealousy has taught them, that is, that refusal to be susceptible to jealousy by absenting oneself from its destructive possibilities is a viable, even desirable option), (3) contrast (while most of the women are undone by jealousy, Thémines and Clèves act in a way that is deconstructive (they throw sand into the gears of a machine that is expected to work in a certain way and then does not). Mme de Clèves's refusal, after her husband's death, to accede to Nemours's desires means that she maintains her love for Nemours in a way different from that experienced by the women in the first three imbricated narratives. The notable exception appears in the fourth: Mme de Thémines. Mme de Thémines's passion, structurally, stylistically, and rhetorically, is a looking glass in which Mme de Clèves's own passion is reflected, structurally, stylistically, and rhetorically. The "mirror in the middle" is not in itself a contrasting image. It is a double: it prepares the reader, as well as the heroine, for repetition. Mme de Clèves is not Mme de Thémines's image in reverse. Yet the repetitive nature of the novel's macro-chiastic and interlocking structure is present in this reflection.

Mme de Clèves's becoming a narrator, in her final dialogue with Nemours, means that she will tell her love for him in its most intense state, and then conclude her narrative ambiguously. "We will see," she says, in essence, to Nemours, and then she will refuse to contribute to change. This was a denial of expectations for most seventeenth-century readers. The narrator of the novel (to be distinguished from Mme de Clèves as narrator) has her love for Nemours eventually disappear after time and proximity to death have taken their toll,[85] but at the moment of Mme de Clèves's narrational confession to Nemours, negation equals its opposite. By *not* having gone to St. André's ball, Mme de Clèves had revealed her nascent love for Nemours. By *not* marrying him after M. de Clèves's death, she exhibits a consistent "same as well as different," or, in other words, a chiastic dialectic. It is her way of telling Nemours, as Mme de Thémines had told the Vidame, that her love for him is something so precious that she will never share it with anyone else.

Mirroring, repetition, reversals, contrasts, all play a role in the micro- and macro-structural and rhetorical design of the novel, as well as in the historical interplay of "reality" with fiction, of history with mimesis. Mme de Clèves's confession and decision, like Mme de Thémines's confession and decision, are declarations – not negations – of passion. As a mirror reverses chiastically the image it repeats, *jamais* equals *toujours* in both Mme de Clèves's and in Mme de Thémines's narrations of their autobiographies to the men they love. The text reverses itself in the reader's expectations (hence the seventeenth-century accusation of implausibility), just as expectations are reversed in the text. The Alpha and the Omega of the text will also meet: the word "inimitable" at the beginning repeats the word "inimitable" at the ending of the novel. Just as Louis XIV wished his realm, his reign, his court to be "inimitable," as well as to endure forever, historically and stylistically, the figure he is asked to look at in the full-sized mirror is that of one whom he believes will attack him. "Magnificence," in that case, just as is the case of the narrative of Mme de Clèves, turns out to be doubled: it not only reveals a "true" image, but also the fear that is consequent to its having been appropriated, on the one hand, and mis-interpreted, on the other.

*   *   *   *

A century and four years after the publication of *La Princesse de Clèves*, a scandalously intriguing epistolary novel burst upon the scene of French letters. As different in tone as are Lafayette's most famous novel and *Les Liaisons dangereuses*, they share numerous narratological factors. The "hinge in the middle" of Laclos's work (the Prévan episode) recalls Lafayette's "mirror in the middle." Contrasts between "appearance and reality," between clock-work order and ever-growing chaos are developed in both. Protagonists read, write, rewrite, and narrate their lives in both novels, emphasizing auto-referentiality and rereading in these texts. "True" versus "a reflection of" a letter (Mme de Thémines's and the imitated copy created by Mme de Clèves and Nemours) is repeated in the "true" versus "false" versions of letters Mme de Merteuil writes in her description of Prévan's adventures. These pivotal epistles, located, structurally, at the core of both works, foreground the centrality of chiastic and imbricated structures in the creation of both of these seventeenth and eighteenth-century narratives.

I

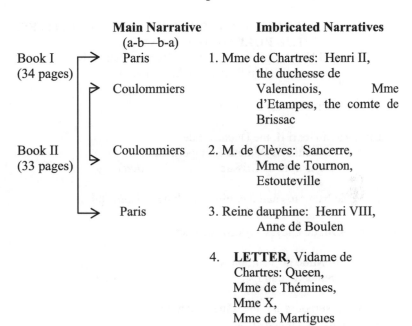

Main Narrative (a-b—b-a)	Imbricated Narratives
Book I (34 pages) → Paris Coulommiers	1. Mme de Chartres: Henri II, the duchesse de Valentinois, Mme d'Etampes, the comte de Brissac
Book II (33 pages) Coulommiers	2. M. de Clèves: Sancerre, Mme de Tournon, Estouteville
Paris	3. Reine dauphine: Henri VIII, Anne de Boulen
	4. **LETTER**, Vidame de Chartres: Queen, Mme de Thémines, Mme X, Mme de Martigues

CENTER OF TEXT

(a-b-a—a-b-a)

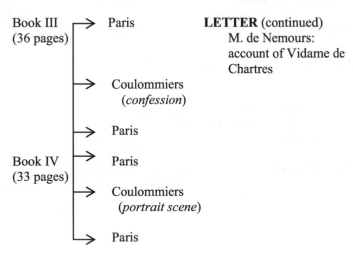

Book III → Paris   **LETTER** (continued)
(36 pages)   M. de Nemours:
                            account of Vidame de
                            Chartres

→ Coulommiers
   (*confession*)

→ Paris

Book IV → Paris
(33 pages)

→ Coulommiers
   (*portrait scene*)

→ Paris

II

PRINCIPAL AND IMBRICATED NARRATORS AND NARRATIVES:
THE ROLE OF JEALOUSY
(Principal Narrators and Narratees in Roman Numerals;
Imbricated Narratives in Arabic numerals)

I.   Mme de Chartres → Mme de Clèves

   Liaisons of Henri II, the Duchesse de
         Valentinois, Mme d'Etampes and
         the Comte de Brissac: *Jealousy*

   1. M. de Nemours and the reine dauphine: *Jealousy*

II.   Sancerre → M. de Clèves → Mme de Clèves

   Liaison of Mme de Tournon with
         Sancerre and Estouteville: *Jealousy*

   2. M.de Nemours and the reine dauphine: *Jealousy*

III. Reine dauphine → Mme de Clèves and ladies
                                 of court

   Henri VIII, Anne de Boulen,
         the Vicomte de Rochefort,
         Jeanne Seymour: *Jealousy*

   3. LETTER: *Jealousy*

IV. Vidame de Chartres → M. de Nemours
      [M. de Clèves]   Mme de Clèves

   Liaisons of Vidame de Chartres with Queen,
         Mme de Thémines, Mme X,
         and Mme de Martigues: *Jealousy*

   4. LETTER (cont.):   *Jealousy*

Notes

[1] See Geneviève Mouligneau: "L'abbé de Charnes affirme savoir de 'bonne part' que *La Princesse de Clèves* a été écrite longtemps avant 1675." In *Mme de Lafayette, romancière*: ed. de l'Université de Bruxelles, Bruxelles, 1980, p. 162.

[2] H. Chamard, and G. Rudler, in particular, study Lafayette's historical meticulousness in regard to the time in which she chose to ground her novel. See "Les Sources historiques de *La Princesse de Clèves,*" *Revue du seizième siècle*, 2, 1914, pp. 92-131, pp. 289-321; 5, 1917-18, pp. 1-20, pp. 231-243.

[3] A. Cantillon states that "Mme de Lafayette utilise l'Histoire comme un univers exemplaire, qui sert de garantie à la vraisemblance de l'univers romanesque." He says that in Lafayette's choice of period, that is 1558-1560, French history furnished the writer with events that common sense could confirm, albeit in a bizarre fashion. Reality went *beyond* fiction in the brutal and fortuitous death of a reigning monarch, whose death is explained as having fulfilled a prediction. In *La Princesse de Clèves*, ed. Nathan, Paris, 1989, p. 98.

[4] *Mme de Lafayette: Romans et Nouvelles*, introd. A. Niderst, vii, Garnier, Paris, 1970. As stated in chapter I, all translations in this book are my own unless otherwise specified.

[5] ibid., p. 53.

[6] Beasley's thesis is that Lafayette's use of "the historical background" made her novel more plausible to readers of her own time, thus advancing an alternative concept of female behavior and rejecting the pervasive patriarchal nature of textual production and reception. These are references to an abridged chapter of Beasley's book, *Revising Memory: Women's Fictions and Memoirs in Seventeenth-Century France* (Rutgers University Press) that she presented at the Renaissance Seminar at Wesleyan University in February 1990. I do not quote directly because that particular version was "not for citation."

[7] Lafayette herself says of her novel: "Il n'y a rien de romanesque et de grimpé: aussi n'est-ce pas un roman: c'est proprement des mémoires [...], c'est une parfaite imitation du monde de la cour et de la matière dont on y vit." (Lettre à Lescheraine, 13 avril 1678), in *Correspondance*, Gallimard, Paris, 1942, p. 21. A. Cantillon also reminds his readers that Lafayette uses History as an exemplary universe that serves to make the novel verisimilitudinous. He reminds us that between 1558-1560 French history furnishes the novelist one of those happenings that makes reality go beyond fiction, that is, the brutal and fotuitous death of a monarch whose death had

been, in fact, predicted. In A. Cantillon, *La princesse de Clèves*, Ed. Nalhan, Paris, 1989, p. 98.

[8] Critics such as M. Turnell have "ascribed part of the novel's immediate success to its readership's awareness of the 'lightly veiled' allusions to the life at the Court of Louis XIV." Quoted by Byron R. Wells in "The King, the Court, The Country – Theme and Structure in *La Princesse de Clèves,*" *Papers on French Seventeenth-Century Literature* 12, 23, 1985, p. 543. In discussing *La Princesse de Montpensier* (1662), Lafayette's first novella, A. Niderst says: "Il est impossible...qu'en deux mois, elle ait pu composer cette oeuvre qui offre un style si étudié et une si adroite fusion de l'histoire et de l'actualité" (xii-xiii). Already in her first work, Lafayette knew how to imbricate chronicle with fiction.

[9] Mme D'Aulnoy, *Le Cabinet des Fées*, introd. Elizabeth Lemirre, I, Mas de Vert , Arles, 1994, p. 13.

[10] See J. Grenier, *Miroirs*, Fata Morgana, Paris, 1980, p. 13.

[11]Gordon E. Slethaug, *Beautiful Chaos: Chaos Theory and Metachaotics in Recent American Fiction*, State University of N.Y. Press, New York, 2000.

[12] In "Truly Inimitable? Repetition in *La Princesse de Clèves,*" MLA, New York,1998. *Approaches to Teaching Lafayette's Princesse de Clèves*, ed. & introd. F. Beasley and K. Jensen, pp. 120-126.

[13] No one, these days, would have the lack of insight to say that the "reader should not be put off by the long list of characters in the first pages of the book. It was a convention of the day to start a novel like that – they can very well be skipped" (N. Mitford, *The Princess of Clèves*, introd. and transl. N. Mitford, New Directions, New York, 1951, xxii. Much thought has been devoted, since 1951, to the role that the imbricated narratives play in *La Princesse de Clèves*. In his study of the "digressions" in the novel, J.W. Scott presents an impressive list of those who objected to as well as approved of the presence of "digressions." Since the publication of Scott's article, in 1957, "The 'Digressions' of the *Princesse de Clèves*" *French Studies* XI, 4, 1957, pp. 293-321, numerous critics have dealt with the subject, including G. Poulet, J. Rousset, S. Haig, L. Horowitz, A. Niderst, P. Stewart, J. Lyons, M.-O. Sweetser, J. DeJean, J. Malandain, D. Judovitz, H. Stone, R. Moye, among others. It is still surprising that a critic as sophisticated as Peggy Kamuf should say that "historical event intervenes as a loosely structuring element marking narrative time at intervals sufficient to signify duration" (67) in "A Mother's Will: The *Princesse de Clèves*," in *Fictions of Feminine Desire*, University of Nebraska Press, Lincoln, 1982. The structure of the novel is not loosely knit around historical events. On the contrary. Lafayette's genius is diminished by such a statement.

¹⁴ In a stimulating article, "Exemplary Teaching in *La Princesse de Clèves*," *French Studies* XI, 4, 1957, pp. 293-321, H. Stone states that the imbrications serve no exemplary purpose in Mme de Clèves's development: "The princess's story emerges from the backdrop of mirrored events. Hers is a story with a difference, a history for which there is no model. The novel's internal narratives mirror the diegetic descriptions of the court against which the princess's own story is set in contrast," n.7, p. 258. There is, certainly, contrast between Mme de Clèves's experiences and those seen in the court, but the mirroring function of the narratives, and, in particular, the tale of the letter written by Mme de Thémines, simply cannot be denied. Mme de Thémines has been primarily ignored as a model for Mme de Clèves.

¹⁵ J. Morel has called attention to this letter in an incisive study entitled "Sur l'histoire de la lettre perdue dans *La Princesse de Clèves.*" *Papers on French Seventeenth-Century Literature* X, 19, 1983, pp. 701-709. Morel states that Lafayette learned of this story from La Rochefoucauld, "qui avait été témoin d'une aventure analogue, mais beaucoup plus simple dans son déroulement, que Victor Cousin a contée dans sa *Jeunesse de Mme de Longueville,* d'après les *Mémoires* de Mlle de Montpensier et de Mme de Motteville," p. 703.

¹⁶ M. Hirsch proposes a feminist interpretation based on psychologically-oriented theory of Mme de Clèves's *non*-acquisition of knowledge. Hirsch is supremely critical of Mme de Chartres: "It is my contention that the mother's lesson is at the center of a nexus of scenes that reflect and echo one another, trapping the heroine in a structure of repetitions which ultimately preclude development and progression." (In "A Mother's Discourse: Incorporation and Repetition in *La Princesse de Clèves*" *Yale French Studies* 62, 1981, p. 73. In Hirsch's view, Mme de Clèves's mother prevents her daughter from growing up, rather than preparing her for what she will find to be true, both historically and affectively, p. 87.

¹⁷ In *Forme et Signification*, José Corti, Paris, 1962, J. Rousset stresses the counterpoint between the imaginary and the "real," saying that the imaginary triumphs over historical reality by making the latter nothing other than a "futile décor." Niderst notes that Lafayette does not move directly from history to private domain but tries to "adroitly fuse both elements," p. 22. While admitting that the historical aspects of the novel give way to Mme de Clèves's affective dilemma, Singerman also stresses the double movement that takes place: "Just as the historical content physically dissolves into the fictional, so the historical content and its events are absorbed, metaphorically, into the context of the psychological and sentimental themes of the novel," in "History as Metaphor in Mme de Lafayette's *La Princesse de Clèves,*" *Modern Language Quarterly* 36, 3,

1975, p. 271. Malandain says it best: "Mais il s'agit en fait d'une structure d'alternance qui fait la signification de l'oeuvre, et d'une écriture, au plein sens que Roland Barthes a donné à ce terme," in *Mme de Lafayette: La Princesse de Clèves,* PUF, Paris, 1985, pp. 103-104.

[18] One edition was published by G.Charpentier et Cie., I-IV, 1886.

[19] *Mémoires de Mme de Motteville sur Anne d'Autriche et sa cour*, ed Riaux. 4 vols., Charpentier-Fasquelle, Paris, 1855. Chapter III, vol. I, pp. 135-143, contains the tale of the lost letter.

[20] I will use the terms "diegetic" and "metadiegetic" in the ways specified by G. Genette in *Figures* II and III. In "D'Un Récit baroque," *Figures* II, Seuil, Paris, 1969, pp. 202-203, Genette discusses modes of amplification of narrative whereby "secondary" récits are inserted into the first. He is quick to point out that "secondary" "est à prendre ici non pas du point de vue d'une hiérarchie d'importance, car un récit second peut fort bien être le plus long et/ou le plus essentiel comme on le voit souvent chez Balzac..., mais quand au niveau de médiation narrative: est récit second tout récit pris en charge par un agent de narration...intérieur au récit premier.... Ce qui est...absolu, c'est la différence de *statut narratif* entre l'histoire directement racontée par le narrateur ("l'auteur") et l'histoire racontée dans cette histoire et par un de ses constituants (personnage ou autre): l'histoire au second degré. Convenons de marquer cette opposition formelle en nommant *diégétique* le niveau premier, et *métadiégetique* le niveau second, quel que soit le rapport de contenu entre ces deux niveaux."

Genette refers again to the above in *Figures* III: "Le préfixe *méta* connote évidemment ici, comme dans 'métalangage,' le passage au second degré: le métarécit est un récit dans le récit, la *métadiegèse* est l'univers de ce récit second comme la diégèse désigne (selon un usage maintenant répandu) l'univers du récit premier," n.1, p. 239.

[21] Mme de Lafayette, *La Princesse de Clèves* Garnier-Flammarion, Paris, 1966, p. 80.

[22] J. DeJean, "Lafayette's Ellipses: The Privileges of Anonymity" *PMLA* 99, 5, 1984, pp. 884-900.

[23] *La Princesse de Clèves*, Garnier-Flammarion, pp. 97-98.

[24] DeJean's argument is intriguing when she says that Mme de Clèves "initiates [the letter's] passage from authentic amorous artifact to literary text," p. 895.

[25] Dällenbach, pp. 24-25. Dällenbach quotes Gide's famous statement: "In a work of art, I rather like to find transposed, at the level of the characters, the subject of the work itself. Nothing sheds more light on the work or displays the proportions of the whole work more accurately. Thus, in paintings by Memling or Quentin Metzys, a small dark convex mirror

reflects, in its turn, the interior of the room in which the action of the painting takes place. Thus, in a slightly different way, in Velasquez's *La Meninas...*" p. 7. Dällenbach quarrels with Gide's "definition" of what constitutes a *mise en abyme,* yet it is Gide who "names" the literary device as a self-conscious and deliberate tactic.

[26] ibid., pp. 24-25.

[27] As stated before, unless specified otherwise, all emphases in this book have been added.

[28] ibid., p. 99.

[29] ibid., p. 100.

[30] ibid., p. 98.

[31] See P. Henry's excellent collection of essays on the subject in his edition entitled *An Inimitable Example: The Case for The Princesse de Clèves,* The Catholic University of America Press, Washington, 1992.

[32] *La Princesse de Clèves,* Garnier-Flammarion, p. 99.

[33] ibid., p. 99.

[34] For an exposition of this motif, see J.R. McGuire's "La Princesse de Clèves dénouant *La Princesse de Clèves,"* *The French Review* 66, 3, 1993, pp. 381-392. By arguing that there is no Christian referent that the Princesse follows, Saint Augustine, in particular, McGuire says that this means that she is "irreprésentable en ce qu'elle n'est la répétition de rien," p. 388. She is, in his view (and this is his definition of "l'écriture féminine"), *sui generis.* I must argue that she is not: Mme de Thémines serves as a precedent, a mirror to Mme de Clèves's own experience.

[35] Along with its principal meaning ("distinction, élégance de manières" etc.), the word "galanterie" had already acquired, in the seventeenth century, meanings it acquired later on: "empressement inspiré par le désir de conquérir une femme; goût des bonnes fortunes" (*Robert*). The *Dictionnaire du français classique,* ed. Jean Dubois, René Lagane, Alain Leroud, Larousse, Paris, 1971, defines "galanterie" as "liaison amoureuse." The *Grand Dictionnaire du 19e Siècle,* Larousse, Paris, calls it a "passion amoureuse," and quotes La Bruyère: "La galanterie n'est qu'un libertinage auquel on a donné un nom honnête." The *Trésor de la Langue Française,* ed. du CNRS, Paris, 1981, says that it meant "goût, recherche des aventures amoureuses, des plaisirs physiques."

[36] *La Princesse de Clèves,* Garnier-Flammarion, p. 98.

[37] ibid., p. 104.

[38] ibid., p. 105.

[39] ibid., p. 98.

[40] ibid., p. 174.

[41] ibid., p. 173.

[42] In "Le Mythe de Tristan et Iseut et 'La Princesse de Clèves'," *Revue d'histoire littéraire de la France*, juillet 1965, pp. 398-414, M.-Th. Hipp emphasizes the role that is played by obstacles in the myth of love in Western literature. Mme de Clèves is quite explicit, herself, when she suggests to Nemours that perhaps it had been the obstacles between them that had kept him faithful to her, p.173.

[43] *La Princesse de Clèves,* Garnier-Flammarion, p. 174.

[44] In *Questions of Interpretation in La Princesse de Clèves*, Rodopi, Amsterdam-Atlanta 1996, p. 36.

[45] N. Miller points this out in "Emphasis Added: Plots and Plausibilities in Women's Fiction," *PMLA* 96, 1981, p. 42.

[46] *La Princesse de Clèves,* Garnier-Flammarion, pp. 98-99.

[47] ibid., p. 63.

[48] N. Miller calls Mme de Clèves's final refusal to marry Nemours "a peculiarly feminine 'act of victory'," p. 39. Miller refers to S. Lotringer's views on the subject, who, Miller says, "has observed that Mme de Clèves leaves the court not to flee passion but to preserve it." Miller adds: "To preserve it, however, on her own terms," p. 43. "Her own terms," argues Miller, makes of this an example of "l'écriture féminine." In "The Ideal of 'repos' in 17th-Century French Literature," *L'Esprit Créateur* 15, 1975, pp. 79-104, D. Stanton deals with the question of Mme de Clèves's final retreat by placing the Princesse's decision in the context of the seventeenth-century's notion of *repos*.

[49] R. H. Moye states that the Princesse's appropriation of the narratives she reads and hears leads to the paradoxical, or ironic ending of the novel. He says that "by forcing the reader to confront the ending as an ironic paradox, Lafayette denies the very appropriation and completion she invites: the story of the Princesse's victory is silence," p. 860. The paradox about which Moye speaks relates, primarily, to the last paragraph of the novel. Moye also argues that earlier in the text Mme de Clèves had departed from society in order to make herself "unnarratable": "Ultimately, the Princesse's conflict is between laying claim to a story that is distinctly and uniquely hers and preserving her anonymity by divorcing herself from a story that now belongs to its audience" (853). This is true. Yet Lafayette has made the narrative of Mme de Clèves one that is, indeed, about passion, and jealousy, and all the horrors accompanying them. The Princesse only retreats from the world, and consequently from the text of *La Princesse de Clèves* itself, *after* Lafayette has her narrate the story of her own love for Nemours to Nemours himself, and consequently, to us.

[50] In his anthology, *Lecture de Mme de Lafayette,* Armand Colin, Paris, 1971, M. Laugaa presents the history of the promotion of *La Princesse de Clèves* by the *Mercure galant.* Fontenelle's letter is on p. 22.

[51] In *Mme de Lafayette: La Princesse de Clèves*, Grant & Cutler Ltd., London, 1983, p. 14.

[52] In *La Princesse de Clèves: Mme de Lafayette*, Hatier, Paris, 1988, pp. 21-24.

[53] In *The Moment,'On re-reading novels.' Collected Essays* II Hogarth Press, New York, 1966, p. 126.

[54] *La Princesse de Clèves,* Garnier-Flammarion, p. 117.

[55] ibid., p. 118.

[56] ibid.

[57] R. Albanese, in P.Henry's edition of *Inimitable Virtue*, calls Mme de Clèves's propensities to reflect, after the fact, the "heroine's retrospective mode of self analysis," p. 94.

[58] *La Princesse de Clèves,* Garnier-Flammarion, p. 176.

[59] ibid., p. 175.

[60] ibid., p. 119.

[61] ibid., p. 119.

[62] I have compared editions of the *Nouveau Testament* dated 1579: ed. Anthoine Harsy, Lyon; 1601: ed. Hieros Haultin, La Rochelle; 1603: Pierre Callas, Rouen, "avec l'approbation dc la faculté de Théologie de Louvain"; 1800: *Les Epîtres de Saint Paul, Les Epîtres Canoniques, l'Apocalypse*; 1975: *La Bible,* Société Biblique Française et Ed. Du Cerf. Translations of Renaissance French into modern French are my own. The vocabulary under consideration varies little. I will quote the relevant phrases in French, and will use the edition that most resembles the syntax of *La Princesse de Clèves.*

[63] Baltrusaitis tells us that a Hellenic ritual of divination frequently employed a young child whose incorrupted look was clearer than that of an adult. Therefore a child ("when I was a child...") is mentioned in I Corinthians 13.11, preceding the text that is related to vision "through a glass," I Corinthians 13.12. This intertext would have been "perfectly understood by Corinthian readers of the epistle," says Baltrusaitis, p. 75.

[64] The 1579 edition of the Epistles states this verse in this way: "Certes je n'approuve point ce que *je fais*: car *je ne fais point* ce que *je veux: mais je fais ce que je hais.*" The 1603 edition states the verse in the following manner: "Car *je n'entends point ce que je fais,* vu que *je ne fais point le bien que je veux, mais je fais ce que je hais.*" The rhyme of *fais* and *hais* was most likely deliberate on the translator's part.

[65] *La Princesse de Clèves,* Garnier-Flammarion, p. 118.

[66] In *Fonction de la narration et du dialogue dans La Princesse de Clèves de Mme de Lafayette*, Lettres modernes, Paris, 1989, 40, n. 51.

[67] ibid., p. 58.

[68] S. Tiefenbrun analyzes four binary structures in *La Princesse de Clèves*, "from which many stylistic and semantic relationships of opposition could be generated," p. 121. One of these is Exterior/Interior, which, she says, provides Mme de Clèves's constant moves from court to country, p. 122. See *A Structural Analysis of La Princesse de Clèves*, Mouton,The Hague, 1976.

[69] See D. Huizinga's *Narrative Strategies in La Princesse de Clèves*, French Forum Publications, Lexington, 1961, where she says that the geography of the novel represents "a woman's struggle for autonomy. Wherever Mme de Clèves goes – parlor or pavilion – her space will be encroached upon by Nemours," p.78. R. Albanese states that the court is "the locus of facticity and a comedy of virtue," while Coulommiers is the world of "sincerity and authenticity," p. 96. Sweetser, too, will say, in a burst of alliteration, that the "two worlds, court and country, are clearly contrasted," p. 216. The Albanese and the Sweetser quotes are found in P. Henry's edition, *An Inimitable Example*.

[70] In "Sur une page de *La Princesse de Clèves*," L'Ecole des Lettres, Paris, 74, 1 oct. 1982, p. 32.

[71] M. Paulson, *A Critical Analysis of La Fayette's La Princesse de Clèves as a Royal Exemplary Novel: Kings, Queens, and Splendor* "Studies in French Literature" 10, The Edwin Mellen Press, Lewiston, 1992, p. 43.

[72] L. Horowitz, *Truly Inimitable*, p. 121-122.

[73] *La Princesse de Clèves,* Garnier-Flammarion, p. 35.

[74] ibid., p. 36.

[75] ibid.

[76] ibid.

[77] ibid.

[78] ibid., p. 37.

[79] ibid.

[80] Although M.-J. Durry does not use the word "hyperbole," she is, perhaps, one of the few critics to call attention to the excessive vocabulary Lafayette uses to describe jealousy: "Quand il s'agit de jalousie, Mme de La Fayette n'use plus de litotes. 'Cuisantes douleurs,' inquiétudes mortelles,' si instructives quand, détrompée, elle se les remémore, ne se reconnaissant plus elle-même, avec une véhemence qui brise, pour la première fois, le style indirect du monologue intime." In *Mme de la Fayette*, Mercure de France, Paris, 1962, pp. 40-41.

[81] *La Princesse de Clèves,* Garnier-Flammarion, p. 37.

[82] ibid., p. 180.

[83] ibid. p. 37.

[84] ibid., p. 37.

[85] In "Silent Victory: Narrative, Appropriation, and Autonomy in *La Princesse de Clèves*," *MLN* 104, 1989, pp. 845-60, R.H. Moye points to the paradoxical ending of the novel: "To see the conclusion as 'either'/'or' is to sacrifice one meaning to the other, to overlook Lafayette's doubleness, her irony," p. 846. By "undercutting the apparent closure of the conclusion," Moye states, "Lafayette invites us to appropriate the story and, in effect, to complete it by passing judgment upon the Princesse's ultimate decision. But by forcing the reader to confront the ending as an ironic paradox, Lafayette denies the very appropriation and completion she incites: the story of the Princesse's victory is silence" p. 860.

Chapter III

The Prévan Cycle as Pre-Text in Laclos's *Les Liaisons dangereuses*

> Le miroir fait toujours plus ou moins office de
> scène théâtrale où chacun se compose à partir
> d'une projection imaginaire, d'un modèle social et
> esthétique et d'une apparence qui se relancent
> réciproquement.
> Sabine Melchior-Bonnet

> La méthode, c'est le chemin après que l'on l'a
> parcouru.
> Jean-Pierre Vernant

Narcissus is a paradigm for chiasmus. He is also a paradigm for auto-referentiality. Narcissus as text, Narcissus as diptych: the juncture (or hinge) occurs at water's edge, between Narcissus and his reflection, between the text and the text repeated. The overall structure of Choderlos de Laclos's *Les Liaisons dangereuses* (1782) is a narcissistic or auto-referential chiasmus. The eighteenth century has been called "the century of fiction" by L. Michel. He says this seems unusual for times associated with the Enlightenment, the creation of the Encyclopedia, for the expansion of philosophical thought, and the guillotine. But Michel emphasizes not only the decorative and the artificial in his analyses of eighteenth-century thought, but he also stresses what he calls the audacious perspectives of fiction," much as the preceding century privileged illusion.[1]

The imbrications of "what seems to be" and "what actually is" characterized *La Princesse de Clèves*. The "artificial" and the "real" would come into play in a most powerful way later on, in 1782, with the publication of *Les Liaisons dangereuses*.

1. The Novel as Diptych

In the original manuscript, *Les Liaisons dangereuses* was composed of only two parts, and the juncture between the completed 175 letters occurred between letters 70 and 71. But whether custom dictated it, the editor suggested it for practical purposes, or Laclos himself decided upon it for reasons of his own, the text was published in four volumes rather than two, and it has been divided into four parts ever since. J.-L. Seylaz points out that far from arbitrary, each part, from the novel's inception, contributed to the dramatic progression of the whole.[2] D. Thelander goes even further than Seylaz when she states that we can assume that Laclos himself did, indeed, have something to do with the decision to divide the novel into four parts and that he arranged the breaks, or parts, so that they would occur "at strategic places in the plot and comply with the requirements demanded by the editor at the same time.[3] In his book on *Les Liaisons dangereuses*, P. Thody remarks that Laclos has all of the elements of his novel fit together "with an economy and elegance which bears witness to his prowess in mathematics and strategy, and this economy is particularly noticeable in the complete absence of superfluous character."[4] He also signals the "formal dance" characteristics of the novel, whereby Merteuil tries to replace Tourvel. In this "dance," both Cécile and Tourvel have something of the same role, since they are both seduced by Valmont even as they try to remain faithful to someone else. They take, as Thody writes, "the same steps" in that each of them writes the exact same number of letters, twenty-four.[5]

One may go further by noticing the extent to which repetition and auto-referentiality occur in the structural creation of the diptych. The text is organized in this manner:

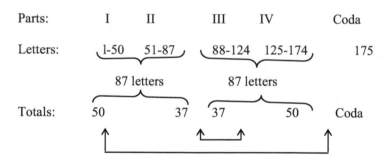

Parts:	I	II	III	IV	Coda
Letters:	1-50	51-87	88-124	125-174	175
		87 letters		87 letters	
Totals:	50	37	37	50	Coda

Letter 175 is a coda, which means that the structural make-up of the entire text is chiastic, and the hinge of the dyptich is placed at the mathematical centre of the work, a-b—b-a, or:

$$
\begin{array}{cc}
50 & 37 \\
& \\
37 & 50
\end{array}
$$

One of Mary Douglas's "rules" about what she calls a ring structure, is this: "The other prime test of a well-turned ring [the first is the chiasmus, which is a 'device that inverts the ordering of words'] is the loading of meaning on the centre and the connections made between the centre and the beginning; in other words, the centre of a polished ring integrates the whole."[6]

The adventures of Prévan are described in the last half of Part II of the novel. They are interwoven among Letters 70-87, which means that these letters lead toward the centre of the text's four-part structure. Letter 87, in which Mme de Merteuil recounts for a *second* time her adventure with Prévan, concludes the Prévan cycle as well as Part II of the novel. The "true" account is made to Valmont in Letter 85. The "false" one is made to Mme de Volanges in Letter 87. As is the case in Lafayette's "mirror in the middle," there is here a "true" letter, as well as a "false" one. One of the differences between Lafayette and Laclos, however, rides on the good will of Lafayette's characters. While Mme de Clèves and Nemours try their best to imitate the letter that is no longer in their possession, Laclos's Merteuil lies, deliberately, creating a dramatic spectacle in her second account of the Prévan incident. Mme de Clèves and Nemours simply imitate the "true" letter poorly, due to their fascination with each other.

References to Prévan are made twice in Part III, in letters 96, 113, and four times in Part IV, letters 125, 168, 169, and 173. The principal cycle of letters about him is found, however, at the end of Part II. Laclos chose to place the Prévan cycle at the juncture of his diptych. Why?

2.   The Central Hinge

Mme de Merteuil manoeuvres Prévan into a disastrous situation: she invites him into her bedroom in the middle of the night, has sex with him, and then loudly summons the servants, making it seem as if he had forcefully intruded. For this he is banished from society, and the entire stratagem is significant in the interplay of themes that deal with manipulation, power, drama, and revenge in the novel. Prévan's adventures with the *inséparables*, however, that are recounted by Valmont to Mme de Merteuil as a warning about Prévan's power, have been thought, by some readers of Laclos, to be extraneous to the main body of the text. Alexandre de Tilly, a contemporary of Laclos, called it one of "several little...stimulating stories" that were incorporated by Laclos to make his novel more titilating and more plausible.[7] Even Seylaz says that he, himself, "neglects to examine" the *inséparables* narrative because it is less significant than other parts of the novel (50). D. Thelander adds her voice to the chorus of detractors of the Prévan tale by saying that two narratives could easily have been left out: the Prévan and the Vressac episodes. That they are "twin" episodes is true, but I cannot agree

with her reasons for stating they are "superfluous." The function of having
Prévan as the hero of this story, she says, is to cover up what might have been
"an obvious and irritating symmetry." Merteuil's episode with Prévan as well
as her epistolary autobiography are simple counterweights to the Vressac
episode, she says, as well as is the story of the *inséparables*.[8] Just as N.
Mitford said that the intercalated narratives in *La Princesse de Clèves* could
be skipped, Thelander says that "Laclos needed something to fill up time
while Valmont could get ready to seduce Cécile while his infatuation with La
Présidente could develop. This negative criticism of structurally important
material is similar to that of numerous critics who misunderstand the value of
the metadiegetic narratives in *La Princesse de Clèves* and call them
"digressions." Thelander goes so far as to suggest that having one's two best
narrators have nothing to narrate would be awkward. Prévan gives them
something to quarrel about, and is a "display piece" that permits the insertion
of Merteuil's autobiographical letter. I claim, however, that there is nothing
gratuitous or lacking in meaning in *Les Liaisons dangereuses*. Laclos plays
only serious games. Each letter, each juxtaposition of letters, is essential to
the whole. The statement Pascal makes about "fitting together of various
parts" in any construction, and the rapport of those "parts" to "the whole" is
perfectly appropriate to Laclos's creation. The Prévan episode is not only
psychologically important, it is crucial to the way in which the novel's
"chess-game" is played out. Could one not suggest that the name *Prévan*
places, in and of itself, emphasis on the *"pre-"* aspect of his character?

     Thody points out that Merteuil needs Valmont to be her mirror and
admirer.[9] Had Valmont not known that she had defeated Prévan, that victory
would not be so grand. But one could also say that Valmont needs Merteuil as
his looking-glass, since he needs her to admire his seduction of la Présidente.
One might add that both mirrors are broken, in the end, resulting in terrible
misfortune for both spectators, for their "looking-glasses," and for others
within their social circles who either admired or detested them.

     The tale of Prévan's "triple adventure" is told in Letter 79, which is
at the centre of the Prévan cycle. The narrative is carefully prepared. In Letter
70, which begins the cycle, Valmont warns Mme de Merteuil about Prévan's
openly stated intentions to seduce her. This reminds one of Mme de
Volange's warnings to Mme de Tourvel about Valmont in Part I, Letter 9: "Je
ne m'arrête pas à compter celles qu'il a séduites; mais combien n'en a-t-il pas
perdues?" In Letter 71 Valmont describes his own adventures with three
seemingly "inséparables," the Vicomtesse de M..., her husband, and her
lover, Vressac. Valmont ends this letter with the repeated admonition:
"Beware of Prévan."

     In Letter 74, Mme de Merteuil responds that she had met Prévan at
the Opéra and that she had already set up a plan whereby she would meet him

at the house of the Marquise de .... She then asks Valmont to describe Prévan's "triple adventure": she states that it must have occurred while she was in Geneva, and Valmont's jealousy of Prévan's glory, she teases, must have prevented him from telling her the story before. She will prepare a grand scheme for Prévan's downfall, she says, thus establishing herself as a "juge entre vous deux." In Letter 76 Valmont responds with alarm to her plan: "Tenez, j'ai peur. Ce n'est pas que je doute de votre adresse: mais ce sont les bons nageurs qui se noient." Narcisse/Valmont is afraid of his double, Narcisse/Prévan. In Letter 79 Valmont has *two* hours to while away before lunch, so he rallies, as he always does when his pen meets paper, and recounts the complicated affair to Mme de Merteuil. During carefully spaced interludes, he says, Prévan had managed to seduce, in one single night, three women who had the reputation of being "inseparable." Rumour had it that each new mistress received, in turn, triple "proof" of Prévan's devotion. Although sceptical, Valmont cannot but admire such a Priapian feat. The following morning, however, Prévan was forced to come to terms with the threesome's outraged lovers. Each had discovered Prévan's betrayal and had arrived in turn at his house, demanding justice. Having arranged with each to meet, the following day, at one of the "portes du Bois de Boulogne," where they were to duel, the lovers arrive at the appointed place at the same time, according to Prévan's plan. Although they are surprised to see each other, they console themselves in their co-fraternity of cuckoldry, and Prévan cheerfully invites them to share a meal with him. Because Prévan knows how to charm, there is soon no question of coming to blows. At the end of the meal all differences are reconciled. Appeased, all three men accept an invitation to dine with Prévan that evening. The *metteur-en-scène* par excellence arranges, during carefully spaced interludes, for each of the *inséparables* to arrive at his house of trysts at the same time as her lover. Each is forced to face the man she had betrayed with Prévan. After each woman begs forgiveness of her jealous mate, the couples, in turn, repair to a back room to "seal" the renewed covenant: "Le traité de paix se ratifia dans un lieu plus solitaire, et la scène, restée vide, fut alternativement remplie par les autres acteurs, à peu près *de la même manière,* et surtout *avec le même dénouement.*"[10] In a grand gesture, Prévan then brings them all together before a dinner table. As he makes his excuses to the *inséparables*, each is apprised of the other's secret, and all become aware of the enormity of Prévan's deception. Prévan is nothing but hyperbolic (as, needless to say, is Valmont). But good will prevails, and all three couples spend the rest of the night at Prévan's having an amicable dinner together. The conclusion of the tale is not so fanciful. Valmont states that:

> Quand on se sépara, les femmes durent se croire
> pardonnées; mais les hommes, qui avaient conservé leur
> ressentiment, firent dès le lendemain une rupture qui n'eut
> point de retour; et non contents de quitter leurs légères
> maîtresses, ils achevèrent leur vengeance, en publiant leur
> aventure. Depuis ce temps, une d'elles est au couvent, et
> les deux autres languissent exilées dans leurs terres.

This ending is proleptic: the novel's own conclusion is inscribed in these words. Prévan is Valmont writ small. Prévan is the reflection of Narcissus at water's edge. If the novel's framework is chiastic, imbricated order has Part IV reflect Part II.

One of the many reasons for Valmont's narration of Prévan's two-day orgy is to even out and give sufficient motive for Mme de Merteuil's narrative of Prévan's ruin. Valmont also wishes to give Mme de Merteuil ample incentive for bringing down Prévan, a desire he has unwittingly created in her by warning her about Prévan's dangerous reputation. While, in Mme de Merteuil's mind, the seducer must be seduced, Valmont continues to warn that Prévan must be reckoned with carefully. Letter 79 gives ample proof of how skilful Prévan is in accomplishing nefarious deeds. A series of mirrors is created within the narrative so that Laclos, the theatrical magician, prepares and thereby reflects the end of his own act: the eighteenth century was as fond of mirrors as was the seventeenth, and Laclos's *Galerie des Glaces* was as scintillating a creation as was Versailles'.[11]

Why does Valmont use *inséparable* as a naming device? It is shorthand, first of all. To name, or to say "Mme de..." three times would prove awkward. The appellation is also an excuse for an obscene double entendre on Valmont's part: the reader is led to believe that society had called the three women *inséparables* to imply that there was a lesbian relationship between them. But the cognomen goes further: it serves as a pretext for Laclos. He is signalling to his reader that this letter is "inseparable" from the whole. This letter is a signifier: the pretext is a pre-text.

The cycle begins with Letter 70, with Valmont's warning Mme de Merteuil that "Prévan, que vous ne connaissez pas, est infiniment *aimable*, et encore plus *adroit*." This description of Prévan could be taken for a description of Valmont himself. The mirror function of Prévan is thus implicit in the first mention of his name. In the concluding stages of Part IV, Mme de Merteuil herself uses the adjective *aimable* to refer to Valmont: "Le Valmont que j'aimais était charmant. Je veux bien convenir même que je n'ai pas rencontré d'homme plus *aimable*" in Letter 152. And there is no question, of course, that he is *adroit*. Prévan, in fact, is so like Valmont that Valmont sees him as a menace, stating that he is the only man he would fear to meet. He expresses the hope that upon his own return, Prévan will be "a drowned man." The end of the novel, in which Valmont himself will be "a drowned man" figures ironically in this pre-text, since, as he says, "it's always good swimmers who drown."

There is no question that Laclos used this metaphor deliberately. Valmont describes to Mme de Merteuil in the second letter of the cycle, Letter 71, his own hilarious adventures of the previous evening when he had spent the night at the chateau of the Vicomtesse de M.... He had managed to have sexual relations with the lady of the house even as her lover, Vressac, occupied the bedroom to one side of hers and her husband occupied the other. Valmont's antics, in other words, *equal* those of Prévan. He finds it necessary to play a macho game of "one upmanship" with Prévan. Valmont had thought it safer for the Vicomtesse to visit *his* room during the night, thus prefiguring Cécile Volange's coming to his bedroom later on. His room was directly across the hall from the Vicomtesse's, but they discover, at night's end, that she had locked herself out. Valmont saves the day or one could say the night, by bursting open the door while she speedily regains her bed and shouts "Au voleur!" Valmont has the effrontery to castigate both husband and lover, who come rushing out of their rooms, for their "lethargic sleep," claiming that he had been trying, for at least five minutes, to smash open the Vicomtesse's door in order to rescue her. Noticing a candlestick that he himself had deliberately knocked over before the arrival of the other two men, he claims that a rodent must have overturned it during the night, scaring the lady of the house. The cacemphaton, or scurrilous double entendre, implied in the conclusion of the anecdote is gleefully related by Valmont when he says that upon returning to his own room the husband requests his wife to have "à l'avenir des rats plus tranquilles." The constant use Valmont makes of sexually ambiguous terms repeats the doubled "fitting together of parts," and the relationship they have to the novel's macro-structure.

Valmont not only brags about his inventiveness; he is also particularly interested in the *details* of the account, stating that even though he has the talent to destroy women's reputations, he can also save them when he so desires. As a mirror reverses its reflected imagery, making left right and right left, revealing sameness as well as alterity, Valmont's picaresque adventure described in Letter 71 serves as a pre-text to Prévan's own wild night, described in Letter 79. But while Valmont "rescues," in this instance, Prévan destroys the *inséparables*. At the end of the novel, however, Prévan, who is destroyed by Mme de Merteuil in Part II, will be rescued, while it is Prévan's mirror image, Valmont, who will be destroyed.

3.   Proleptic Encounters of a Close Kind
One of the clues to the recounting of these adventures is found in the

relationship between their details and other parts of the novel. Both Valmont and Prévan are braggarts. The first boasts that he will seduce Mme de Tourvel while the second brags about the fact that even though he might have to "wear out six horses" in the process, he will seduce Mme de Merteuil. Prévan is hyperbolic in that during one night alone he grants sexual "favours" three times each to each of the *inséparables*. Valmont is never loath to withhold the fact that, like Casanova, he can "perform" multiple times during one night. Just as Prévan goes to meet the outraged lovers of the *inséparables* at one of the gates of the Bois de Boulogne, which is located at one end of Paris, Valmont, at the conclusion of the text, will go meet Danceny, who demands justice, at one of the gates of the Bois de Vincennes, at the *other* end of Paris. Their fates are reversed: while Prévan is prepared to duel but avoids doing so, in the middle of the novel, Valmont will die, in the end, as a consequence of the wounds he suffers in his duel with Danceny.

Even as Prévan is able to reconcile himself with the outraged lovers "si bien que ce ne fut pas assez de n'avoir plus de rancune, on se jura *amitié* sans réserve" (Letter 79), so does Valmont, at death's door, reconcile himself with Danceny: "Il lui a pris la main, l'a appelé son *ami*, l'a embrassé devant nous tous" (Letter 163). The words *amitié* and *ami* appear in both middle and end of the novel.

The theatrical thematics, which play such an important part throughout the text, are especially significant in the *inséparables* letter. As each couple leaves the scene to repair the damaged relationship in the wings, the "stage" is alternatively occupied "à peu près de *la même manière*, et surtout avec *le même dénouement*." The doubled insistence on "the same ending" points to the ending of the novel: "Les hommes, qui avaient conservé leur ressentiment, firent dès le lendemain une rupture qui n'eut point de retour." This will be the case of Valmont himself. His own *rupture* with Mme de Tourvel, and Mme de Merteuil, and Cécile Volanges, *n'eut point de retour*. Nor is there any reconciliation between Danceny and Cécile Volanges. But Prévan & Company go beyond leaving their mistresses: "Ils achevèrent leur vengeance en publiant leur aventure." In the end, Valmont/Danceny do just that. They "publish" abroad two letters, both from Mme de Merteuil. The first, Letter 85, in which Mme de Merteuil recounts her adventure with Prévan, thereby exonerating Prévan, and the other, which is Mme de Merteuil's infamous autobiography, or "Profession of Faith" (Letter 81), puts the final touch upon her downfall.[12] Both of these letters are structured into the Prévan cycle, and are "published abroad." The choice of *two* letters undergirds the dyadic textual production of the *Liaisons*.

Even more pre-textual is the last phase of the punishment meted out to the *inséparables*: "Depuis ce temps, une d'elles est au couvent, et les deux autres languissent exilées dans leurs terres." At the conclusion of *Les*

Liaisons dangereuses, Cécile Volanges enters the convent. The other two women in the novel's triad of principal female characters, Mme de Merteuil and Mme de Tourvel, end up "in exile." The former's exile is literal, as she will be forced to flee her country and go to Holland in order to save, stealthily, the last vestiges of her wealth. Mme de Tourvel's "exile" is metaphorical in that she abandons society, retreats to the convent, and dies. The three women's fate in Part II prefigures the fate of the three principal women at the end of Part IV., and Prévan's "triple adventure" is mirrored in Valmont's "triple adventures" with Merteuil, Tourvel, and Volanges.

4.   The Title in Text and Pre-Texts

Letter 79 ends with a coda. Valmont thus concludes his epistle to Merteuil about Prévan: "*Adieu, ma belle*; méfiez-vous des idées plaisantes ou bizarres qui vous séduisent toujours trop facilement. Songez que dans la carrière que vous courez, l'esprit ne suffit pas, qu'*une seule imprudence* y devient un mal sans remède. Souffrez enfin que la prudente amitié soit quelquefois le guide de vos plaisirs." Since the last letter of *Les Liaisons dangereuses*, 175, may be considered as a coda to the entire novel, the first two and the last two parts of the novel are equally composed of 87 letters. Valmont's own coda, in Letter 79, then, will be echoed in the final prescription Mme de Volanges makes in the novel's coda. As she bids her friend *adieu*, Mme de Rosemonde says: "Qui pourrait ne pas frémir en songeant aux malheurs que peut causer *une seule liaison dangereuse*?" Valmont's *adieu* is repeated by Mme de Rosemonde's *adieu,* and his *une seule imprudence* is echoed by Mme de Rosemonde's *une seule liaison dangereuse*. Mme de Volanges is repeating herself as well, for she had used *une seule imprudence* in Letter 165, while decrying what had happened to Mme de Tourvel, stating that all was lost due to *une seule imprudence*.

The novel's title is repeated three times in the singular within the work itself: once in Part I, *une seule liaison dangereuse*, Letter 32, once in Part II, *une liaison dangereuse*, Letter 63, and once in the coda, Letter 175, *une seule liaison dangereuse*. It appears, interestingly enough, twice more in reversed form: such as in Letter 22: "M. de Valmont n'est peut-être qu'un exemple de plus du *danger des liaisons*," and Letter 32: "Quand il ne serait, comme vous le dites, qu'un exemple du *danger des liaisons*, en serait-il moins lui-même une *liaison dangereuse*?" The chiasmus makes the title of the novel appear as in juxtaposed sets of mirrors, thus mirroring the content of the whole.

L.Versini, in *Laclos et la tradition*, brings to our attention many of the commonplaces of eighteenth-century literature that are found in *Les Liaisons dangereuses*. The title is one of them: it had been used previously in 1763 by Mme de Saint-Aubin in her *Danger des liaisons*.[13] Laclos had initially called his manuscript *Du danger des liaisons*. He reversed it, however, using a title that was less moralizing, less didactic.[14] But he repeats, nevertheless, Mme de Saint-Aubin's title when he uses, twice, *le danger des liaisons*. One of Mme de Saint-Aubin's conclusions is that *on ne badine impunément avec l'amour*. There are intertextual reflections in this house of mirrors[15] since *Les Liaisons dangereuses* was also the title of a short story written by Marmontel.[16]

The danger, as Mme de Volanges states, of *une seule liaison dangereuse* echoes Valmont's warning about the danger of *une seule imprudence*, but the irony of Valmont's coda in Letter 79 is that even as he writes the warning, he is blind to the disaster that will result from his own *imprudence*. As J. Rousset states: "C'est que les livres dialoguent entre eux, se lisent les uns à travers les autres. Nous voilà tout près de l'intertexte généralisé de Borges ou du palimpseste de Genette."[17]

5.   Blindness and In-Sight

The text reads the reader as the reader reads the text. In order to see this methodological principle as chiastic, the reader must reflect upon the rhetoric of the reading act itself. Narcissus is both text and reader; but he has also been condemned into being nothing other than an appreciative critic of his own text. At first he does not take a step backward, so to speak, outside of the play of juxtaposed mirrors. He sees only his double, and not his own dupery. For all his binocular vision, he is disposed to look at his text in a singular fashion, even after he recognizes himself. It is appropriate that, at the end of the text, Laclos has Mme de Merteuil lose one of her eyes as a punishment for her misdeeds. The blindness or the lack of self-perception that the master-minds in this novel possess, even as they build their elaborate machinery for the deception of others, is one of the mainstays of the text. Valmont and Merteuil are finally undone because their passions are reflected in their reflections, that is, their letters. They are examples of Narcissus being condemned to repeat himself. The dialectical movement from vision to blindness is constant in Laclos, and the mirror-structure of the novel carries that message.

If Valmont's Letter 79 is a pre-text of the ending of *Les Liaisons dangereuses*, Mme de Merteuil's Letter 85, in which she describes Prévan's downfall, is a response to Valmont's worries about Prévan. But Mme de Merteuil's description of Prévan's downfall is also a pre-text of that which precipitates the novel's conclusion, Mme de Tourvel's downfall. Her seduction is recounted by Valmont in Letter 125, the first letter of Part IV. Letter 125 thus mirrors Letter 85.

Mme de Merteuil begins her epistle, Letter 85, by bragging: "J'ai mis à fin mon aventure avec Prévan; *à fin!*..[italics in text] A présent vous allez juger qui de lui ou moi pourra se vanter." So will Valmont, in Letter 125, brag about his victory over Mme de Tourvel. It was no simple capitulation, but a victory of which he is extremely proud, at least at the beginning.

Mme de Merteuil's adventure with Prévan begins at the theatre. In Letter 74 she reports having stood next to Prévan at the Opéra, and having loudly made a rendez-vous with the marquise, her friend, for the following Friday. There are also various references to the theatre in the letter in which she recounts Prévan's undoing, such as "ce coup de théâtre passé" or "le jeu dura plus que je n'avais pensé." Valmont's affair with Mme de Tourvel, too, ends in the theatrical mode: "Je marquai de l'oeil le théâtre de ma victoire...car, dans cette même chambre, *il se trouvait une ottomane.*" The end of Valmont's and Mme de Merteuil's own affair, which is only referred to as having taken place in the past, had also been concluded "*sur [une] ottomane.*" Similar "details," as Valmont is wont to call them, appear in both letters 85 and 125. Prévan kneels down before the Maréchale, near whom Mme de Merteuil is seated during their first visit to her house, and engages in a conversation filled with double entendres that are directed to Mme de Merteuil. Valmont, the master of the double entendre, falls to *his* knees in *his* theatrical coup before Mme de Tourvel, and tells her many flattering and tender things.

When Prévan offers Mme de Merteuil his hand, she breathes deeply to mark her emotion. She kept, she says, "les yeux baissés et *la respiration haute.*" Mme de Tourvel, too, breathes deeply when she gives in. She had "le maintien mal assuré, *la respiration haute....*" Sameness versus difference: Merteuil's hard breathing is fake. Tourvel's is an expression of genuine emotion. Theatrical thematics accentuate the role of masks, which hide, conceal, change, distort the wearer's identity. Masked balls were frequent occurrences in the King's courts. They were highly prized by Louis XIII's and by Louis XIV's courts, and throughout the eighteenth century. Their ancient provenance is not discounted, neither is their ever-present role in calling intrigue to mind. Ballets and theatrical productions of all kinds, as we know, were replete with extravagant masks and costumes. Molière, Corneille, and Quinault created a tragi-comic ballet in five acts entitled *Les Amours de Psyché*. The music was composed by Lully, and it was a great success in Louis XIV's court. But their pre-text had been a poem composed by La Fontaine in 1669, entitled "Les Amours de Psyché," a work in which one of the accoutrements was a mirror that, when placed on a frame, could be moved at different angles on the stage.

Another intriguing aspect of Protean "heroes" or "villains" was Dom Juan. J. Rousset quotes one of the dancers in a play/ballet as saying:

Et je ne me suis déguisé
Que pour me faire mieux connaître.

Rousset comments that this is how Dom Juan comes into his own, that is, in disguise. He is always on the run, always Protean, always in a state of metamorphosis.[18] One of the pleasures of the spectacles was precisely the making and *un*-making of the heroes' quick retreats into and out of reality. A more appropriate statement could not be applied to Valmont.

The ultimate "coup de glace" appears at the end of both letters 85 and 125. Near the conclusion of her letter, Mme de Merteuil says that after Prévan left her house in disgrace, the news of his downfall was sounded abroad. By late afternoon his superior had arrived to "faire ses excuses, de ce qu'un officier de *son corps* avait pu me manquer à ce point. Il...avait sur-le-champ envoyé ordre à Prévan de se rendre *en prison*." Valmont's final statement occurs in a post-script: "Savez-vous que Prévan, au bout de son mois *de prison*, a été obligé de quitter *son corps*?" While Mme de Merteuil first uses *son corps*, then *prison*, in her conclusion, Valmont reverses the order. This chiasmus is separated by an interlude of 40 letters: "corps-prison—prison-corps." The echo does not reverse any meaning, such as the one that occurs when the March Hare argues with Alice. It is, rather, of the same order as the Dormouse's "breathing when he sleeps" and "sleeping when he breathes."

With mirror-production becoming prolific in eighteenth-century France, mirror "spectacles" in literature increase as well. While it was expensive and rare for literal mirrors to be acquired under Louis XIV's reign, one hundred years later mirrors were found in 70% of Parisian houses and in the provinces as well. S. Mercier came out with this quip: "Bientôt le boudoir de la marchande de draps sera tout en glaces... Où n'en met-on pas?" Large mirrors, however, were still a sign of wealth, and only the aristocracy possessed full-sized or large ones. At the end of the eighteenth century the "psyché" was subject to many improvements and variations; it would have neither table nor drawer, and would frequently have several mirrors on closets attached to it.[19] J. Eymard says that it "comes into its own" around 1810, and becomes an indispensable auxiliary to beauty during the Empire and the Restoration.[20] The ever-developing expansion of "the mirror stage" would lead to the creation of dramas such as those sighted in the *Liaisons*.

6.   Ceci n'est pas Narcisse (non plus)

It is expected that repetition of vocabulary should occur in letters that are exchanged, since the situation is in itself chiastic: writer-reader—reader-writer. The verisimilitude that is built into epistolarity is significantly furthered by the mirror imagery that results from Laclos's deliberate usage of repetition. His choice of the epistolary form was clearly influenced by the eighteenth-century's fascination with mimesis. By choosing a vehicle that would allow letters to seem "real," Laclos insisted, even further, on the Magritte-like *ceci n'est pas une pipe* quality of his text. It is as if this message were handwritten under Narcissus: *Ceci n'est pas Narcisse*. This is especially true when one remembers that Narcissus is a representation, a text, or multiple texts (Ovid's, Conon's, Pliny's, Pausanias's, Guillaume de Lorris's, and many others.) As E. Said says of Foucault: "A discourse...simply repeats, in a different mode, another discourse."[21]

Laclos begins his manoeuvres with mimesis by employing a double tactic: not only is there an *éditeur* of this compilation of letters; but the *rédacteur* disagrees with the editor, and each has a distinct personality and style. And even *they*, by their choice of vocabulary, reflect each other and upon each other in their initial quarrel. In the opinion of H. Duranton, they cancel each other out perfectly.[22] In their initial annulment of each other, they preview the final deconstruction of the carefully wrought mechanism that Merteuil/Valmont try to create. P. Villani states that the Preface of the *Rédacteur* returns the reader to the grand tradition of mirrors that existed in literature since the Middle Ages. Those edifying tomes were called *specula*, such as *speculum doctrinale, speculum historiale, speculum morale*, this last one having been written by Vincent de Beauvais, the son of Saint Louis. These books were pedagogical in tone and tenor.[23] Villani also quotes Baudrillard who, in *De la séduction*, says that in the Narcissus myth, it is not a question of a mirror's being proffered to Narcissus so that he might find himself ideally alive. All seduction, says Baudrillard, is in a sense narcissistic, and the secret lies in the deadly act of being absorbed, or taken in, by the mirror.[24]

In the first sentence of his *avertissement* to *Les Liaisons*, the editor warns us: "Nous croyons devoir prévenir *le public*, que, malgré le titre de *cet ouvrage* et ce qu'en dit *le rédacteur* dans sa *préface*, nous ne garantissons pas l'authenticité de *ce recueil* et que nous avons même de fortes raisons de penser que *ce n'est qu'un roman*." Under Narcissus II, his representation in the water, an inscription should read: *Ceci n'est pas Narcisse non plus*.

On the opposite page from that of the editor's, many of the same words are used by the *rédacteur* to contradict the idea that *ceci n'est qu'un roman*: "*Cet ouvrage*, ou plutôt *ce recueil*, que *le public* trouvera peut-être trop volumineux, ne contient pourtant que le plus petit nombre des lettres qui composaient la totalité de *la correspondence* dont il est extrait."[25]

In the case of juxtaposing mirrors, quadruplicate (if not infinite) reflections occur. Just as Valmont's letter about Prévan, Letter 79, contains a coda that is reflected in the novel's coda, Letter 175, so does Mme de Merteuil's statement about Prévan in Letter 85 prefigure Valmont's post-script in Letter 125. The post-script of Letter 125 reflects the coda of Letter 175, just as the coda of Letter 79 reflects the Prévan statement in #85. The work turns back upon itself, reflecting itself in the act of turning back. In so doing, the geometry of its construction exhibits the two principal characters' mirroring and repeating themselves.

Villani foregrounds the claustrophobic nature of copying and recopying. He personalizes the letters by calling them mirrors that have their own personalities. He says that these mirrors spend their time copying and re-copying themselves, which is, after all, their primary function. This closed milieu "delights" in a permanent redundancy of communication and is addicted to "photocopying": "one makes rough drafts that are kept, that one re-copies, that one sends if the occasion presents itself, or one regrets not having done so...One may even double the narcissistic rapports between letters, word for word, or regrets not having done so....".[26] After all, a letter is always addressed, first, to oneself. In the section of his chapter, which is called "The Mirror's Seductiveness," the comparison is made between mirrors, letters, and Don Juan: "Don Juans seduce...because they are at first seduced by their proper selves, which means that in order to seduce an other, one must first produce in them an auto-erotic desire. Seduction and writing, then, go hand in hand." To describe seduction, Villani again quotes Baudrillard when the latter uses the expression (for Don Juan): "I will be your mirror."

Thody points out how certain characters in the novel have predilections for certain words, and ceaselessly repeat them. Merteuil is fond of the word "humeur," while Tourvel uses "bonheur." Merteuil and Tourvel as rhyming mirrors: not only does Merteuil's "humeur" reflect the opposite of Tourvel's "bonheur," but the values surrounding their opposing representations reach the core of the novel's reflective meanings.

7.   Double Keys to the Kingdom

The double key motif contributes to the conflation of mirrors in *Les Liaisons dangereuses*. Already in Letter 10 Mme de Merteuil refers to possessing two keys to her house of trysts. While she has given one to Belleroche, making him think that he is the sole possessor of that key, she is quick to tell Valmont that she owns a *double clef*. Mme de Merteuil accentuates the motif even further when she says that although Belleroche does not know that she plans to leave him soon, she, herself, knows that fact well enough for *both* of them.

In Letter 84, which is also structured into the Prévan cycle, Valmont gives most precise instructions to Cécile Volanges on how to secure the key to her room. Mme de Volanges keeps the key on her mantlepiece: "Tout deviendra facile avec cette clef...Mais à son défaut, je vous en procurerai *une semblable,* et qui la *suppléera.* Il me suffira, pour y parvenir, d'avoir l'autre *une heure ou deux* à ma disposition... J'en *joins ici une à moi,* qui est assez *semblable,* pour qu'on ne voie pas *la différence.*" The verb *supléer* recalls what Laclos said about the reading act in his *L'Education des femmes*: "Reading is, actually, a second education that fills in what was lacking in the first."[27]

Valmont points to both similarity and difference in his trickery. These can be perceived when two objects are brought into contiguity one with another, which is one of the meanings of metaphor. But one could say that the double key motif reveals a desire to "confound" metaphor by making the perceiver believe that both entities *are* the same. Mme de Volanges hopefully will not perceive *la différence.*

In writing about the poetry of E.Jabès, J. Derrida employs the following chiasmus: "On ne sort du livre que dans le livre puisque pour Jabès le livre n'est pas dans le monde, mais le monde dans le livre."[28] Valmont's phrase "j'en joins ici une à moi, qui est assez semblable, pour qu'on ne voie pas la différence" is a description of Laclos's own activity. Laclos uses Valmont's writing of letters to show how his writing is similar to and yet different from the act of writing a novel. Referentiality occurs within the realm of auto-referentiality. Writing is celebrating writing.

In the act of writing his letter to Cécile, and in telling her that there *is* a difference between the two keys that he wishes to hide, Valmont points to an artificial device. By using the epistolary form, Laclos too uses an artificial device. And artificial devices cannot deny their own artifices: Valmont's instructions to Cécile reveal, in encapsulated form, the novel's technique. The formula for chiasmus, "a-b" is both like *and* different from "b-a." To say "man does not live to read; he reads to live" is to say something that is both similar *and* different. Likeness as well as difference are built into the trope. P. Ricoeur stresses the tension that exists between sameness and difference: "To see the like is to see the same in spite of, and through, the different. This tension between sameness and difference characterizes the logical structure of likeness."[29]

8.   Citings

In Letter 110 Valmont describes to Mme de Merteuil the double affair in which he is involved: he is in the process of seducing both Mme de Tourvel and Cécile Volanges. In this letter, as throughout the book, he makes constant use of the words *à la fois, deux, même, second, double* (and its double, *quatrième*). He begins with a quotation from *La Nouvelle Héloïse* (which just happened to have been published 22 years before *Les Liaisons dangereuses*):

> 'Puissances du Ciel, j'avais une âme pour la douleur: donnez-m'en une pour la félicité!' C'est, je crois, le tendre Saint-Preux qui s'exprime ainsi. Mieux partagé que lui, je possède *à la fois* les *deux* existences. Oui, mon amie, je suis, *en même temps*, très heureux et très malheureux; et puisque vous avez mon entière confiance, je vous dois *le double* récit de mes peines et de mes plaisirs. Sachez donc que mon ingrate dévote me tient toujours rigueur. J'en suis à ma *quatrième* lettre renvoyée. J'ai peut-être tort de dire la *quatrième*; car ayant bien deviné dès le premier renvoi, qu'il serait suivi de beaucoup d'autres...j'ai pris le parti de mettre mes doléances en lieux communs, et de ne point dater: et depuis ce *second* courrier, c'est toujours *la même lettre* qui va et vient; je ne fais que changer d'enveloppe.

The initial reference to and quotation by Saint-Preux reveals one of the pre-texts Laclos chooses to have his characters constantly read and cite. *Clarissa Harlowe* and *La Nouvelle Héloïse* are quoted frequently by both Valmont and Mme de Merteuil. *Les Liaisons* reflect and distort previous epistolary novels. Like reflecting images depicted in the convex or concave mirrors of a funhouse, citations from previous works are deformed by being re-formed. They are transformed, since the new contexts give the truncated texts new meanings.

Laclos's manuscript contains a note that was suppressed in the printed edition. It stated that Valmont seemed to love to quote Rousseau, but profaned his usage by changing his quotations to suit his needs.[30] Quotation is itself something of a profanation, an abuse. It means repeating the original by putting it to a use for which it was not originally intended. In *La Seconde main: ou le travail de la citation*, A. Compagnon says: "The subject of citation is an equivocal character who contains, simultaneously, a bit of Narcissus and a bit of Pontius Pilate within him. He is an index finger, a traitor — he points his finger in public to other discourses and other subjects — but his denunciation, his summons, are both a calling-forth and a solicitation: a request for recognition."[31] One could also call it a seduction, in the sense of what seduction means to Valmont. As Cécile is "wrenched away" from her initial state by means of a double key, so does Valmont, with duplicity, wrench Saint-Preux's words away from their original surroundings. The same words acquire new and perverse meanings when Valmont repeats them, when he interrupts their initial flow of discourse, when he cuts them off from their contexts.

There is no better example of Valmont's being a master of the *textus interruptus* than the famous letter he writes to Mme de Tourvel during intermissions between sexual performances with the courtesan Emilie, in Letter 48. Using Emilie's naked body as a desk, thus celebrating sexuality and "double" writing at the same time, he says: "Pardonnez, je vous en supplie, au désordre de mes sens... Il faut vous quitter un moment pour dissiper une ivresse qui s'augmente à chaque instant, et qui devient plus forte que *moi*." After he takes time out, he says: "*Je* reviens à vous, Madame..." We are to understand that the space, the white inviolate space between the words *moi* and *Je* is being used for other than inviolate purposes. The *plaisir du texte* occurs between two words, between Narcissus's mirror-words: *I* and *me*.

An interesting point is made by P. Bayard in regard to the Emilie "incident."[32] He points out that dictation is underscored in the *Liaisons* in order to substitute one's self for the other. In Valmont's letter to Mme de Tourvel in which he uses Emilie's naked back as a desk, Valmont is putting himself in Mme de Tourvel's place as a reader. And when Valmont dictates letters to Danceny via Cécile Volanges, he is quick to brag about his multiple personality: he is lover, scriptor, seducer, and scriptee. He becomes Danceny's "lover" as well in that he is dictating a letter that the latter will read and assume that it was written by Cécile.

In Valmont's citing Saint-Preux he reveals a desire to collapse the distinction between pain and pleasure. While Saint-Preux used antithesis while saying: "j'avais une âme pour la douleur: donnez-m'en une pour la félicité!" Valmont says: "Mieux partagé que lui, je possède *à la fois* les *deux* existences. Oui, mon amie, je suis, *en même temps*, très heureux et très malheureux." He then offers to recount "*le double récit* de mes peines et de mes plaisirs."

Valmont's variation of the "love *and* hate" theme reveals one of the main premises of the poetics of sadistic eroticism. Like Sade's Dolmancé, who appears on the literary scene after Valmont, Valmont tries to collapse love and hate, pleasure and pain, into one. In Letter 100 Valmont says that he both hates and loves Mme de Tourvel with equal intensity. But he cannot be satisfied until he has collapsed these distinctions for Mme de Tourvel as well. He does not wish the experience to be love *and* hate, but love/hate. He does not desire it to be pleasure *or* pain but pleasure/pain. Valmont wishes to do away with *la différence*.

Simply put, Valmont wishes to be God. Baudelaire thought of Valmont as the devil, but then it is God that the devil tries to emulate. Valmont's language expresses his desire to abolish the space between words, the space that exists between juxtaposed mirrors. The letter Valmont keeps sending back to Mme de Tourvel is not dated. Valmont would abolish time itself. But his intention fails, since language and time are inextricably related. Time has one word follow another, diachronically. Despite the fact that the letter is the same, Valmont must, perforce, change envelopes. One might use what Antonio Tabucchi places as an epigraph to his modern epistolary novel, *Il se fait tard, de plus en plus tard* to describe the "movement" of Valmont's letter: En avant, en arrière/ En avant, en arrière/ On s'amuse vraiment/ En avant, en arrière/Ainsi va la vie." This refrain, that is taken from a popular Italian song, seems to capture the essence of Valmont's "mono-correspondence," or of his sending one epistle forth and back.[33]

9.   Of Mirrors and of Time
        The function of a mirror is not only to reflect, in reversed form, but also to reveal. Among the many things Laclos reveals in his eighteenth-century "Hall of Mirrors" is that no matter how much Valmont wishes to collapse the distinction and the tensions that exist between words, he does not succeed. Even as he repeats himself, even as the undated letter he keeps sending back to Mme de Tourvel is the same one, each sending of it is diachronically consecutive. Only through his death, which follows his realization of the fact that he has lost Mme de Tourvel forever, does he come to know metamorphosis, for he is then, finally, transformed, Narcissus-like, into the work of art: his letters will be "published" after he allows himself to be brought down, in a suicidal act, by Danceny. He will become text itself -- since that is all that is left. But of course, *that* says it all. Another way of expressing this thought is to say, as does P. Bayard, that the prime object of the *Liaisons*, a book composed of letters, is to be read.
        Laclos also shows that dis-order is the mirror-image of order. Through manipulation and contrivance, the dynamic duo Merteuil/Valmont create a Manichean dis-order that is symmetrical to the semblance of "order" that kept in tension the eighteenth-century society in which they lived, at least before it was undone by the advent of the guillotine.

10.   The Diptych's Unhinging
        Laclos goes beyond Narcissus. Had chiastic and interlocking symmetry alone prevailed in *Les Liaisons dangereuses*, the novel would not be the grandiose text that it is. It would have remained what Villani calls a "claustrophobic text."[34] one that remains closed, locked into itself in the act of barren specularity. But hidden within the carefully crafted construction of their schema and their texts is an element that undoes everything for which Merteuil/Valmont have worked with such diligence, an element that is beyond their control and that is instrumental in dis-assembling their careful construction of parts. While the novel exhibits what is typical of the eighteenth-century's intelligence and rigor in its construction, and while Valmont and Merteuil try to build a system that is actually more powerful than that of the society in which they live, the structure will "unhinge,"

despite their perspicacity, in the end. The well-equilibrated pendulum-clock, the symmetrical system that is operative in the structural chiasmus of the text contains, within its core, an element that goes beyond the passion that Narcissus has for himself. His passion, after all, is a false alterity in that it is merely self-reflective. What happens to both Valmont and Merteuil is the surprising discovery of true alterity, of love for an *other*, for a *different* human being. This love for an other becomes a magnificent disruption of the overall syntax of the text. In his study of Laclos in *The Novel of Worldliness*, P. Brooks notes that in Valmont's loving Mme de Tourvel he is "committing a major infidelity to his system of lucidity, intelligence and power. His *odi et amo* admits to a strength of emotion that both he and the Marquise have continually denied to be possible."[35] The crumbling of the "system" crucially affects the rhetorical structure of the text. One could compare textual dismantlement with political dismantlement, much like the structure of the French political system that would soon be crumbling, falling apart, with chaos at its core.

Love, in *Les Liaisons dangereuses*, proves to be a grandiose anacoluthon that succeeds in changing the systematic arrangement of the epistles between Merteuil and Valmont: Merteuil's full answer to Valmont's throwing down the gauntlet in Letter 153 ("vous voyez que la réponse que je vous demande n'exige ni longues ni belles phrases. Deux mots suffisent.") is scribbled at the bottom of his own letter, which she simply sends back to him: "Hé bien! la guerre." This inconsistent or anomalous change in the structure and form of their letter-writing announces the end.

There are only two letters exchanged between them after this telegraphic, or non-discursive message: Letter 158 (from Valmont to Merteuil), and Letter 159 (Merteuil's immediate response, which ends with "Adieu"). T. Todorov notes, as well, that a change in narrator occurs when Valmont and Merteuil turn to hostility from having been each other's confidants of one another: "Chaque lettre ici est un acte (du performatif autonome). C'est exactement à ce moment que Mme de Volanges prend le relais de la narration. Après la première lettre 'narrative' (constative) de Mme de Volanges à Mme de Rosemonde, il n'y a plus une seule lettre de confidence entre Valmont et Merteuil: le récit n'a pas besoin de plus d'un narrateur."[36]

Because Prévan prefigures Valmont, he indicates what will transpire in the conclusion of the text. But because he is also the opposite, or the mirror-image of Valmont in that he will "succeed," in the end, whereby Valmont will "fail", he represents, as well, the contrast that exists between manipulative seduction and the verity of passion. That Valmont comes to know love through Mme de Tourvel is not usually disputed, but that Mme de Merteuil loves Valmont as much as he loves Mme de Tourvel is not so frequently admitted.[37] The letter in which this is made strikingly clear, nevertheless, is Letter 131. In the last paragraph of this letter Mme de Merteuil makes a most poignant declaration of passion:

> Savez-vous que je regrette quelquefois que nous en soyons réduits à ces essources! [She is referring to "une infidélité réciproque," or the request of a letter from Mme de Tourvel that would prove that the latter had succumbed to Valmont.] Dans le temps où nous nous aimions car je crois que c'était de l'amour, j'étais heureuse; et vous, Vicomte!... Mais pourquoi s'occuper encore d'un bonheur qui ne peut revenir? Non, quoi que vous en disiez, c'est un retour impossible. D'abord, j'exigerais des sacrifices que sûrement vous ne pourriez ou ne voudriez pas me faire, et qu'il se peut bien que je ne mérite pas; et puis, comment vous fixer? Oh! non, non, je ne veux seulement pas m'occuper de cette idée; et malgré le plaisir que je trouve en ce moment à vous écrire, j'aime mieux vous quitter brusquement. Adieu, Vicomte.

The aposiopesis says more than what Mme de Merteuil actually puts into words. By means of ellipsis she is saying "we were happy once and could become so again" (despite the rhetorical negations that follow). Here, again, is an interruption in syntax that cries out Mme de Merteuil's absolute love for Valmont. The same reasons Mme de Clèves gave Nemours for refusing to see him again are those that Mme de Merteuil evokes in her elliptical declaration of passion to Valmont. She would not be able to abide Valmont's being unfaithful to her. She knows her man - only too well. She would not be able to "le fixer" - to have him to herself alone, to retain his fidelity. Two characters could not possibly be more different one from another than Mme de Clèves and Mme de Merteuil. And yet they are similar in requiring fidelity from the man they love above all others. They are also similar - yet different - in another important aspect, and that is in their intertextual references. The Princesse would subtly allude to Saint Paul's statement about not being able to do what she knew she should do. Merteuil uses the Scriptures many times, but she does so ironically.[38]

Within the symmetry of chiasmus and of imbricated order, within the seeming closure of mirror-imagery that is omnipresent in both *La Princesse de Clèves* and in *Les Liaisons dangereuses*, absolute passion plays a disruptive role. The *Liaisons* "unhinge" because of the novel's very negation of symmetry: passion, the love for one who is *not* oneself, undercuts Narcissus, and does him, finally, in.[39]

*   *   *   *

1782 was the date of publication of *Les Liaisons dangereuses*. 1789 was the "official" date of the beginning of the French people's dismantling of their political system. It does not seem surprising that both of these grandiose "systems" should falter in such proximity one to another. Fifty-four years after Laclos's masterpiece was published, as we shall see in the next chapter, Balzac's *Facino Cane* became available to readers fascinated by embedded narratives. In his chapter on the epistolary novel in *Forme et Signification*, and in his comments on Balzac's own epistolary work, *Mémoires d'une jeune mariée*, J. Rousset uses the formula "life by means of proxy" to describe one of the grand themes of the *Comédie Humaine*.[40] The formula applies to epistolarity in Laclos as well as to Balzac because Valmont, Merteuil, and all of the other characters in *Les Liaisons dangereuses* actually live their lives by proxy, in chiastic and imbricated ways, sending and taking back messages through which they participate, vicariously, in the lives they shape as well as undo. The same formula applies to embedded narratives, to Balzac's *Facino Cane*, because Narrators I and II in frame narratives experience a "vie par délégation": they live, through others, the narratives they hear and tell.

The mirroring figures in embedded tales, the micro- and macro-dispositions of the rhetoric, and the structure of those narratives provide an illustrative model of the reading act itself. The frame and the framed are in a dynamic dialogue, just as epistolarity and reading are.

Notes

[1] L. Michel, *La Mort du libertin: agonie d'une identité romanesque*, Découvrir, Paris, 1993, p. 3.

[2] In *Les Liaisons dangereuses et la création romanesque chez Laclos*, Minard, Paris, 1958, p. 38. Various ideas in this chapter first appeared in *Modern Language Studies*, Winter, 1988.

[3] In *Laclos and the Epistolary Novel*, Droz, Génève, 1963, pp. 24-25. See, also, Mary Douglas's *Thinking in Circles: An Essay on Ring Composition*, Yale UP, New Haven and London, 2007. This learned anthropologist makes ample use of the chiasmus in her analyses of ancient literatures of the *Iliad* and the *Bible*, in particular. In her preface, she refers to John Myres's use of the words "pedimental writing." By this, she says "pedimental means writing that goes up to a central point, makes a turn, then comes down step by step on the other side, like wide-angled pediments or doorways." In other words, she says, "pedimental" is another name for a

chiasmus." While Myres applies achitectural expression to short compositions, Douglas herself uses "ring compositions" to describe the structues of longer texts, such as epics or Biblical books. pp. xii-xiii.

[4] French and German Publications, University of Glasgow, 1994, p. 18.

[5] ibid., p. 490.

[6] ibid., p. 32.

[7] Quoted in *Choderlos de Laclos*, Appendices aux *Oeuvres Complètes*, ed. Maurice Allem, Bibliothèque de la Pléiade, Paris, 1951, p. 734.

[8] ibid., pp. 58-59.

[9] ibid., p. 22.

[10] As in all previous chapters, underlinings in citations have been added, unless otherwise noted.

[11] In preparation for the re-opening of *La galerie des glaces* at Versailles on 25 June 2007, *Le Figaro, hors-série* printed an entire edition, with a cd-rom, on the completely restored *galerie des glaces*, entitled *Versailles Retrouvé: La Renaissance de la galerie des glaces*. It is worth admiring, as much as Valmont and Merteuil mirror each other.

[12] In *Studi sulla letteratura dell'età preromantica in Francia*, Libreria Goliardica Editrice, Pisa, 1956, A. Pizzorusso calls attention to the fact that in Mme de Merteuil's self-created education (Letter 81), she fashions herself into becoming exactly the opposite of *la femme naturelle*. "Her purpose," he says, "is to unhinge [deconstruct] and then reconstruct the proportions of the real; to revolutionize matter, to render the implausible true and the true implausible," p. 23. In Pizzorusso's words, Mme de Merteuil wished to render "l'inverosimile vero e il vero inverosimile." The critic naturally uses chiasmus to describe Mme de Merteuil's intentions. The trope unconsciously foregrounds the strength of the armature in the overall structure of the novel.

[13] L. Versini, *Laclos et la tradition*, Librairie Klincksieck, Paris, 1968, pp. 150-151.

[14] G. Poisson, *Choderlos de Laclos, ou, l'obstination*, Grasset, Paris, 1985, p. 127.

[15] In the first chapter of *Fiction and Repetition: Seven English Novels*, Harvard UP, Cambridge, 1982),J. H. Miller identifies a number of different forms of repetition that occur in prose fiction: "Any novel is a complex tissue of repetitions and of repetitions within repetitions, or of repetitions linked in chain fashion to other repetitions," pp. 2-3. One among other types identified by Miller (repetitions of other works by other authors) is, in part operative in Laclos's repeating Mme de Saint-Aubin's title.

[16] Poisson, p. 127.

[17] In *Passages, échanges, et transpositions*, José Corti, Paris, 1990, p. 14.

[18] Rousset, 1968, p. 137.

[19] Melchior-Bonnet, p. 94.

[20] ibid., p. 89.

[21] In "Michel Foucault as an Intellectual Imagination," *Boundary 2*, I,1, Binghampton, SUNY, 1972, p. 14.

[22] H. Duranton, *"Les Liaisons dangereuses* ou le miroir ennemi," *Revue des sciences humaines*, XXXIX, 153 (janvier-mars 1974). Duranton says: "L'oeuvre s'offre donc comme un reflet amplifié de l'ironique jeu de face à face des deux préfaces qui s'annulent si parfaitement," p. 126.

[23] In "Le Miroir: La séduction vertigineuse," published in *Analyses et Réflexions sur Laclos: Les Liaisons dangereuses* (Paris: Edition Marketing, Paris, 1991, p. 59.

[24] Cited by Villani, p. 63.

[25] In *Rereadings: Eight Early French Novels*, Summa Publications, Inc., Birmingham, Alabama, 1984, P. Stewart states succinctly the literary self-consciousness that is brought about by the disagreements existing between the *éditeur* and the *rédacteur*: "For all its roundabout patter, the 'forward'-matter of *Les Liaisons dangereuses* grounds the text in literarity," p. 223.

[26] Villani, p. 60.

[27] Choderlos de Laclos, *Les Liaisons dangereuses*, notice et notes de J. Papadopoulos, Gallimard [Folio], Paris, 1977, p. 488.

[28] J. Derrida, *L'Ecriture et la différence* , Seuil, Paris,1967, p. 113.

[29] P. Ricoeur, "The Metaphorical Process as Cognition, Imagination, and Feeling," in *Metaphor*, ed. Sheldon Sacks, Chicago: Chicago UP, Chicago, 1979, p. 146.

[30] Folio ed., p. 492.

[31] Seuil, Paris, 1979, p. 40.

[32] P. Bayard, *Le Paradoxe du menteur*, Ed. de Minuit, Paris, 1990, p. 183.

[33] A. Tabucchi, *Il se fait tard, de plus en plus tard*, trad. Lise Chapins et Bernard Comment, Christian Bourgois, Paris, 2001, p. 9.

[34] Villani, *op. cit.*, p. 60.

[35] In *The Novel of Worldliness: Crébillon, Marivaux, Laclos, Stendhal* , Princeton UP, Princeton, 1969, pp. 194-195.

[36] T. Todorov, in "Choderlos de Laclos et la théorie du récit" *Tel Quel* 27, automne 1966, p. 23.

[37] P. Brooks himself does not admit this. He says: "She remains

faithful to her system, and this means that she must ever remain distant from us: there is no self-betrayal nor, until the end, any weakness, and even this is a function of her last desperate attempt to preserve her letter system," *op. cit.* p. 208.

[38] See her references to Samson and Delilah [letter 81], to the poor man who picks up crumbs from the rich man's table [letter 113], to her comparison of Cécile to Mary Magdalen [letter 63], to visiting a friend in affliction [letter 63], to Valmont's being "rich" in hubris [letter 137], to Tourvel's thinking of Valmont as "The Prodigal Son" [letter 127].

[39] In John Ruskin's reflexions upon the subject of subject-matter, he says that he had never met a question of any importance that did not need both a positive and a negative answer to it, "like an equation of the second degree." Most important topics, he says "are three-sided, or four-sided, or polygonal...." Cited by Mary-Ann Caws *op. cit.,* p. 4. Ruskin speaks in a postmodern way, or to quote A. Tabucchi on the question of epistolarity, "a letter is a questionable messenger," p. 290.

[40] Rousset, p. 103.

Chapter IV

The Frame and the Framed:
Mirroring Texts in Balzac's *Facino Cane*

> Parmy tant d'emprunts, je suis bien aise d'en
> pouvoir desrober quelqu'un, les desguisant et
> difformant à nouveau service.
> Montaigne, *Essais*

Elements found within framed narratives may refer to elements outside the frame. They refer, according to M.A. Caws, to the larger or whole text. The passage may also represent something outside of itself, as if it were an indication of elements that have larger significance.[1] Links that exist between the "frame" and the "framed" in embedded narratives are multifarious and complex, more complex, even, than intratextuality, such as Valmont's referring to Rousseau and to Richardson. Works sighted in Balzac's *Facino Cane* (1836) reveal how real and implied authors and narrators use intra- and intertexts to mirror basic segments of frame stories. The orchestration of these elements also shows that the narratives themselves are frequently homologous, in their structures, to the texts with which they are in dialogue. Balzac's and his narrators' direct and indirect references to libraries, books, *1,001 Nights*, the *Divine Comedy, the Odyssey, Childe Harold's Pilgrimage*, Diderot's *Lettre sur les aveugles* et al., build bridges between the two parts of *Facino Cane* and reflect acts of narrating and decoding texts.

1.   The Structure of the Text

Facino Cane is a short story that was written by Balzac in one night. It was published for the first time on 17 March 1836 in the *Chronique de Paris*. It is thirteen pages long in the Pléiade edition, and its final resting place is with the other *Scènes de la vie parisienne*. The initial part of the frame, told by Narrator I, as I shall call him since he is given no name, occupies the first five pages. Two pages are then devoted to a bridge/dialogue between the first and the second narrator, and to a description of the latter. Facino Cane, who is Narrator II, takes up five pages with his embedded narrative, and one page of commentary and dialogue rounds (or squares) off the frame. The transitional dialogue and description is in a chiastic relationship to the final description and dialogue, and the structure is strikingly balanced.

The two stories exist in such a way that works sighted in them participate in the reflexive aspects of the narratives themselves. The process of analyzing the layers upon layers of allusions is spellbinding. Due to the complexity of these narratives, a summary of them is in order.

In the frame, or the *histoire enchâssante*, as T. Todorov calls it,[2] Narrator I describes the poor section of Paris in which he lives, as well as his love of *la science*.[3] Like the real author, he has a veritable passion for observing the customs and lives of others, and while taking breaks from the Royal library where he studies, he follows people and "substitutes" himself for them, participating, second-hand, in their lives. He follows a couple and their child down the street, listening to their discussions. They talk about the play they have just seen at the Ambigu-Comique, and about their finances, their wages, the high price of food. The Narrator then analyzes his own capacity to empathize with others to the point of identifying himself with them.

While attending the wedding of his housekeeper's daughter, Narrator I becomes fascinated by one of the three blind musicians hired to play for the assembled crowd, and engages him in dialogue. The extraordinary old man is Marco Facino Cane, a Venetian from the royal house of Varese. That he is from "the city of mirrors" is a strategic textual ploy. The blind man becomes aware of a mutual affinity he has with Narrator I, and after finishing his playing, he tells the young man *his* story.

In this embedded narrative, Facino Cane describes how, at the age of twenty (which is also Narrator I's age at the time of the events he has been describing thus far), he fell in love with a young married Venetian woman. Found with her, he is attacked by the husband, and in self-defence, kills the older man. Bianca refuses to flee with her lover to Milan, where he goes to escape his pursuers. Returning to Venice when his funds run out, Bianca hides him in her house where they live together happily for six months. Because a government official becomes interested in Bianca, he discovers Facino Cane, captures him, and throws him into a dark prison dungeon. Deciphering a message cut into a stone, Cane finds an escape route that the previous occupant had begun to dig. A broken piece of his sword helps Cane carve his way out of the passageway, and it happens to lead into the room of the palace where the treasures of Venice are stored. He buys off his jailer and they escape, taking with them as much of the treasure as they can carry. The jailer dies; Cane goes blind. He ends up in London, where "Mme du Barry's friend," with whom he had become involved, robs him and abandons him. Finally making his way to Paris, penniless, he spends his days with other blind men from the Quinze-Vingts, a home for the blind, telling his story to anyone who will listen. His intention is to entice someone, through narrative's appeal, into taking him back to Venice, where he is sure to find the treasure by intuiting its location, by sniffing it out, by "smelling it," as he says of his monomania for gold.

At the end, in the *histoire enchâssante's* final dialogue between both narrators, Narrator I agrees to lead Facino Cane back to Venice. But the old man dies abruptly, not long after, "of a catarrh."

2.   History and Fiction

References of import appear immediately in the first two sentences of the text. Narrator I is the encoded implied author who most resembles Balzac in his work. He lives on the Rue de Lesdiguières, near a library. The signifier "Lesdiguières," having to do with dams or dikes, is a bridge leading toward Narrative II, since Venice is the principal locus of Facino Cane's narration. The signified also relates to the real author because Balzac had lived at no. 9, rue Lesdiguières, in 1819 and 1820. Narrator I spends many hours during the day working "in a near-by library, that of MONSIEUR."[4] This became the Arsenal Library in which Balzac, too, had worked. In this intratextual referent, the books in the "bibliothèque," a *royal* library, are in relation to the *Livre d'or* in which the historical figure, *Bonifacio* Facino Cane,[5] the fictive *Marco* Facino Cane's "ancestor," had had his name inscribed in order to protect himself from the Visconti[6]. The Golden Book was the register, destroyed in 1797, in which noble families of Italy had their names written. This was done in golden letters, which explains the title of the book.[7] The words "Facino Cane" must have fascinated Balzac, whose delight in onomastics is evident throughout his work: *Facino* is close, in sound, to the Italian word *fascino* (fascination), and the word *cane (dog)* may have inspired Balzac to endow his character with the ability to smell, to sniff out gold. "Une *cane*" is also associated with a blind man's walking stick.

According to A. Lorant, the name "Cane," was that of an Irish family with whom the Balzacs had shared a house in Tours. The English name was pronounced "Canet" in the Touraine, and Balzac may have transformed it, says Lorant, into an Italian one[8]. But this explanation does not, in any way, account for the *Marco* or the *Facino* in Marco Facino Cane's name. The fictive first name *Marco* is obvious, since Balzac's personage is Venitian. Marco also evokes the 13th-century paradigmatic Venitian traveller and gold seeker, Marco Polo. He too was an author, having narrated descriptions of the East that were, throughout the Renaissance, the principal if not only source there was for the exotic lands he describes. Not only is the inscription of a proper name in a book a *mise en abyme* of the text, but the "real" and the "fictive" are confounded in the referent. The *bibliothèque de MONSIEUR*, Bonifacio *Facino Cane*, and the *livre d'or* are all historically referential. The geographic and topographic semes in the text are historical, in the main, even though Balzac had not yet seen Venice when he wrote the short narrative.[9] As is the case in *La Princesse de Clèves*, history is used to valorize as well as highlight the fictive. Facino Cane is doubly fictional in serving as title to the short story that the real author wrote, and in becoming a narrator in his own right, he reflects both author and Narrator I as well. Relationships between "reality" and fiction, between libraries, books and reading, between the structure of this text and its "conversations" with other texts are established from the beginning, and continue to mirror each other throughout the narrative.

In his discussion of the opening paragraph of *Le Père Goriot*, V. Brombert calls attention to the references that are "structured around contradictory signals of surface realism and of simultaneous subversions of the realistic discourse."[10] Perhaps one could say that instead of undermining surface realism, *Facino Cane's* "reality effect" is in *tension* with the fictive. Balzac, in fact, had some hesitation when it came to the title he was to give his short narrative. The original edition, published in 1837 under *Etudes philosophiques,* bore the royal name, *Facino Cane*. In the Souverain edition of *Mystères de Province,* the text became plebeian (i.e., "realistic" in title): it was called *Le Père Canet*. In the Furne edition of 1844, the royal lineage was recovered, and *Facino Cane*, from then on, has figured in *Scènes de la vie parisienne.*

For a practical reason the implied reader is encoded in the first sentence of the frame: "Je demeurais alors dans une petite rue que *vous* ne connaissez sans doute pas."[11] Because the street indicates the quarters of the poor, the implied readers are thought to be above living in such an area. They are required to be literate, or, to say the least, to be sufficiently endowed with knowledge to understand the literary allusions in the text.[12] Literacy seems to be related to financial means (despite both narrators' poverty), and to the ability to live in an area other than the one beginning with "la rue Saint-Antoine." The first sentence distances readers, on the one hand, but succeeds in "instructing" them, on the other, about how another part of the world lives. There is, consequently, pedagogical and moral value placed on narrative.

In her study of the history and theory of the frame narrative, K. Gittes states that certain organizing devices are constant throughout the genre's development. As she traces the history of the genre (that frame narrative *is* a genre is only one theory among others[13]) Gittes observes that over and above the obvious motifs of a "controlling narrator or a pervading travel or wisdom theme," organizing devices include: intelligence as a means of survival in the world; tension between the framing story and the enclosed tale; the rebirth theme, and the open-endedness of the framing story.[14] All of these are present in *Facino Cane*.

Narrators I and II are both intelligent, even though the "lesson" of the story undermines this quality of mind. Learning is not rewarded, at least in monetary terms: Narrator II goes blind, loses his fortune, and dies, while Narrator I continues to expend "la puissance destructrice de la pensée" by telling tales. Balzac encodes one of his favourite ideas into this short story.

As he describes his intuitive powers at the end of the first paragraph, Narrator I says that this gave him the capacity to live the life of the person observed. It permitted him to substitute himself for the other, as the dervish of *1,001 Nights* would take the body and soul of persons after having pronounced magic words.[15]

The simile Narrator I uses in his literary allusion is an important one because he has recourse to the exotic, to the realm of fantasy, when he compares himself to the dervish in *1,001 Nights* (the "Chinese box" narrative par excellence). This reference builds a mirror-image of Narratives I and II in regard to the exotic elements present in the latter. Palaces, bridges, prisons, vast fortunes, excessive monomanias for gold, cloak-and-dagger details, symbolic aspects of blindness versus sight (and in-sight), narrative repetition, all relate to the sign that is deliberately encoded in the text by the reference made to the Oriental stories told by Scheherazade to her husband, Schariar, legendary king of Samarkand, in order to save her life. A further link is established, as well, between Parts I and II, because Facino Cane himself will also mention *1,001 Nights*, thus reflecting the narrative's frame.

By citing this work, Balzac mirrors his own activity: he, a narrator, has created Narrator I, who leads us to Narrator II, who will return us to Narrator I. But the *dialogic* function of the frame is almost subverted by Narrator I when he announces that he is something of a succubus. Narrator as vampire: in a strange twist given to the Narcissus paradigm, he imbibes the identity of the other, substituting the other for himself. We have seen this in the event of natives who are afraid to have their pictures taken, lest their souls be taken along with pictures. Dialogic tension between the frame and the embedded narrative would be reduced to a univocal account if both were to become one, and the dynamism of the tale's double structure would be rendered less powerful in that case. This is only a latent temptation in *Facino Cane*, yet it signals the empathy that exists when meaningful dialogue occurs in the reception of texts.

In his introduction to *Facino Cane*, Lorant reminds us that the idea of intuitive observation was one in which Balzac's contemporaries were acutely interested. Balzac, says Lorant, may have been influenced by the physiologist named de Jouy, who claimed to penetrate those he observed. He was able to figure out their most intimate thoughts, to understand people's looks, gestures, and even their silences.[16]

The interpretation of "body language" and expression was a matter that deeply concerned Balzac and his generation. This interest was not only due to the influence of Lavater and Gall, but came about through nineteenth-century developments in urban conditions of life. It became necessary and desirable to be able to classify those one did, as well as did not know when one met them on the street. Balzac's own interest in street encounters results from their being a source for his creative imagination. Intense interest in the body's representation, if not to say presentation, came about in the late eighteenth century, when full-sized mirrors not only became available to the middle class, but became part of the decorative motifs of salons, restaurants, cafés, and department stores. Mirrors moved from private to public spaces, and viewers' bodies were reflected everywhere. One did not have to wait until the twentieth century to sight the "forests of mirrors" that happen to exist seemingly everywhere in Paris, in France, in Western Europe in general. The proliferating perception of the body went hand in hand with the importance of appearance - as it contrasted with "reality" and with the social codes involved in such perceptions.

Another source of Balzac's ideas about identification with others, according to Lorant, was Thomas De Quincey's *Confessions of an English Opium Eater*, published in 1822. De Quincey's statements (which had been translated by Alfred de Musset in 1828) referred to a couple who had one or two children. After having "experienced" an opera under the influence of opium, De Quincey describes sharing the concerns of an impoverished family with them. He claims to share their pleasures and pains as he discusses, with them, the price of every-day life. He says he shared their desires, their difficulties, their opinions.[17] These statements resemble closely the description of the family that Narrator I follows down the boulevard after they had attended a performance at the Ambigu-Comique. Facino Cane, too, will "follow the traces" that lead to gold. Identification leads to narration and to interpretation, in all of these cases: De Quincey's, the real and the implied authors', and those of Narrators I and II.

Readers follow lines of influence of texts within texts, says A. Reed, especially in De Quincey's mention of Coleridge in *Confessions of an English Opium Eater*. Just as he (Reed) was happily discussing lines of influence in that text, he tells us that the text itself sent him elsewhere, inscribing, thereby, a labyrinth, doubling and redoubling the line, "folding it over and in on itself.[18] This remark is most appropriate because in the text discussed, Coleridge tells De Quincey the story of Piranesi. Not only are Piranesi's *Carceri* related to prisons, they clearly evoke the birth and initiatory symbolism present in *Facino Cane's* progression through the prison's "womb," towards deliverance. It would be difficult to find a closer identification between Balzak, Coleridge, De Quincey, Piranesi, and Facino Cane's escape from his "carcere," or "prison." Coleridge tells De Quincey that in the delirium he had experienced, resulting from a fever, his "dreams" were mostly architectural. After describing the overlappings of staircases, such as those one observes in Piranesi, he [Coleridge] says: "and I beheld such pomp of cities and palaces as was never yet beheld by the waking eye, unless in the clouds."

Because *ambigu* alludes to "double" and also signifies "ambiguity," the name of the theatre mentioned by Narrator I foregrounds the binary tensions and bridges that exist between the "plebeian" and the "royal" dimensions of the text, its "realistic" and simultaneously fictive elements, as well as the characters of Narrators I and II. Both are young, in their twenties, at the time of the adventures they relate, yet one is younger and the other old at the time of the diegeses themselves. Both have a passion, or a monomania; Narcissus-like, both want to "lose themselves" in their passion, whether it be persons, gold, or the narrative act. Both allude to other texts, but Narrator I is the more learned of the two.

Narrator I further enhances the tension between the poor and the elite (the Ambigu-Comique being a boulevard theatre specializing in vaudevilles and light comedy) when he says that he follows the couple down the *Pont-aux-Choux* to the *Beaumarchais* boulevard. In the *publication préoriginale* of *Facino Cane* in the *Chronique de Paris*, the story was "précédé d'une chronique consacrée à l'adaptation de *Gil Blas*, due à Sauvage et de Lurieu".[19] Once again, the mundane leads towards and incorporates the "literary." The boulevard that begins with cabbages (Pont-aux-Choux) ends with the name of a writer who had criticized kings (Beaumarchais: "Of cabbages and kings..."). As in *Les Liaisons dangereuses*, theatrical motifs form part of the mirror structure under consideration.

While describing his adventures, Narrator I's intertextual usage of one of Dante's phrases becomes another link between Paris and Venice (or Italy). Narrator I calls Paris "cette ville de douleur."[20] thus referring to the *Inferno:* "Per me si va nella *città dolente*" 'Through me you enter into the city of grief'.[21] Since Facino Cane experiences all manner of *douleurs*, Paris and Venice are in relation with each other in the text by intra- and intertextual means. The *città dolente* motif also brings to mind the famous opening pages of *La Fille aux yeux d'or* in which the physiognomy of Parisians is called "presque infernale," and Paris "un enfer." As the *two* travellers in the *Divina Commedia* move towards the Inferno, they approach the gate and read the words inscribed upon it. The words of the best-known line of the *Inferno* depict what lies within, pain eternal and beings who have lost all hope: "Lasciate ogni speranza, voi ch'entrate" 'Abandon all hope, you who enter here' (Part III, third stanza). The loss of hope and its renewal characterize Facino Cane. The renewal occurs whenever Facino Cane meets Narrator I (or any virtual guide). In fact, the end in view of his tale is to "fascinate" Narrator I into travelling back with him to Venice to find the gold hidden in the Doges's Palace. He wishes to re-enact his narrative, to repeat it, as it were. But Cane's death in the realist mode ("Le pauvre homme avait un catarrhe" [22] puts an end to all hope, and to this particular narrative as well.

There is open-endedness, or lack of closure, however, in the finale, since Narrator I states that he possesses many more tales in his bag of tricks. What could be interpreted as another intertextual reference to Scheherazade's telling of stories in order to save her life (Balzac also told stories for a living) is the metanarrative statement Narrator I makes: "[l'histoire] fait partie de ces récits curieux restés dans le sac d'où la mémoire les tire capricieusement comme des numéros de loterie: j'en ai bien d'autres, aussi singuliers que celui-ci, également enfouis [like the treasure Facino Cane finds buried in the subterranean vaults of the palace], mais ils auront leur tour, croyez-le." [23] The comment upon taking narrations, as it were, "out of a sack" is suggestive of the magical or dervish-like quality of the narrator.

Narrator I creates a dichotomy between elevated and mundane music just as he had between social ranks when he describes the tunes the blind men play at the wedding. Because they were paid a flat fee of 7 francs per night, the blind men played popular music: "sur ce prix-là, certes, ils ne donnaient ni du Rossini, ni du Beethoven, ils jouaient ce qu'ils voulaient et ce qu'ils pouvaient." [24] The contrasts between Rossini and Beethoven and popular music are placed in the text for several reasons. They emphasize the discussion in which Balzac was engaged concerning the value of Italian vs. German music. They also prepare the readers for comparisons of Facino Cane to names of such importance as Dante and Homer. In the 1837 Delloye et Lecou edition, Balzac confounded the reference to Homer with the previously noted intertextual statement from Dante (*la città dolente*). He called Facino Cane "ce vieil Homère des douleurs." [25] By conflating Homer with "la ville des douleurs," his "Homère des douleurs" became a metonymic signal of the entire Greek and Roman body of literature. But perhaps Balzac found this excessive, and excised it from later editions. [26]

As he begins to describe Facino Cane, Narrator I asks the implied reader to imagine what one of these "phénomènes qui arrêtent tout court l'artiste et le philosophe" would look like: "Figurez-vous le masque en plâtre de Dante, éclairé par la lueur rouge du quinquet et surmonté d'une forêt de cheveux d'un blanc argenté." [27] He goes on to compare the old man to the writer of epic: "Quelque chose de grand et de despotique se rencontrait dans ce vieil Homère qui gardait en lui-même une Odyssée condamnée à l'oubli." [28]

Narrator I contradicts the diachronicity of his narrative by making this negative proleptic statement. Facino Cane had not in the past, and will not in the future, keep his Odyssey to himself. And neither will Narrator I. Balzac would use Narrator I to "penetrate" *ce vieil Homère*, and he would have recourse to all manner of frame narrative devices (mirrored narrators, implied readers, implied listeners, double narratees, different levels of narrative, dichotomies, contrasts, bridges, tensions, links, specular themes and techniques) i.e., the entire spectrum of dyadic and chiastic ingenuity and artifice so that Facino Cane's story would *not* be "condemned to oblivion." It would, in fact, come to form part of Balzac's own "epic," *The Human Comedy*, which is "in dialogue" with Dante's *Divine Comedy*. Each small part of the *human* comedy, including *Facino Cane*, stands in a synecdochic relationship to the whole of Balzac's opus, and to all of the works sighted (and uncited), including the *Odyssey*. We recall that in the *Odyssey*, Ulysses became a narrator in his own right in no less than four books (IX to XII) when he presented his own account to the Phaiákians. Frame narrative reflects the epic genre.

Balzac's not having seen Venice at the time of writing *Facino Cane* did not keep him (1) from creating it in his mind, and (2) like Marcel, in *A la recherche du temps perdu*, from learning about it in visual representations and in literary texts. After describing the blind old man, Narrator I "sees" Venice and the Adriatic: "Je voyais Venise et l'Adriatique, je la voyais en *ruines* sur cette figure *ruinée*."²⁹ Since he has the capability of looking into the souls of others, he will also "see" into the inner recesses of a city, in a similar way to Facino Cane's being able to "see" gold, even after having gone blind, or so he believes, from having spent so much time in the darkness of a prison cell. Like blind Tiresias, Narrator II can "see." He "sees" the treasures called "narratives."

The chiastic phrase "Je *voyais* Venise et l'Adriatique, je la *voyais*..." foregrounds the visionary talents of Narrator I, his identification with Narrator II, and Facino Cane's own abilities to "see" hidden treasure. Balzac himself is also "seeing" into another text, that his own text will echo, *Childe Harold's Pilgrimage*, which had been published in 1818. Balzac would allude directly to *Childe Harold* in *Massimilla Doni*, which was revised in 1837. There he states: "...un grand poète anglais était venu s'abattre sur Venise comme un corbeau sur un cadavre, pour lui coasser en poésie lyrique, dans ce premier et dernier langage des sociétés, les stances d'un *De Profundis*."³⁰ Byron has Childe Harold begin the fourth Canto with these words:

> I stood in Venice, on the Bridge of Sighs;
> A palace and a prison on each hand:
> I saw from out the wave her structures rise
> As from the stroke of the enchanter's wand.³¹

At this point we, the readers, see Facino Cane's palace and his prison "on each hand." We also see "the stroke of the enchanter's wand," that of a dervish from *1,001 Nights* who brings persons, cities, and visions of all types into "sight." The magical quality of writing, reading, and perceiving is mirrored in *Facino Cane's* intertext.

In Stanza II of *Childe Harold*, the poetic persona depicts the gold, the jewels, the riches of Venice that become Facino Cane's monomania:

> From spoils of nations, and the exhaustless East
> Pour'd in her lap all gems in sparkling showers.
> In purple was she robed, and of her feast
> Monarchs partook, and deem'd their dignity increased.

In the third stanza, the ruined, decadent Venice will appear. Although stated negatively, the literary allusion to Tasso creates "echoes" between Byron and a literary figure of the past. Music is also intermittently "present" in Stanza III:

> In Venice Tasso's echoes are no more,
> And silent rows the songless gondolier;
> Her palaces are crumbling to the shore,
> And music meets not always now the ear.

The *ruins* make their unequivocal and repetitive appearance in stanza 25:

> But my soul wanders; I demand it back
> To meditate amongst decay, and stand
> *A ruin amidst ruins.*

Balzac's own phrase is poetic, and may be rendered in poetic form:

> *Je voyais Venise* et l'Adriatique,
> *Je la voyais en ruines* sur *cette figure ruinée.*

In the anaphora (the repetition of the first person, *je*, and of the verb *voir* in the imperfect at the beginning of the successive clauses), in the repetition, or substitution, in the second clause of the pronoun *la* for *Venise,* in the repetition of the noun *ruines* in its adjectival form *ruinée*, in the alliteration of "*v*oyais *V*enise," we see how Balzac poeticized his phrase, echoed Byron's verse, and created an interlocking microtext (je voyais Venise-je la voyais: a-b-c—a-c-b) of the whole frame narrative at the very heart of his macrotext through his uses of repetition and substitution.

In *Childe Harold*, the poetic persona is the "ruin amidst the ruins" of Venice; in Balzac's text, Venice's ruins are imprinted upon Facino Cane's face and are envisioned by Narrator I. The Balzacian credo whereby the exterior is a mirror of that which lies within is doubly reified in the poetic expression. The frame of the narrative is also mirrored in the embedded narrative because Narrator I, who had called Paris a Dantesque "ville de douleur," now "sees" an Italian city in ruins upon the face of Narrator II. When the blind man leads Narrator I outside to tell him his story, begging the latter to take him to Venice, he entices him with the promise of an enormous fortune: "vous serez plus riche...que les Rothschild, enfin riche comme *Les Mille et Une Nuits.*"[32] As we enter into Cane's own luring *incipit*, we begin to see the frame in another light, for it seems to undergo metamorphosis: the border begins to mirror its own "picture." The metadiegesis repeats the diegesis. Narrator I had referred to *1,001 Nights*. One cannot help observing that "1001," in Arabic numbers, is a chiasmus, a frame seme, and that "nuits" not only recall Narrator I's nightly pilgrimages but is also a metaphor of Cane's incarceration and blindness. Narrator II refers to *1,001 Nights* with no prompting, with no connection whatsoever being established between Narrators I and II. It is left to the reader to see how one reflects the other. It is the reader who sights the bridge that will link both allusions. It is the reader, as well, who recalls that Marco Polo's *Book of Marvels* was commonly referred to as *Il Milione.*

Intratextuality is as demanding as intertextuality in requiring participation, or dialogue, between the reader and the text. Implied readers must not only recognize Beaumarchais, Beethoven, Rossini, Dante, and Homer, but they must also look at the mirror in the text in order to see, like Alice, what lies behind the looking glass. To realize that the *Divine Comedy, Childe Harold's Pilgrimage* and the *Odyssey* are all "voyages" forms part of the "pleasure of the text." Epic "voyages" are reflected in Narrator I's passion for walking, for locomotion, for following people; in Facino Cane's passion for Bianca and for gold, which takes him from Venice to Milan, then back to Venice, and then on to Smyrna, London, and Paris. The pleasure of reading is enhanced when one remembers that Homer was blind, that the libretto to Rossini's *Barber of Seville* came from Beaumarchais's play, and that both *The Barber* and *The Marriage of Figaro* poke fun at the aristocracy. Literary allusion has been defined by Ziva Ben-Porat as "the simultaneous activation of two texts."[33] One could extend that definition to say that it is the simultaneous activation of multiple texts.

3.   Sightings in the Embedded Narrative

Cane begins *his* tale with "que je meure sans confession...si ce que je vais vous dire n'est pas *vrai*. J'ai eu *vingt* ans comme vous les avez en ce moment...."[34] One hears echoes of the first paragraph of *Le Père Goriot*, in which the narrator makes this statement: "Sachez-le: ce drame n'est ni une fiction, ni un roman. *All is true.*" While discussing the beginning paragraphs of *Le Père Goriot*, V. Brombert reminds us that on 10 August 1831, Philarète Chasles informed his public, the readers of the *Revue de Paris*, that Shakespeare's *Henry VIII* had been called *All Is True* when it was first produced. "The extreme signal of realism (*all is true*)," says Brombert, "thus places the elaborate disclaimer of literarity under the sign of literature."[35] In *Le Père Goriot* and in *Facino Cane*, Balzac is mirroring the authentications used by eighteenth-century authors to disclaim (and reclaim) "literarity." Prévost, Diderot, Laclos *et al.* used the notion that Magritte illustrated memorably in his painting, *Ceci n'est pas une pipe*, to say "ceci n'est pas un conte" ("ni une lettre, ni un roman"). Facino Cane, a fictive narrator, is doing the same thing. But instead of saying *ceci n'est pas un récit* in order to claim "truth," he is saying, directly and positively, *que je meure si ceci n'est pas vrai*. The nineteenth-century narrator is repeating, in a chiastic or mirror-like image, the eighteenth-century dictum that prompted plausibility.

The same interplay between mimetic and fictive with which Narrator I began his tale is repeated in the metadiegesis by Narrator II. "*Ceci est vrai*," he says. The insistence upon fictionalized "realism" or "truth," in his case, may have something to do with what comes next: his monomania is made more plausible if we know that he himself is aware of it. After all, it is not Narrator I who tells us about it. Facino Cane himself is telling it *viva voce* (or so we read). He even takes time out from his narrative to explain what might be interpreted as a superstition. When a woman is pregnant, he says, her "fantasies" influence her foetus. "*Il est certain*," he insists, that his mother had a passion for gold during her pregnancy.[36] At this juncture the word *or* (*gold*) is repeated six times in five sentences (or eight times, if one includes the *deux ducats* he takes out of his pocket as proof of his own passion), making of the recurrent signifier a syntactic, tactile, and initiatory obsession. As Lorant states, the word *or* appears 17 times in the story, and the word *trésor* six times. Many other semes containing the phonemes *or* appear or reappear throughout the narrative.[37]

Diderot's *Lettre sur les aveugles*[38] is another among many works of import sighted in the embedded narrative. When Diderot reedited his works in 1782, he reread his *Lettre sur les aveugles* (1749) and remembered the criticism that had been addressed to him by Sophie Volland's niece, Mélanie de Salignac, when the work first came out. She was blind. Instead of revising his main text, he added a series of notes to it entitled *Phénomènes*, and called the whole *Additions à la Lettre sur les aveugles*.[39] In his introduction, the implied author excuses himself for not redoing *La Lettre* itself, "de peur que la page du jeune homme n'en devînt pas meilleure que la retouche du vieillard." As is true of the Narcissus paradigm, the *jeune homme* vs. *le vieillard* theme is carefully elaborated in *Facino Cane*.

Diderot's *Phénomène* no. 2 states: "On m'a parlé d'un aveugle qui connaissait au toucher quelle était la couleur des étoffes."[40] The idea of *correspondances* is evoked here in the sense that is given the word by Swedenborg, Balzac, Nerval, Baudelaire. Diderot, in fact, goes on to use the word after a conversation the implied author reports having had with Mlle de Salignac about geometry. He asks himself: "S'était-il établi à la longue une sorte de correspondance entre deux sens divers?"[41]

The number of rapports between *Facino Cane* and Diderot's *Additions* are numerous:

    1. *Correspondences*

    Diderot: "Un aveugle...connaissait au toucher...la couleur des étoffes";[42] "Quand elle entendait chanter, elle distinguait des voix *brunes* des voix *blondes*."[43]

    Balzac: "Je sens l'or."[44]

    2. *Reading as deciphering or decoding*

    Diderot: Mlle de Salignac learns how to read (and write) by using a pin to puncture a certain *écriture* upon paper. She decodes this writing "en promenant le bout de son doigt sur les petites inégalités que l'épingle ou l'aiguille avait pratiquées au *verso* du papier."[45]

    Although Louis Braille, the inventor of braille, lived from 1809 to 1852, the idea of decoding writing with one's fingers was already present in the eighteenth century. Mlle de Salignac, for example, "lisait un livre qu'on n'avait tiré que d'un côté. Prault en avait imprimé de cette manière à son usage."[46]

    Balzac: Facino Cane deciphers, with his fingers, the message inscribed in Arabic upon a stone in his dark prison cell: "Je parvins à déchiffrer, en tâtant du bout des doigts la superficie d'une pierre, une inscription arabe par laquelle l'auteur de ce travail avertissait ses successeurs qu'il avait détaché deux pierres de la dernière assise, et creusé onze pieds de souterrain."[47]

    3. *Blind animals that see*

    Diderot: Mlle de Salignac says: "Je me figure quelquefois qu'il y a des animaux qui sont aveugles, et qui n'en sont pas moins clairvoyants."[48]

    Balzac: Facino Cane compares himself to a mole (a blind animal) as he works in his underground cave.[49]

    4. *Fate*

    Diderot: Sophie Volland's niece believed that the energy expended in trying to escape "destiny" simply leads one, magnetically, into its clutches: "Elle était fataliste; elle pensait que les efforts que nous faisons pour échapper à notre destinée ne servaient qu'à nous y conduire."[50] (*La Peau de chagrin* echoes in the wings.)

    Balzac: the theme of abusing passions (or expending energy) is Balzacian to the core. Facino Cane's monomania reflects this notion. Narrator

Il believes he becomes blind either from having spent too much time in a dark prison cell, or as a punishment for abusing his visual capacity to see gold. He wonders "si ma faculté de voir l'or n'emportait pas un abus de la puissance visuelle qui me *prédestinait* à perdre les yeux."[51]

5. *Mirrors*

Diderot: Mlle de Salignac says that were the interlocutor to draw, upon her hand, any representation, she would recognize it: "ma main deviendrait pour moi un miroir sensible."[52] And yet the eye is superior to the hand: "Si la peau de ma main," she says, "égalait la délicatesse de vos yeux, je verrais par ma main comme vous voyez par les yeux."[53]

Balzac: while he does not use the word *mirror* itself, Balzac employs doubles and the number two (as well as their multiples) throughout *Facino Cane*. Uneven numbers are rare in the narrative. Balzac creates mirrors through his use of doubles and through mirroring structures, vocabulary, rhetoric, and syntax. There are, of course, two narrators, two narratives. In Narrative I there are: "deux boulevards;"[54] "deux époux," "vingt manières différentes," "une seconde vue;"[55] "quarante sous," "dix sous," "quatre francs," "dix sous," "dix francs," "quatre-vingts personnes;"[56] "Quinze-vingts," "deux compositeurs," "l'embrasure d'une croisée," "tous deux," "l'artiste et le philosophe."[57]

In Narrative II there are a series of binary contrasts: "grandeur vs. Abjection,"[58] "despotisme vs. Pauvreté," "bien vs. Mal," "forçat vs. héros," "ombre vs. lumière," "incendie vs. lave refroidie," "chaudes vs. froides." And then doubles and multiples of two appear again:[59] "quatre-vingt-deux ans"; "vingt ans;"[60]; "millions," "mille maux," "vingt ans," "dix-huit ans," "deux chérubins," "deux mains," "deux cents ducats;"[61] "deux ducats"; "vingt-deux ans;"[62] "deux pierres;"[63] "quatre tomes," "deux tas," "deux mille livres," "six voyages," "deux gondoliers," "vingt millions;"[64] "six millions," "Bianca et l'amie de Mme du Barry," "Quinze-Vingts," "deux ans;"[65] "millionnaires," "Quinze-Vingts," "deux ans;"[66] "deux mois."[67]

That the eighteenth-century scholar Lavater influenced Balzac's theories of physiognomy is unquestionable, and that his ideas were in the background of the author's description of Facino Cane's Dantesque face is more than likely. Lavater believed that "second sight" and the ability to perceive gold through "the eyes of the soul" are part of the same phenomenon. They have their source in the physiological and psychological "fluids" that nourish the mind. Excessive use of these "fluids" can lead to psychic and physical deterioration.[68] Narrator I wonders whether his talent contains dangers: "A quoi dois-je ce don? Est-ce une seconde vue? Est-ce une des qualités dont l'abus mènerait à la folie?"[69]

Une seconde vue: the expression has hermeneutic structural resonances. Narrator I can "see," second hand, as it were, into the psyche of another. In the structure of the text the term acquires an embedded as well as a reflexive presence: Narrator I > Narrator II < Narrator I.

4.   Ali Baba: Reading and Finding Hidden Treasure

Narrator I "sees into" Narrator II, who can "see" gold through the eyes of his soul, and, in the end, Narrator I sheds tears after having been momentarily reduced to silence by Cane's narrative and by the final tune he plays upon his clarinet, *Super flumina Babylonis*. The first words of Psalm 137, a lament of the Jews in exile, begin with: "By the rivers of Babylon, there we sat down, yea we wept, when we remembered Zion."[70] The "rivers of Babylon" are related (1) to the frame (the men are seated on stones from the Bastille near the place where, later, the bridge was built joining the Canal Saint-Martin to the Seine); (2) to the embedded narrative (the Bridge of Sighs joined the prison to the Doges' Palace); and (3) to the exile motif. After the moment of silence, the dialogic element prevails, "difference" is ascertained, and the young man cries out, almost as if he were shouting "Open Sesame": "nous irons à Venise,"[71] since the narrative, in his mind, had taken on "les proportions d'un poème" (the *Odyssey? Childe Harold?*). "Second sight" means perceiving, "second hand," or vicariously, the literary motifs within the paradigmatic structure of the text. Narrator I is ready to embark upon an epic voyage. The narrative has enchanted him, as the sirens had enchanted Odysseus with their music, as Narcissus was enchanted by a vision in the water.

In *La Seconde main*, A. Compagnon states that quotations bring together two texts, two discourses. A given *énoncé* is displaced from an original source and located in a second one. The displacement creates a bridge, a dialogue (to use Bakhtine's word), a relation between the two.[72] The "seconde main" is a constant factor employed in *Facino Cane*. Texts cited (as well as uncited) mirror other texts that reflect the narrative's tensions between visibility and invisibility, mimesis and the fictive, sight and blindness, imprisonment and freedom, realism and fantasy. They also reflect the dialogic structure of the frame narrative *per se*.

A dialogue is established not only between the narrators, but also between them and the reader (real and implied). Reading thematizes and foregrounds the *récit*. Since Balzac himself had read some of the same works as his Narrators and readers, the references sighted offer insight into the real author's own views of explicit and hidden texts.

The act of narrating in *Facino Cane* is reflexive. It emphasizes, twice, the importance of the power there is in the telling of tales, be they "verbal" or written. A. Moger says: "Like most people, I am held hostage by narrative."[73] Narrator I is "held hostage" by Narrator II, just as the various readers of *Facino Cane* are "held hostage" by both. The only encoded person who claims to escape from being taken hostage by Facino Cane is one of the blind men who is metonymically called *le violon*. He says to Narrator I: "Ne lui parlez pas de Venise...ou notre doge va commencer son train; avec ça qu'il y a déjà *deux* bouteilles dans le bocal, le prince!"[74] But *le violon* protests too much. Were he not blind, he, too, might have yielded to the temptation to lead Facino in his quest back to Venice.

Because Venice's gold was embedded in the recesses of the Doges's Palace, there is a link between reading, deciphering, and "finding hidden treasure." The knowledge and effort that it took to decode the Arabic inscription and to dig through the passageway that led to the gold is mirrored, in many ways, in the initiatory quest motifs that come into play in allusions made to *1,001 Nights*, the *Odyssey*, the *Divine Comedy, Childe Harold's Pilgrimage*. Facino Cane's monomania is symbolic of mirror-making between embedded narratives and their frames, of micro-chiastic reflections, of the act of reading and decoding, of establishing bridges and rapports between binary structures, of finding ("sniffing out") and deciphering the significance of intra- and intertexts in literature. Like the Doges' Palace, *Facino Cane* is replete with treasures, and there are, no doubt, many more in that *châsse*, waiting to be discovered.

*   *   *   *

In chapters II, III and IV, I have shown how the formula "une vie par délégation" applies to epistolarity as well as to frame narrative (in Mme de Thémines's letter, in the entire text of *Les Liaisons dangereuses*, and in *Facino Cane*). "Living by proxy" applies equally well to what Barbey d'Aurevilly, whose *Une Page d'histoire* was published forty-six years after *Facino Cane*, created in various ways throughout his work: a poetics of incest. To live by proxy is to live in and through the other.

A "vie par délégation," or "to live by proxy" means living through, by means of others. J. Starobinski carefully analyses one of the incidents in Rousseau's *Confessions* in which the narrator is caught spying on Mme Basile, his hostess, through the half-opened door, then throws himself down passionately, his arms extended, believing that she could not possibly see him. But the chimney-piece mirror betrays his behaviour. Mme Basile simply uses her finger and beckons him, to show him the mat at her feet. The mirror had revealed all: it was an intermediary between the narrator, who is timidity itself, and Mme Basile, who is exhibiting herself knowingly. In the culpable joy of having been discovered spying, there is a doubled reaction: the narrator sees without having been seen (or so he thinks), and this is followed by the guilty delight of having been caught doing so. Both Mme Basile and the young man's feelings are mediated by the mirror. For Starobinski, this scene is a paradigm of writing. The immodesty, or to go further, the shameless behaviour of revealing one's soul (as Jean-Jacques does in his *Confessions*) brings in the "spectator" or "sighter" of this scene, who becomes an accomplice.[75]

One could add to this example the scene in Gide's *L'Immoraliste* in which Michel observes the young Arab stealing his wife's sewing scissors by looking in the mirror above the chimney-piece. Nothing is said by either of them, which means that Michel's friends, whom he has gathered around himself to hear *his* "confessions," or narrative, as well as the reader, live an incident of spoliation by proxy. Sighting, seeing, as well as "vocal specularity" (to reverse the expression, Echo's "specular vocality") that is, writing what one wishes to "confess," are all mediated by mirrors and combined "by proxy."

Narcissus is not only interpreted as solipsistic, in certain texts. He was also interpreted by Pausanias as transgressively incestuous. Pausanias gives us pause - since his paradigm will be encountered again, hundreds of years later, in the work of a writer whose full name is Jules-Amédée Barbey d'Aurevilly.

Notes

[1] In *Reading Frames in Modern Fiction*, Princeton U.P., Princeton, 1985, p. 4.

[2] T. Todorov, *Poétique de la Prose*, Seuil, Paris, 1971, p. 82.

[3] A. Béguin, among others, does not view *Facino Cane* as an embedded text. He identifies Narrator I with the real author, Balzac, and calls the *histoire enchâssante* a prologue. See *Balzac lu et relu,* Seuil, Paris, 1965, p. 154.

[4] Honoré de Balzac, *La Comédie Humaine*. Texte présenté, établi et annoté par A. Lorant, Gallimard, Paris, Bibliothèque de la Pléiade, 1977, VI, p. 1019.

[5] Bonifacio Facino Cane was a flesh-and-blood Piedmontese who was a leader of mercenary troops in the thirteenth century. He wrested Genoa from the French and died, shortly thereafter, in 1412. See *Balzac Short Stories*, ed. A.W. Raitt, Oxford UP, Oxford, 1964, n. 238. Unless otherwise noted, references to textual commentary and notes are found in the Pléiade edition of *La Comédie humaine.*

[6] See n. 2, 1539: "Ces indications topographiques imprécises révèlent que Balzac ne connaissait pas Venise avant la rédaction de sa nouvelle." But he had read *Venezia la Bella* (Renduel, 1834), by Alphonse Royer, who also collaborated in *L'Italie pittoresque* (1835). In a letter to

Mme Hanska (15 July 1834), Balzac made a disparaging remark about Royer: "Pauvre Royer qui a fait *Venezia la Bella* et qui, en 2 volumes, n'a pas su m'en dire autant que vous m'en dites sur Venise en 2 pages" (n. 2, p. 1027).

[7] Lorant, ed., p. 238.

[8] ibid., p. 1013.

[9] ibid.

[10] V. Brombert, *The Hidden Reader: Stendhal, Balzac, Hugo, Baudelaire, Flaubert*, Cambridge: Harvard UP, 1988, p. 20.

[11] See "Histoire du Texte" in the Pléiade edition, pp. 1535-1536.

[12] ibid., p. 1022.

[13] See K. Gittes, "The Frame Narrative: History and Theory;" diss. California Univ., San Diego, 1983, p. 122, and pp. 188-189.

[14] ibid., p. 1019.

[15] Lorant, p. 1011.

[16] ibid., p. 1011.

[17] ibid.

[18] In "Abysmal Influence: Baudelaire, Coleridge, De Quincey, Piranesi, Wordsworth," *Glyph*, The Johns Hopkins UP, Baltimore, 1979, IV, p. 190.

[19] Lorant, p. 1030.

[20] Balzac, p. 1020.

[21] III, 1; see Pléiade n. 2, p. 1020.

[22] ibid., p. 1032.

[23] ibid., pp. 1020-1021.

[24] ibid., p. 1022.

[25] ibid., p. 1539.

[26] See the Pléiade note: "Dans la dédicace des *Parents pauvres* (1846), Balzac associe également Dante à Homère," p. 1539.

[27] ibid., p. 1022.

[28] ibid., p. 1023.

[29] ibid., p. 1025.

[30] Honoré de Balzac, *Oeuvres complètes*, texte présenté, établi et annoté par R. Guise, Gallimard, Editions de la Pléiade, Paris, 1979, X, p. 553.

[31] Lord Byron, George Gordon, ed. Robert F. Gleckner, *The Poetical Works of Byron* IV, Houghton Mifflin, Boston, 1975, p. 1.

[32] Lorant ed., p. 1025.

[33] Z. Ben-Porat, "The Poetics of Literary Allusion," *PTL* 1, 1976, p. 107.

[34] Lorant ed., p. 1026., p. 1026.

[35] V. Brombert, 1988, p. 21.

[36] Lorant, ed., p. 1026.

[37] ibid., p. 1016.

[38] See Lorant's n. 1, 1027: "Balzac, lecteur de la *Lettre sur les aveugles*, se souvient vraisemblablement des observations faites par Diderot, d'après lesquelles l'aveugle, capable de reconnaître au toucher la couleur des étoffes et de discerner les vraies médailles d'avec les fausses, *voit par la peau*. Dans l'addition à sa *Lettre*, Diderot rapporte les propos d'une jeune aveugle selon qui 'l'or, l'argent, le fer, le cuivre polis, deviennent propres à réfléchir l'air.' Ce phénomène de la *réflexion de l'air* peut donner une explication rationnelle à la faculté de "voir" l'or chez le passionné Facino Cane."

[39] See the introduction to Diderot's *Additions à la lettre sur les aveugles* in *Oeuvres philosophiques de Diderot*, textes établis, avec introductions, bibliographies et notes par P. Vernière, Editions Garnier, Paris, p. 1956. Various comparative elements in this chapter were published by *French Forum*, vol. 15, no. 2, May 1990.

[40] ibid., p. 152.

[41] ibid., p. 161.

[42] ibid., p, 152.

[43] ibid., p, 156.

[44] Balzac, p. 1027.

[45] ibid., p. 1027.

[46] Diderot, p. 161.

[47] ibid., p. 162.

[48] ibid., p. 1028.

[49] ibid., p. 164.

[50] Balzac, p. 1028.

[51] Diderot, p. 163.

[52] Balzac, p. 1030.

[53] Diderot, p. 163.

[54] Balzac, p. 1019.

[55] ibid., p. 1019.

[56] ibid., p. 1020.

[57] ibid., p. 1021.

[58] ibid., p. 1022.

[59] ibid., p. 1023.

[60] ibid., p. 1024.

[61] ibid., p. 1025.

[62] ibid., p. 1026.

[63] ibid., p. 1027.

[64] ibid., p. 1028.

[65] ibid., p. 1029.

[66] ibid., p. 1030.

[67] ibid., p. 1031.

[68] See Lorant's Introduction, pp. 1015-1016.

[69] ibid., p. 1020.

[70] Raitt, p. 239.

[71] Balzac, p. 1031.

[72] A. Compagnon, *La Seconde main ou le travail de la citation* , Seuil, Paris, 1979, p. 56.

[73] A. Moger, "Working Out (Of) Frame(D) Works: A Study of the Structural Frame in Stories by Maupassant, Balzac, Barbey, and Conrad," diss., Yale U, 1980, p. 2.

[74] Lorant ed., p. 1024.

[75] Starobinski, *L'Oeil vivant*, Gallimard, Paris, 1961, 218.

Chapter V

Barbey d'Aurevilly's *Une Page d'histoire*: Incest as Mirror Image

> Un monde se dédouble, le tain du miroir
> Emprisonne une vision dont il demeure
> Le seul détenteur.
> Antonia Yasmina-Filali

> A tous égards, la répétition c'est
> la transgression. Elle met en question
> la loi, elle en dénonce le caractère
> nominal ou général, au profit d'une
> réalité plus profonde et plus artiste.
> Gilles Deleuze

The serpent biting its tail that remains iconographically intact so as to signify unity, the end in the beginning, the Omega in the Alpha, that is symbolically depicted as the ourobouros, will not do as a symbol for Barbey d'Aurevilly's short story, *Une Page d'histoire* (1882). But the witticism about two snakes seen devouring each other that concludes with the punch line, "and when I looked again, they were *both* gone," will do. One could even say that it is an appropriate emblem for several of Barbey's most intriguing short stories, narratives about social and sexual transgression in which the real author elaborates what might be termed a "poetics of incest." This is particularly true of the shortest of these tales.

Very few facts about Julien and Marguerite de Ravalet can be uncovered in the chronicle of their fate, we are told by the narrator of *Une Page d'histoire*. What is known, we are told, is that at the end of the sixteenth century, during the reign of Henri IV, the beautiful Marguerite and Julien were incestuous brother and sister in a family infamous for its crimes ever since it had come from Brittany to the chateau of Tourlaville in Normandy around 1400. Mme de Lafayette chose the last part of Henri II's reign (1558-1559) as an historical armature for her novel. Barbey moves forward chronologically to the end of the sixteenth century, the reign of Henri IV (1589-1610) for context. If we are looking for literary context, one might even hear the Queen, in *Alice*, shouting "Off with their heads!"

After Marguerite and Julien de Ravalet fell in love, their imperious father exiled his son and married off his daughter to Jean Le Fauconnier.

Like Laclos and Balzac, Barbey was fond of onomastics: the old man's name recalls the falcon, the bird of prey. Julien returned from exile, abducted Marguerite from the clutches of the old "Fauconnier," and their traces were lost for more than a year. They were found in Paris, on a sad day at the end of the year, the 2nd of December 1603. They were being taken to the scaffold, to be beheaded, and their death concluded their family's lineage. The most vivid historical detail available is that of Marguerite's being so beautiful that when she climbed the steps of the platform where she was going to die, she lifted her skirts so as not to trip on them, thereby revealing her bright red stockings. The executioner became distraught, and she slapped him smartly to bring him to his senses.[1]

Barbey's short story is symbolically "undone" in the tale of the Ravalets. As a decadent writer, Barbey was extremely fond of ambiguity and duplicity. This penchant was translated, semiologically, into a fondness for double entendres. The seme *Ravalet* recalls the verb *ravaler*, and, as such, it emphasizes the termination of the family's race: "La famille qui vivait là [in the chateau of Tourlaville] portait sans le savoir un nom fatidique. C'était la famille de Ravalet... Et de fait, elle devait un jour le *ravaler*, ce nom sinistre! Après le crime de ses deux derniers descendants, elle s'excommunia elle-même de son nom."[2]

The incestuous crime of Julien and Marguerite led them to their deaths, under the executioner's axe. It led to the end of the Ravalet family, and to the conclusion of the narrator's story as well. It also happens that *Une Page d'histoire* was the last narrative written by Barbey d'Aurevilly, in 1882.[3]

Barbey clearly plays with the polysemy of words: *Ravalet - Ravaler*. *Ravaler* means *descendre, jeter à bas, faire descendre*. Its first and second meanings relate to masonry ("travaux d'achèvement des parois extérieures d'une maison"), a work that goes from top to bottom, signifying "descent." Its figurative meanings are "abaisser, déprécier, avilir, dépraver, salir, dénigrer, vilipender." In the sixteenth century the word acquired the meaning of *avaler de nouveau*, or simply, "to swallow," as in *ravaler sa salive,* or metaphorically, *je lui ferai ravaler ses paroles*. (In English, people are made to *eat* their words - in French, to swallow them). Barbey has the last descendants of the *Ravalets* "swallowing their own name," - gone, gone - as well as "lowering, vilifying, denigrating, depraving" it. This was a perfect word for a decadent writer, since "decadence" comes from the medieval Latin word *cadere,* to fall.[4] It is not improbable that Lafayette, herself, in *La Princesse de Clèves*, wished to signal the decadence of the final years of the reign of Henri II. Barbey situates his text on decadence and incest at the *end* of the sixteenth century, even though he makes a deliberate historical mistake by having Henri IV still be married to Marguerite de Valois in 1599. That was the year he repudiated her, divorced her, and married Marie de Médicis.

Une Page d'histoire's narrator not only plays with double meanings. He is, himself, ambivalent about the crime. He finds himself identifying with the protagonists of his story. Though the narrator states that incest is "une honte et la fin d'une race," he will also say that the protagonists "se sont enfoncés en moi comme si je les avais connus."[5] Symbolic "incest" thus occurs between the narrator and his characters. Barbey uses the word "charme" twice, as he refers to a troubling charm that renders the happiness of the brother and sister "enviously shared [by the narrator]" who prays, "may God forgive us for that." He and his characters swallow each other up, as it were. The surrealist notion that was introduced later, in Breton's Vases communiquants, of "the one in the other," is clearly at work in the metaphorically incestuous relationship that exists between the narrator and his heroes.

Lafayette, Laclos, Balzac, and Barbey all weave the threads of History into their stories, using, for the most part, History as an intertext. As a reflection in a mirror never reproduces a completely "authentic" image of the original, intertexts are changed as they are imitated, referred to, or transmogrified. As P. Auraix-Jonchère says: "On peut avancer de même que le jeu intertextuel, dans les cas poétiques dominés par la première personne, engendre une forme de 'neutralisation,' dans le sens où si le 'je' guérinien se perçoit en filigrane à travers la parole de Barbey [the reference is to the work of Maurice de Guérin] il s'en trouve modifié, de même que s'altère le 'je' aurevillien."[6]

1.   History and Story: Prologue and Parts
        The tale of Tourlaville is divided into five parts. In the "Prologue" (Part I), the narrator talks about himself, about "ma terre natale de Normandie," about the spectres that haunted the land. He talks about his town, which he calls "la ville de mes spectres," and about the two specific spectres whose story he will tell and who will, he says, join "the company of the others."

        After what I entitle the narrator's "Prologue" (Part I), the family's place in history is told in Parts II and III.[7] The Ravalet saga took place at the end of the sixteenth century, the century that brought to the fore Catherine de Médicis and the race of the Valois, "the Borgias of France," as the narrator calls them. This also became the age of "la reine Margot," whose scandalous adventures were made famous by Dumas, and more recently, by Patrice Chéreau's film, "La Reine Margot." It is no accident that the narrator alludes not only to Marguerite de Valois's incestuous past, but poetically foregrounds the names "Marguerite de Valois" and "Marguerite de Ravalet."

Both share first names, and their last names share similar sounds, namely, "*Val*ois" and "Ra*val*et." The reader is made to think of the connotations of the word "*val*" or "valley," or of the expression *à val*, which means "down dale," or "to go downhill." Does one not think of the oxymoronic name of *Val*mont, as well? In Chapter VI, which is devoted to Georges Rodenbach's short story entitled *Le Crapaud*, the setting, or "vale," where the protagonist comes to know a devastating experience, is rich with symbolic meanings. The name of the chateau in which the Ravalets had lived was called "le château de Tourlaville." a name that includes the consonants and vowels of "val," in the center, spelled backwards.

Marguerite de Valois, the narrator tells us, "avait à son compte, sur son âme, assez d'incestes pour se punir elle-même dans l'inceste de Marguerite de Ravalet."[8] The narrator is referring to the beheading of the Ravalet brother and sister, which, he states, occurred during the reign of Henri IV. While Henri IV hesitated to execute them, his wife Marguerite de Valois, (or so we are told) had no pity. Barbey performs his historical sleight of hand, as stated earlier, by having Henri IV married to Marguerite de Valois at this time. It would not be surprising if Barbey performed this feat in order to equate the scandals of Marguerite de Valois with those of Marguerite de Ravalet, as well as make a word-play with their names. To expiate her own incestuous past, Barbey says, Marguerite de Valois encouraged her husband to effectuate justice upon the guilty pair. One incest precedes the other, making of incest a repetitive or doubled act in the historical structure of the tale.[9] Incests in European history were sources of particular interest to Romantic and Decadent writers.

The Ravalet's family history had more than its share of murders, rapes, debauchery and sacrilege, all of which could not but whet the appetite of the real author of *Les Diaboliques*. Many of these crimes are named and described briefly by the narrator in Parts II and III. But, he says, while the public awaited some new monster to come forth from the bloodied and sullied Ravalets, two beautiful roses appeared instead, Julien and Marguerite, who were as "beautiful as innocence." [10] The family crest, in fact, carried "une rose en pointe." When the two roses became one, "Marguerite/Julien," the family's history came to an end, and the tale alone is left to be told.

2.   First Chiastic Part

Parts II and III emphasize the place in *history* of the Ravalet family. The narrator then says he must use his imagination to tell their *story* in Parts IV and V. Since the meanings of both *history* and *story* are contained in the word *histoire*, as noted in chapter II, ambiguity is present in the short story's title, *Une Page d'histoire*. The story will consist of a "*page d'histoire*," a metonymic way of accentuating its fleeting presence, as that of a brief reflection in a mirror, or that of a piece of paper's standing in for the entire reign of Henri IV. It will be a fiction based upon an historical event, a "page d'*Histoire*." Both meanings are made distinct by the narrator. When he writes *History* with a capital "H" he talks about his *spectres* coming to him after "*trois siècles d'Histoire*." When he writes *story* with a lower-case "h," he speaks of "*l'histoire de ces deux spectres*," or "the *tale* of two spectres."

"Spectres-Histoire—histoire-spectres": this first chiasmus, used in the Prologue of the narrative, accentuates, through its disposition of words, both the duality of *histoire*, on the one hand, and the unity of both, on the other. After all, the story is based upon the history of an incestual relationship, sparse though the historical details may be. Placing "Histoire" at the center of this chiasmus is one way of legitimizing it as "real."

In frustration, the narrator says in Part IV: "Et voilà tout ce que l'on sait de cette triste et cruelle histoire. Mais ce qui passionnerait bien davantage serait ce que l'on n'en sait pas!... Or, où les historiens s'arrêtent, ne sachant plus rien, les poètes apparaissent et devinent. Ils voient encore, quand les historiens ne voient plus." It is up to the poet to use imagination to turn the tapestry of history inside out, "to find out what is behind that tapestry, fascinating precisely because of what it hides from us...." A mirror is appropriate for this imagery, since the narrator's task is that of coating glass on the underside with aluminum or silver so that it will reveal what has been hidden so far. Their purpose is to repeat "the interior in the exterior, and the exterior in the interior"[11] Even then, the narrator indicates uncertainty by asking one question after another, and each question mark is followed by suspension points: "Qui a jamais su l'origine de cet amour funeste, probablement déjà grand quand on s'aperçut qu'il existait?... A quel moment de leur enfance ou de leur jeunesse trouvèrent-ils dans le fond de leurs coeurs la cantharide de l'inceste, souterrainement endormie, et lequel des deux apprit à l'autre qu'elle y était?..."[12] Six questions ending with suspension points appear in one paragraph.

P. Bacry reminds us that an ellipsis means, etymologically, "a lack, or a need for something." It consists in suppressing elements of a phrase without modifying or lessening its significance.[13] One might call an ellipsis, then, a rhetorical expression of desire, or of want, a device used not only by Lafayette but also by Laclos.

3.   Krieger's Artifact Before Fact

In his essay on "*Ekphrasis* and the Still Movement of Poetry; or *Laokoön* Revisited" (1967),[14] Murray Krieger shows how a number of factually based questions in Keats's "Ode on a Grecian Urn" end in suspension points: "What men or gods are these? What maidens loth?... Who are these coming to the sacrifice? To what green altar...?" For Krieger, "these ellipses have guaranteed the poet's exasperation at the inadequacy of empirical data before beauty's archetypal perfection, the inadequacy of fact before artifact." [15]

Like Keats's poem on a Grecian urn, but in a more deliberate fashion, Barbey's narrator also expresses his impatience at the lack of historical data available to him, so much so that in Part IV, he will opt for artifact (in this case literature) before fact. He begins by using poetic custom to evoke those writers and poets who had gone before him for whom the question of incest was unquestionably provocative. He mentions, intratextually, Chateaubriand's *René*, and Byron's *Parisina* and *Manfred*, all texts dealing with incest.[16] Barbey's text is grounded primarily in literary textuality, even as it narrates historical incest intratextually. The writer himself was fascinated by incest, and elaborated a poetics of incest not only in *Une Page d'histoire* but also in *Ce qui ne meurt pas* (written in the 1830's but published in 1883), in the novella *Léa* (1832), and in the poem "Treize ans" (dated approximately around 1869-1870). P. Auraix-Jonchière remarks that the poem "Treize Ans," exhibits a taste for death. The poem was inspired by an autobiographical incident, Barbey's having fallen in love with his cousin, Ernestine du Méril, who was nineteen years old, in the poem, and the young man [or the poetic persona, the "I" or the "moi"] was thirteen. The word "incest" appears explicitly in the poem, and for Auraix-Jonchière, this confirms the proximity, or rather, the identity of the two biographemes.[17]

Reflections in a mirror, and a mirror is a literal as well as a literary "artifact," have their own fugacity, their own transient, fleeting and short-lived "life." In 1668, during the "war of mirrors" between Colbert and the city of Murano, Venice's mirror-making "capital," du Fresnoy makes statements, in his *De Arte graphica*, that were clearly inspired by da Vinci. It was da Vinci, we recall, who suggested looking at one's painting in a mirror in order to see the defects or faults in verisimilitude that were reflected therein. It was he, as well, who developed writing from right to left, in "mirror-writing." Du Fresnoy's text was translated and annotated by Roger de Piles, who said that the mirror is the ruler and the master of painters because they see the defects in their work by means of a distance being established between the objects depicted and the work represented, as well as by seeing them in reverse. It follows that references to mirrors are not veritable art...but an artificial mechanism.... J. Eymard, who quotes du Fresnoy, concludes: "A mirror's marvel is that it reveals the fugacity of images, and thereby, the flight of objects.... The pleasure of recognition presupposes an obscure recognition that loss will soon follow."[18] Finding and losing: seemingly contradictory, both characterize images reflected in mirrors, as literature signals life as well as death. Closing a book (or a computer screen) can only represent a halt in the lives of those depicted in words. And Lacan reminds us that the Freudian game of "fort" – and "da" that children play is an anguishing as well as reassuring game for a child.

4.   Traces

The narrator/poet will use the well-known topos, *captatio benevolentiae* (which might be interpreted as a friendly seduction), in Part IV, to disavow rhetoric, only to use it to pull in his readers, thereby rendering them sensitive to rhetorical strategies: "In order to follow spectres" he says, "one must have more faith in [those spectres] than in rhetorical figures."[19] As Lévi-Strauss would say, the narrator testifies that he found "traces" of "les beaux Incestueux," and he will use anaphora to show what those traces are. The usage of antimetabole inverts the order of repeated words [a-b—b-a] to sharpen their sense or to contrast the ideas they convey. Chiasmus and commutatio sometimes imply a more precise balance and reversal, while antimetabole implies a looser usage of reversal. They are, nevertheless, virtual synonyms. The usage of repetition is a basic element of Barbey's poetics of incest: "same into same" as well as "different into same" translate the structural, albeit contradictory, significance of such a poetics.

The phrase the narrator first uses in the *middle* of his first sentence, and then at the beginning of four successive phrases, is the following: *je les ai retrouvés*. He begins: "Les spectres qui m'avaient fait venir, *je les ai retrouvés* partout dans ce château, entrelacés après leur mort comme ils l'étaient pendant leur vie."[20] In the first usage of *je les ai retrouvés* at the beginning of a sentence, the narrator mentions the scattered poetic inscriptions found on the walls throughout the chateau: "*Je les ai retrouvés* errant tous deux sous ces lambris semés d'inscriptions tragiquement amoureuses...".[21] He cites those inscriptions in a footnote. It is as if, together, they formed a prose poem: "Un seul me suffit. — Ce qui donne la vie me cause la mort. — Sa froideur me glace les veines et son ardeur brûle mon coeur. — Les deux n'en font qu'un. — Ainsi puissé-je mourir!"

The inscriptions are poetically rendered: "un *seul* me suffit" is echoed in "les *deux* n'en font qu'*un*." The long sentence in the middle uses repetition and contrast: "froideur"/"glace"/"veines" contrasts with "ardeur"/ "brûle"/"coeur." The second and fifth sentences echo each other in their references to death.

The second anaphora, *je les ai retrouvés*, "finds" traces of the lovers in the octagonal tower of the chateau, where the narrator opposes "des tiédeurs absentes" to the "satin glacé" of the blue boudoir in the tower. Octagonal towers are fraught with symbolic symmetry. Like Keats's Grecian urn, the tower of Tourlaville stands archetypically cold in its reminder of warm life and loves past.

5.   Within the Mirror

In the third *je les ai retrouvés* the narrator "finds" the incestuous lovers in a mirror of the chateau, "dans la glace oblongue de la cheminée, avec leurs grands yeux pâles et mornes de fantômes, me regardant du fond de ce cristal qui, moi parti, ne gardera pas leur image!"[22] As J. Frappier says: "Narcissus is the patron saint of mirrors. Their thematics are twins."[23] The "literal," or referential mirror in *Une Page d'histoire*, the "oblong mirror above the fireplace" raises two questions: that of focalisation and that of historical veracity. As for the question of focalization, of "who sees?" of point of view, the narrator reflects the reader in and of the text, the doubled "eyes" of the "I." The lovers "exist" insofar as the reader-spectator is in dialogue with their *imago*. Reader criticism, and Iser in particular, has taught us that the book exists *in relationship* to its reader. There is no clearer example of this than in Barbey's having his narrator/poet's spectres "come to life" so long as he, the spectator, sees them in the mirror in the text. Once he has stopped "reading" them, they are gone. They can be "re-found," so to speak, once we readers "read" the spectator's "reading" them in the oblong mirror he describes. The mirror is in the text as the text is in the mirror. One could use the ending of Baudelaire's sonnet, "La Mort des amants," as a fitting statement that reflects the lovers' death:

> Et plus tard un Ange, entrouvant les portes
> Viendra ranimer, fidèle et joyeux,
> Les miroirs ternis et les flammes mortes.

When the narrator looks into "les miroirs ternis" (one could add "of the text"), he brings the lovers back into literary existence. Just as Barbey uses a sleight of historical hand to equate the two Marguerites (de Valois and de Ravalet), he creates "an oblong mirror" above the chimney-piece that is most likely too large for the time to which it is attributed. Mirrors large enough to be placed above chimney pieces did not exist until the seventeenth century. It was Louis XIV who was able to afford to have large looking glasses placed in his Galerie de Glaces. Before that time, in the historical "reality" that Barbey uses as a context for his tale, it would have been impossible to have a large oblong mirror placed above the fireplace. Readers of Barbey, during his own time, in the late nineteenth century, had become accustomed to seeing large mirrors grace the spaces of Paris and beyond, so that the question of verisimilitude would, most likely, not have been posed by his readers.

6.   Double Viewing Points Within the Portrait

The spectator/poet's fourth and final *je les ai retrouvés* is an admirable exercise in *ekphrasis*: "*Je les ai retrouvés* enfin devant le portrait de Marguerite, et le frère disait passionément et mélancoliquement à la soeur: "'Pourquoi ne t'ont-ils pas fait ressemblante?'"[24] It has been said that Narcissus dies from not being able to attain himself because that which is identical cannot be attained.[25] This statement renders Julien's remark about his sister's painting doubly profound. Julien's question could apply to his finding a breach between his own vision of his sister and her mimetic representation. It might simply apply, as well, to his wishing to become one with his sister. But since "the identical cannot be attained," he, like Narcissus, will succumb because difference exists. Julien follows the example of Pausanias's Narcissus, rather than Ovid's. He worships his own reflection in the water, since he and his twin looked alike, but difference always remains.

Again, the question of point of view and mimesis is raised. To the brother/lover the portrait of his sister/lover cannot possibly "resemble" her. To him, the lover, the mimetic qualities of painting are a failure. But this will not keep the narrator from painting, ekphrastically, a portrait of Marguerite for his readers. *His* "painting" will supposedly "resemble" her because it is semiologically engraved. An interesting historical detail reveals that, as she quoted Brantôme, Marguerite de Valois noted in her *Mémoires* that, having renounced looking in a mirror ever since her husband had died, Mme de Rendan saw herself, accidentally, at a later time, in one, and asked who was the person she saw therein.[26]

So, to the portrait of Marguerite de Ravalet. Just as the "reader" gazed at the lovers in the oblong mirror and they returned his gaze ("me regardant du fond de ce cristal"), so does Marguerite de Ravalet look at the spectator, in the narrator's version, rather than at the Cupids surrounding her: "Elle est debout, en pied, dans ce portrait, - absolument de face, - et elle ne regarde pas les Amours qui l'entourent (preuve de plus qu'ils ont été ajoutés au portrait), mais le spectateur.... Elle semble...faire les honneurs, de sa belle main droite hospitalièrement ouverte, *à la personne qui regarde le portrait.*"[27]

There is a difference between the gaze in the mirror and the gaze described in the painting. While it is the narrator who finds the lovers in the oblong mirror, and they gaze back at him, the initiative comes from *within* in the ekphrastic depiction. Were one to juxtapose them, the point of view of the eyes in the mirror and those in the painting would be chiastically related. In the painting Marguerite looks at the generic spectator, or at "la personne qui regarde le portrait." She thus encodes that person in the portrait. Semiologically that person is as much a part of the portrait as are King Felipe IV and Queen María Ana in Velásquez's painting of *Las Meninas.*[28] In Velásquez, most of the persons represented gaze at the King and Queen, who are "spectators" being "spectated," to use a neologism. They are looking at each other, in one way or another, even as we "sight" both sides. Although in Velázquez the King and Queen are supposedly "outside" of the painting, their supposed representation in the mirror places them "inside" of the painting as well. Colie, Foucault, Kahr, Vaizey, Searle, Snyder, Cohen, *et al.* agree on this point, even though they disagree on other interpretations of that famous painting.[29]

While there is no "literal" mirror represented within the *portrait* of Marguerite, the ekphrastic "painter" of *Une Page d'histoire*, its narrator, that is, also becomes "the spectator" who is being observed. He becomes the object of Marguerite's gaze as well as the equivalent of the real and implied readers of *Une Page d'histoire*. He becomes a mirror of the reflexive activity that takes place in the act of reading, in the act of reading about a portrait in which the subject gazes at her "reader" to the point that her "reader/spectator" is pulled into the text. On 4 February, 1995, in *Le Figaro Magazine* (17), Anne Sinclair, a popular television personality in France at that time, made the following statement about herself: "On vous consomme...parce que l'on vous voit." Marguerite "consumes" *her* spectators, reversing the relationship just described between television viewer and viewed. Another citation of a citation that has to do with "sighting" is M. Thévoz's, who quotes Lacan's having quoted Merleau-Ponty who says, in *Le Visible et l'invisible*: "Je ne vois que d'un point mais, dans mon existence, je suis regardé de partout."[30]

J. Eymard raises the interesting question of esthetic theory from the sixteenth through the nineteenth centuries when he says (1) that Ronsard believed that the poet was like Narcissus in that he examines his work and is consumed by it so as to leave place for the flower of his poetry, and (2) that the text of Marco Girolamo Vida, entitled *Manuel de Poétique*, was preeminent in classical and poetic theory following the classical age because it was in a direct rapport with the concept of metaphor. For Vida, image was the source and substance of language. It was the end in view of poetic expression. Around 1550, most poetic and artistic manifestos bore the imprint of Vida, and when it came to the question of "painting" versus "imitation," the hesitation between both of them was maintained, due to the fact that painting itself referred to mirror-imagery. Eymard claims that this tension was at the heart of French classical esthetics.[31]

7.   Second Chiastic Sighting

One of the two most deliberate and evident uses of chiasmus in *Une Page d'histoire* is located at the conclusion of Part IV. While it is not found exactly at the "hinge" of the text's structure, as we saw Mme de Thémines's letter being placed strategically at the center of *La Princesse de Clèves*, and Prévan's narrative being placed at the "hinge" of *Les Liaisons dangereuses*, it concludes the most self-consciously tropological section of the text, the most rhetorically charged, because it opposes "la Chronique" to "l'imagination des poètes."[32]

Part IV began with opposition between history and poetry, and it ends there as well. This appears in the intentionally striking chiasmus: "La Chronique, qui dit si peu de choses, a dit seulement qu'elle prononça que c'était elle [Marguerite de Ravalet] qui avait entraîné son frère. Elle accueillit, sans se plaindre et sans protester, l'échafaud, comme elle avait accueilli l'inceste, et simplement, parce que la conséquence de l'inceste était, dans ce temps-là, l'échafaud."[33]

In the chiasmus "échafaud-inceste—inceste-échafaud," the historical consequence of incest is placed before the cause in the first part ("échafaud-inceste"), and cause precedes effect in the second part ("inceste-échafaud"). It is as if the narrator (1) reverses, rhetorically, in the chiastic disposition, the natural order of things, since incest at least calls into question "the natural order of things," and (2) mirrors his own ambiguity in his condemnation of but fascination with incest. By being repeated in the center of the chiasmus, "inceste" is thus valorized. It is also framed by death because it leads to l'échafaud.

*Ravale*r: to swallow twice, *avaler de nouveau*. The chiasmus does that. As R. Lahnam says, "chiasmus seems to set up a natural internal dynamic that draws the parts closer together, as if the second element wanted to flip over and back over the first...."[34] A poetics of incest does that too: it is the interpenetration of two similar entities.

M. Krieger, as well as many other commentators upon *ekphrasis* (including Lessing), emphasize the relationship that exists between the imitation of a spatial work and the question of temporality.[35] One of the principal objects Krieger studies is the urn in literature (Keats's, T. Browne's, Shakespeare's, Donne's, etc.). Due to the urn's being a container of ashes for the dead, it represents both life and death, both movement and stillness. Its circular shape emblematizes the beginning and the end. Krieger states that the circularity of the urn adds complex dimensions to the temporal aspects of *ekphrasis*. It is an "always-in-motion but never-to-be-completed action." "As with Keats' urn," Krieger says, "it accompanies the introduction, in accordance with the ekphrastic principle of spatial forms within literature's temporality."[36] It brings to the literary work a doubleness that reveals "continual, deliberate advance, a 'succession,' yet a forever movement, 'without progress'".[37] Mary Douglas's *Thinking in Circles* is most appropriate as it relates to Krieger's analysis of Keat's poem.

Time is integral to the ekphrastic portrait painted by the narrator of *Une Page d'histoire*. When Marguerite "semble faire les honneurs, de sa belle main droite hospitalièrement ouverte, à la personne qui regarde le portrait,"[38] she is represented as making a living, loving, inviting gesture to the percipient.[39] The bloodied-winged Cupid painted next to her, however, was painted "après coup," *after* her death. The linear movement of her life and death are inscribed in the painting in several ways: both love and death are portrayed, the passage of time is represented because it was painted both before and after her death, and the static description of a static object is "brought to life" by focalization. Even though *ekphrasis* is related to a descriptive pause, it forms part of a narrative that moves through time, that has a beginning and an ending.[40] This, however, does not mean that it has only closure, or only openness. It has both. The lovers die. The narrator lives on, remembering their "story." The passage of time and the lasting elements of art are not only in tension - they are deliberately "woven" and "unwoven," like Penelope's tapestry. In his introductory chapter to an issue of *Nineteenth-Century Fiction*, J.H. Miller uses his own 1976 article on "Ariadne's thread" as an intertext to what he has to say about "The Problematic of Ending." He develops Aristotle's suggestion of the existence, or the possibility of a narrative "which would be all unraveling or denouement, in which the 'turning-point' from tying to untying would be the beginning of the narrative proper and all the complications would lie prior to the action as its presupposition."[41] The History/story dichotomy could be contained in what Miller calls "ending and beginning at once, a beginning/ ending which must always presuppose something outside of itself, something anterior [History] or ulterior [story], in order either to begin or to end, in order to begin ending."

The inviting gesture Marguerite de Ravalet makes with her right hand contrasts with the one depicted by her left hand. Through both of her gestures, Marguerite de Ravalet seems to be inviting the reader to a hermeneutical task, and, at the same time, her left hand, like the arm and hand painted by Parmigianino in his "Self-Portrait in a Convex Mirror" may also be viewed as a barrier to interpretation. In Marguerite's portrait, she crumples up a handkerchief with her left hand "avec la contraction d'un secret qu'on étouffe...".[42] The right hand knows but does not reveal what the left hand is doing. While the right hand invites - the left one hides, in what one is led to assume is either a guilty or obsessive, but in any case, highly symbolic contraction.

M. A. Caws is thought-provoking when she juxtaposes John Ashbery's poem on Parmigianino's painting to the painting itself. While Caws says that Ashbery sees the arm as a barrier, as if it were painted there "to protest what it advertises," she then suggests another interpretation. The hand, she says, can be viewed as a pointer, pointing inwards, back *into* the convex "mirror" of the self-portrait.[43] Both Marguerite de Ravalet's hands manifest a visible disparity in the manner in which they are depicted. One invites the outsider in, while the other manifests the tension of that which is private. The portrait as mirror shows the tension existing in the nineteenth century between private and public domains - with the private coming to weigh more in Romanticism, in Symbolism, and in Decadence.

In the ekphrastic description of Marguerite's dress, the narrator says she is wearing "une robe de *cérémonie* blanche et rose, dont l'étoffe semble être tressée et dont les couleurs sont de *l'une en l'autre*, comme on dit en langue de blason."[44] We return to the surrealist injunction to join "one in the other." But "l'une en l'autre," as J. Petit says, is also heraldic language, meaning "alternance des émaux entre les pièces et les partitions."[45] While *alternance* appears in heraldic vocabulary, the word *tressée* the narrator uses seems equally appropriate to the meaning he is giving to his ekphrastic description: two colours, pink and white, are woven together so as to form one iridescent colour. One imagines the material looking pinker at times and whiter at others, depending upon the point of view of the spectator, as well as the folds of the material itself. The colours of Marguerite's iridescent dress are emblematic of a narrative that is, simultaneously, a neat knotting that leaves no threads hanging out (brother and sister both die, leaving no issue behind them, thus ending the family's sequence), and an "un-knotting," or untying, that does leave a narrator "hanging out" to comb the narrative threads so that both colours, pink and white, are seen, shining, side by side, all mystery and complexity foregrounded in this poetics of one in the other.

Ovid's narrator intertwines the colours pink and white in the description of Narcissus's admiring "the glorious beauty of his face, the blush mingled with snowy white."[46] After he comes to know himself and despair, Narcissus beats his breast until it becomes pink, "just as apples sometimes, though white in part, flush red in other part, or as grapes hanging in clusters take on a purple hue when not yet ripe."[47] In the end, before he dies, the "ruddy colour" no longer mingles with the white.

The "mingling" of colours or the braiding of two entities into one in *Une Page d'histoire*, the colours of which go "de l'une en l'autre," not only describes, ekphrastically, the colour of Marguerite's dress, but also has some readers return to Ovid's paradigmatic myth. The "mingling" of the desire to join two in one is a metaphor for both life and death. It is also a metaphor for chiastic rhetoric, achieving further import in Barbey's story by being a metaphor for a poetics of incest itself.

There are two ekphrastic scenes in *La Princesse de Clèves*. In one, Nemours steals the Princesse's portrait, thus symbolizing his desire to "own" the beautiful woman depicted therein. The other is the famous scene at Coulommiers, in which Mme de Clèves gazes at the portrait of Nemours while he gazes at her, just as the "eyes" of M. de Clèves are represented by his servant who gazes at Nemours as he gazes at Mme de Clèves as she gazes at Nemours's portrait. Both progression and regression are present in that crucial scene, thus indicating the forward or accumulated advance of Mme de Clèves's affective development, and the retrogressive arrow that points back to her husband, creating a tension that will lead to a jealousy so strong that it will kill him, causing her to reject Nemours's offer of marriage after M. de Clèves's death. Love's arrow goes both forward and backward, much as a chiastic movement causes a sentence to "fold" over itself.

8.   Of Time and Contestation
         The notion of difference in similarity brings us to Barbey's having his narrator call into question various aspects of narrative, mainly, verbal incriptions and ekphrastic description: "Ces inscriptions et ce portrait ont été contestés."[48] Both of these "callings into question" have to do with the idea of time. The inscriptions were most likely added to the wall panellings *after* the lovers' deaths, we are told. It would be most implausible, in the narrator's mind, for them to have been placed there at a time in which the lovers were trying to hide their passion:

> Quant aux inscriptions, moi-même je ne pourrai jamais admettre qu'elles aient été tracées par eux, les pauvres misérables! et que deux amants qui se savaient coupables, et dont la vie se passait à étouffer leur bonheur, sous les yeux d'un père qui avait le droit d'être terrible, aient plaqué avec une si folle imprudence sur les murs le secret de leur coeur et la fureur de leur inceste.[49]

The inscriptions were added, the narrator surmises, after Marguerite's death.
         The same is true of the Cupids depicted in the painting. They are called a "suspicious detail."[50] This is especially true of the Cupid with the bloodied wings: "Ce sang aux ailes indique par trop qu'il a été mis là après la mort sanglante de Marguerite."[51]
         Poetic inscriptions and the use of *ekphrasis* affirm literary and artistic creation and call them both into question. The narrator both "constructs" and "deconstructs" his tale. Marguerite and Julien both live their love and die because of it. The narrator both creates and undermines, both condemns incest and envies it, both decries rhetoric and uses it. The painter of Marguerite's portrait has her invite and reject the viewer who gazes at her portrait.

9.   The Third Chiasmus
         The relationship of the text's two principal uses of chiasmus to the contexts of Parts IV and V is compelling. The first, located in the

"Prologue," is of less consequence than are the second and third. Part V begins by referring, as did Part IV, to textuality, when the narrator mentions having read a few printed letters that the brother and sister had exchanged. But even here there is contradiction. Although "on ne trouve pas dans ces lettres un seul mot qui indique le genre d'intimité qu'on y cherche."[52] words of passion are found in the quotations from Marguerite's letters that are italicized by the narrator: "votre lettre que j'ai *brûlée*," "*vostre passion à mon bien dont les* FELICITES me sont encore présentes au coeur..."; "Vos récits de Paris me mettent en joie sur les *marques seures de vostre passion qui me sont plus chères que la vie...*"[53] After noting the existence of the epistolary communications and reading quotations from them, the reader learns how Marguerite's father forced her to marry the old but rich "messire Le Fauconnier" and at this point the two words *adultère* frame the two uses of the word *inceste*, making, once again, *inceste* the principal part of the third chiasmus: "Plus tard, on la força d'épouser ce messire Le Fauconnier, et c'est ainsi qu'elle introduisit *l'adultère* dans *l'inceste*; mais *l'inceste* dévora *l'adultère*, et des deux crimes fut le plus fort."[54]

Adultery is first introduced into *incest*, but then *incest* wins out, "devouring" *adultery*. The frame of the chiasmus is "consumed" - swallowed twice, as it were - since the word *adultère* appears at both beginning and ending of the "a-b—b-a" structure. As in the second usage of chiasmus, in Part IV, emphasis is placed upon the central part of the trope. The narrator's doing this in two locations of the text creates for the word an epistemological instrument that gives seeming ontological status to incest. In the first instance the trope undermines incest's consequence, *l'échafaud*, and in the second it states that of the two crimes, incest or adultery, incest is the strongest, a plus in Barbey's mind. The real author of *Les Diaboliques* believed that the worse the crime the "better" it was.

The incest taboo led to decapitation, at least in Barbey's narration of the ending of the Ravalet family. Barbey wrote during a century in which the guillotine was still used on a regular basis, but since Marguerite and her brother were executed on 2 December 1603 (was the number "2" chosen deliberately by Barbey?) they could not have been decapitated by the guillotine, which was not invented by Dr. Guillotin until 1789 and put into official use until 1791-92. In the notes Barbey took on the history of the Ravalets, he states, simply, that they died "la tête tranchée en place de Grève, 1603." In his "story," the narrator states, simply, that it was a "coup de hache" that brought about their demise. Personally, Barbey sympathized with the perpetrators of a taboo that was as old as humanity. He also took perverse delight in an esthetics that celebrated representations of Judith and Holofernes, Salomé and John the Baptist, David and Goliath. J. Clair states it well: "Narcissus changes into Medusa, the reflection reversing its properties, the reflection no longer offering one a gratification of the self but thrusting one into the horror-pangs of death. This was, indeed, to become one of the major esthetic themes of the *fin de siècle*."[55]

Immediately after using the chiastic phrase "adultère-inceste—inceste-adultère," the reader is told that Marguerite had children from both "crimes," from M. Le Fauconnier as well as from her brother, but that both children had died. She was thus able to climb the steps to the scaffold without looking back. Her eyes were riveted upon her brother, instead, who went before her, preceding her into death.[56] While this leads to "closure" in terms of the ancestry of the Ravalets, the "story" remains "open" in that its narrator is left to tell the tale.

Marguerite's having conceived children from both husband and brother creates echoes with another one of Barbey's tales of incest, *Ce qui ne meurt pas*. Although it was written in the 1830's, Barbey did not publish it until 1883. Its writing, then, precedes *Une Page d'histoire*, but its publication follows it. In this novel, Allan de Cynthry falls in love with his adoptive mother, Yseult de Scudemor, who is disillusioned with life and love, and is unable to reciprocate Allan's sensual desires. She does, however, become his mistress, out of pity for him. Her aim is to destroy the boy's passion by revealing to him her own boredom and sense of affective sterility. After having achieved her purpose, because Allan's own passion for her dies, Allan falls in love with Camille, Yseult's daughter, his adoptive sister. They marry, but Allan loses his passion for her as well. The climax, as it were, of the story, takes place when both mother and daughter give birth to children conceived from Allan. At the end of the novel, Yseult de Scudemor dies soon after childbirth, and Allan and Camille are left with two children, Jeanne and Marie. Allan has no love left, but intends to be faithful to his adoptive sister/wife and to both of his children. *Ce qui ne meurt pas* was written in two parts, a structure that is appropriate for what is double incest. As an *Epilogue*, Allan writes a letter to his friend, André d'Albany, a name that rhymes with his own, Allan de Cynthry (another semantic mirroring), to tell him that life holds no meaning for him. Epistolarity, or writing, is, once again, foregrounded.

Barbey frequently reminds his readers, particularly in his correspondence, that he was born on All Saints' Day, the day devoted to the celebration of the dead. He makes of his own birth a pattern that is repeated over and over again in his poetics. He lives to construct, to imprint, to make permanent the prose he creates, even as he reminds his readers that he was born on the Day of the Dead and that death is part of life. His life and work, then, repeat binary formulations and ideas, the attraction and repulsion of opposites, or, as we see in *Une Page d'histoire*, the contestation of one by the other.

If we consider the last paragraph of *Une Page d'histoire* as a coda that the narrator adds to his tale, we find that it reveals another facet of the tale of Tourlaville. Having recently visited the castle, the narrator had seen two swans glide by on the lake next to it. Their description brings to mind the Narcissus paradigm, as related by Pausanias, of Narcissus falling in love with the imagined reflection of his twin sister. It is as if the swans were the boy and his Other, close together, with nothing separating them. They were "pressés, tassés l'un contre l'autre comme s'ils avaient été frère et soeur, frémissants sur cette eau frémissante. Ils auraient fait penser aux deux âmes des derniers Ravalet, parties et revenues sous cette forme charmante."[57] But even the analogy to metamorphosis is immediately disavowed: "ils étaient trop blancs pour être l'âme du frère et de la soeur coupables. Pour le croire, il aurait fallu qu'ils fussent noirs et que leur superbe cou fût ensanglanté...".[58] Analogy and its immediate disavowal represent both circularity and its negation, both closure and openness.

This ending mirrors a scene in one of Barbey's *Diaboliques*, "*Le Bonheur dans le crime*." When Hauteclaire Stassin is first seen with her former lover, now husband, in the Jardin des Plantes, and faces the panther, whom she resembles, according to the second narrator, the "good doctor Torty," he exclaims: "panthère contre panthère." This remark leads to the event that is generative of the tale that will follow, which is the narrative of Hauteclaire's having poisoned the Countess Serlon de Savigny in order to marry her husband. After Hauteclaire takes off her long violet-coloured glove and strikes the panther's nose with it, thus endangering her own hand when the panther strikes back and devours the glove, the couple moves away. Torty's description is telling: "Ils passèrent auprès de nous, le docteur et moi, mais leurs visages tournés l'un vers l'autre, *se serrant flanc contre flanc*, comme s'ils avaient voulu se pénétrer, entrer, lui dans elle, elle dans lui, et ne faire qu'un seul corps à eux deux, en ne regardant rien qu'eux-mêmes."[59] They would like to be two in one, much as the swans, who are "tassés l'un contre l'autre," or, like Marguerite de Ravalet's dress, whose iridescence shows both pink and white colours woven together.

When he gave his courses on Baudelaire at the Collège de France, J. Starobinski published a seminar on "Le Cygne" that he entitled "figures penchées." He was faithful to the history of the poem, to the poem in history, to *ekphrasis*, as well as to the poetics of Baudelaire. Starobinski pays especial attention to the structural dimensions of the poem. It is divided into two parts. In the first stanza we perceive the axis of symmetry, the central part (I would say "hinge") around which both parts are organized, as in a mirror. The poet uses the word "miroir" in the second line, after his apostrophe to Andromaque: "Ce petit fleuve/Pauvre et triste miroir où jadis resplendit/ L'immense majesté de vos douleurs de veuve..." We recall that even though it was an axe that decapitated Marguerite and Julien de Ravalet, the guillotine, two centuries later, came to be known as "la Veuve"....

In the second part, as a mirror reverses imagery, Baudelaire's "homme d'Ovide," Narcissus, cannot look at his reflection because the pool is dry. Instead, he looks up reproachfully to God, to a sky that is "ironique et cruellement bleu."[60] Starobinski points out that in the first stanza of the second part, the words "mélancolie" and "allégorie" (he had already studied Dürer's and George de la Tour's portraits of *Melancolia*), add a dimension of auto-reflexivity to the work. Even as the poem contains socio-political dimensions, he says, it would be unfortunate to reduce it to those. The same is true of *Une Page d'histoire*, and yet the way in which the narrator approves of the decadent elements of the Valois dynasty seems more striking than Baudelaire's socio-political allegory on the emptiness of his time.

In "Le Cygne," Narcissus, who is called "l'homme d'Ovide" leads to the rhyme "avide," that evokes the word "vide," "nothingness" or "emptiness," that will appear in the third stanza of Part II of the poem. One may read Baudelaire's "cygne," as does Riffaterre in his studies of the same poem, as a "signe," as a supreme example of intertextuality. The semiotics of incest seem to be manifest in the narrator as a wish that the swans, in *Une Page d'histoire*, be black instead of white, with red bloodied feathers on their gracefully curved necks. One wonders whether Barbey was not tempted to use red ink when he wrote his "signes."

One stanza of Baudelaire's "La Mort des amants" seems a fitting epigraph (if not "epitaph") for *Une Page d'histoire*:

Usant à l'envie leurs chaleurs dernières
Les deux coeurs seront deux vastes flambeaux,
Qui réfléchiront leurs doubles lumières
Dans nos deux esprits, ces miroirs jumeaux.[61]

The reader cannot but be aware of the word-play implicit in the name of "*Tour*-la-ville." The word evokes a tower, solid and stable, as well as movement in a circumference. As E.Souriau says, "le chiasme part dans un sens; puis, tout en continuant dans une même dimension linéaire irréversible, celle de la suite de la phrase, il retourne cependant en arrière en ce qu'il fait défiler de nouveau les mêmes éléments, dans un autre exemplaire, en sens inverse."[62]

Readers of this story cannot "faire le tour" of *Une Page d'histoire* without encountering transgression, ambiguity, both closure and lack thereof, hermeneutic challenges, inscriptions, ekphrastic depictions, interpretative contestations, and chiastic framing devices that are both reflexive and reflective. This text foregrounds other texts in its use of rhetoric and in the negation of its usage. The text reflects itself in itself, and causes the reader to reflect upon what is reflected in the text. The reader says to herself, in the end: "And when I looked again, they were both gone..." and no one but the narrator was left to indulge in, repeat, and pass forward the narrative. The narrator was to the incestuous couple what Horatio was to Hamlet. Hamlet refused to allow Horatio to commit suicide, perhaps, as he himself was dying, because he wanted his tale to be told. It's very telling would justify, in his own mind, the numerous deaths that surround him as he dies, as well as remind the viewers of the original death, that of his father, whose demise preceded Hamlet's coming onto the stage.

While much has been written about "openness" and "closure" in literature, with "openness" being assigned, primarily, to twentieth-century texts, D. Richter contests the dichotomy that assigns "open-endedness" to modern novels and closure to older forms. He studies Richardson's *Pamela*, and concludes that even as traditional a novel as that one could be considered as having an "open form."[63]

The narrator of *Une Page d'histoire* tells his readers, in his *incipit*, that he made an annual visit to his "native land," which is Normandy. This year, he says, as he foregrounds the *writing* of his tale, he had found the story of two siblings who had the power of spectres. He calls his town a "*veuve*," thus announcing, proleptically, a metonym of the decapitation that would bloody the necks of the swans he describes in his final paragraph.

*   *   *   *

Decadents and Symbolists might be sighted as blood-brothers and sisters. The ambiguities created between male and female in their writings are powerful returns to Plato's androgyny myth as well as to a wish to obliterate the distinction between the One (I) and the Other (II).

In Chapter VI, I will show how the Belgian Symbolist writer, Georges Rodenbach, deals with the attempt to abolish differences (or the establishment of *différance*) in various guises. In the short story *L'Ami des miroirs*, published posthumously, he creates a twice-told tale leading to Nothingness (effacement, ambiguity, and death), and we think of Baudelaire's swan, once again. The narrator will even deny giving names to the principal personages in his tale. In Rodenbach, like Baudelaire's implied critique of the emptiness of French society at the time of his writing "Le Cygne," I have called the protagonists Narcissus I and II since their identities are not otherwise known, and Ovid is the clear intertext. But Narcissus I's love of Narcissus II does not lead to adulation. The narrative moves from Narcissus I's jealousy to his making nefarious suggestions to Narcissus II that will lead the latter to commit suicide. In Rodenbach's short story, once again, only Narcissus I, like the narrator of *Une Page d'histoire*, will be left to tell the tale.

In Rodenbach's novel *Bruges-la-morte*, duplicity dominates the rhetoric, structure, and pathology of the text. That Rodenbach situated the expression "à rebours" at the center of his work is significant (and one cannot but think of Huysmans at this point), of a twice-"lived" tale that will also lead to effacement - effacement that is a prelude to many of the twentieth-century's eventual literary tendencies that move "against the grain," if not back upon themselves, chiastically. Some might consider the "decapitation" of the author as present, in an embryonic state, in Symbolism, as well as in multiple *mises-en-abyme* that become overtly self-conscious. The transgressive "one in the other" motifs that are present in Decadent and Symbolist ambiguity lead to a denial of traditional logic that the Surrealists later embraced with fervour and delight.

The future is in the past, or as C. Martindale says in *Redeeming the Text*, what we call "our" time is always made up of fragments of the past. Barbey, Rodenbach and his fellow Symbolists simply (and not so simply) paved the way for chiastic and imbricated rhetoric, structure, and meaning to become, eventually, a passage, if not a "rite of passage" from one way of looking at the world of texts to other ways.

Notes

[1] Page references in this chapter, unless otherwise noted, are to vol. II of the Pléiade edition, *Barbey d'Aurevilly, Oeuvres romanesques complètes*, ed. J. Petit, Gallimard, Paris, 1966, p. 372.

[2] ibid., p. 369.

[3] ibid. See J. Petit's *Notice* of *Ce qui ne meurt pas*: "D'autres éléments interviennent. L'inceste, par exemple, thème qui deviendra obsédant dans les dernières pages écrites par Barbey: *Une Page d'histoire*..." p. 1366.

[4] See *Le Robert*, Société du Nouveau Littré, Paris, 1966, for meanings of both *ravaler* and *decadence*.

[5] Barbey, p. 368.

[6] P. Auraix-Jonchière, éditeur et essai sur Jules Barbey d'Aurevilly, "Un Palais dans un labyrinthe," *Poèmes*, Champion, Paris, 2000, p. 245.

[7] J. Petit reminds one that the characters in the story belonged to Norman history, and that Barbey had doubtlessly known about them for a long time. Around 1872, Barbey noted, in *Disjecta Membra*, that he needed to read up on the subject. A while later, he took copious notes on it, from a *Notice* by M. de Pontaumont. He calls it "Ravalet de Tourlaville." He begins

his notes in this manner: "La famille de Ravalet venue de Bretagne en 1480 en Normandie. Seigneurs de Tourlaville. Terribles! L'un d'eux assassine son frère, un autre fait pendre ses vassaux parce qu'ils n'ont pas fait moudre leur blé au moulin seigneurial. Un troisième enlève la femme d'un écuyer voyeur de Tourlaville…etc." Barbey then places the brother and sister in this context: "Et enfin, c'est Marguerite et Julien de Ravalet de Tourlaville, frère et soeur incestueux, qui meurent la tête tranchée en place de Grève, 1603. Ce fut Marguerite de Valois, soupçonée elle-même d'inceste, qui empêcha son mari Henri IV de pardonner (voir P. de l'Etoile)."

[8] ibid., p. 372.

[9] J. Petit reminds the reader in a note that although Barbey did not invent this fact, in 1599 Henri IV and Marguerite de Valois were divorced. Petit also doubts the veracity of "la reine Margot's" incest: "si la vie de Marguerite de Valois fut aventureuse, il ne paraît pas qu'on l'ait accusée d'inceste" (1361). J. Petit is at odds with Dumas, Barbey, and others on this question.

[10] ibid., p. 371.

[11] Melchior-Bonnet, *op.cit.*, p. 106.

[12] Barbey, pp. 371-372.

[13] P. Bacry, *Les figures de style, op. cit.*, p. 150.

[14] Krieger's essay was reprinted as an Appendix in *Ekphrasis, The Illusion of the Natural Sign,* The Johns Hopkins UP, Baltimore, 1992, pp. 263-288.

[15] ibid., p. 284.

[16] The reference to *René* is obvious. The one to Byron is less explicit. In *Barbey d'Aurevilly et l'Imagination*, Droz, Génève, 1978, Berthier reminds us that *Parisina* raconte les amours incestueuses de Hugo, fils naturel du prince d'Este à Ferrare, avec la femme de son père; Hugo sera décapité, Parisina mourra folle." As for *Manfred*, says Berthier, "on devine que les tourments du héro proviennent en partie de ses rapports incestueux avec sa soeur Astarté. Mais on songe aussi à *La Fiancée d'Abydos*, où les amours de Sélim et Zuleika sont d'abord d'allure très incestueuses, puisque Sélim passe pour le frère de Zuleika; et nous savons par Bourget que c'était justement ces passages que Barbey préférait chez Byron, ces nuances 'les plus tendrement mystérieuses et coupables'" p. 169. Byron's biography contained incest, just as did Barbey's, in the latter writer's early love for his cousin, Ernestine du Méril.

[17] P. Auraix-Jonchière, *op. cit.,* pp. 187-188.

[18] J. Eymard, *op. cit.*, p. 62.

[19] Barbey, p. 374.

[20] ibid.

[21] ibid.

[22] ibid.

[23] Cited by Eymard, p. 388.

[24] Barbey, p. 374.

[25] Melchior-Bonnet, p. 249.

[26] Marguerite de Valois, *Mémoires*, Paris: Société de l'Histoire de France, Paris, 1824, p. 2.

[27] In the notes Barbey takes from the *Notice de M. de Pontaumont*, it is obvious that he never saw the portrait the narrator of *Une Page d'histoire* describes: "Château Renaissance. Quand on le visite, on aimerait mieux voir que ce château le portrait de Marguerite de Ravalet qu'on en a enlevé. Elle était, dit-on, représentée debout, entourée d'amours aux yeux bandés qu'elle repousse pour sourire à un seul dont les yeux sont sans bandeau et les ailes *tachées de sang*. De la bouche un mot sort: "*un seul me suffit*."" It is obvious that Barbey's ekphrasis betrays or changes the ekphrasis in the notes he took from M. de Pontaumont. While Pontaumont has Marguerite smile at the Cupid whose wings are bloodied, Barbey has Marguerite face the spectator, p. 375.

[28] Interpretations of *Las Meninas* are multiple and complex. Some of the most interesting include R. Colie's chapter entitled "Problems of Self-Reference" in *Paradoxia Epidemica*, Princeton UP, Princeton, 1966, pp. 354-350; M. Foucault's *The Order of Things*, in French, *Les Mots et les Choses*, Harper & Row, N.Y., 1976; H.W. Janson's *A Basic History of Art*, Harry N. Abrams, N.Y., 1971, p. 250, and rev.ed. 1977, 518-19; M. Vaizey's *One Hundred Masterpieces of Art*, Putnam, N.Y., 1979; J. Searle's "*Las Meninas* and the Paradoxes of Pictorial Representation," *Critical Inquiry* 6, Spring 1980: pp. 477-88; J. Snyder and T. Cohen's "Reflexions on *Las Meninas*: Paradox Lost," *Critical Inquiry* 6, Spring 1980: pp. 429-47.

[29] The authors of the last two articles listed in note 28 (Searle's, and Snyder and Cohen's) disagree with each other in their interpretations of *Las Meninas*. All three authors have profound things to say, nevertheless, about point of view, about where the King and Queen are located, about what they are doing on "this side" of the picture, about the reflection in the mirror, and about what the painter is painting on the represented canvas. While I shall not take sides in these authors' disagreements, I do wish to say that, in my view, one of the most interesting remarks Searle makes is that "the painter is painting the picture we are seeing: that is, he is painting *Las Meninas* by Velásquez," p. 485. Snyder and Cohn's conclusions are also illuminating. They say the following about what Velásquez probably wished. He wanted: "the mirror to depend upon the unseeable painted canvas for its image. Why should he want that? The luminous image in the mirror appears to reflect the

king and queen themselves, but it does more than just this: the mirror outdoes nature. The mirror image is only a reflection. A reflection of what? Of the real thing – of the art of Velásquez. In the presence of his divinely ordained monarchs…Velásquez exults in his artistry and counsels Philip and María not to look for the revelation of their image in the natural reflection of a looking glass but rather in the penetrating vision of their master painter. In the presence of Velásquez, a mirror image is a poor imitation of the real,"(p. 447." What interests me particularly is that most people who have written about *Las Meninas* agree that the King and Queen are on "this side" of the painting, and that the image in the mirror is that of Felipe IV and Queen María Ana. I agree with Searle, as well as Snyder and Cohn, who come to a meeting of minds on the notion that it is the art of Velásquez that matters.

[30] The Lacan quote is found in his *Séminaire* XI, 69, and Thévoz's in *Le Miroir infidèle*, Ed. de Minuit, Paris, 1996, p. 9.

[31] Eymard p. 553-613.

[32] Barbey, *op. cit.,* p. 373.

[33] ibid., p. 376.

[34] In *A Handlist of Rhetorical Terms*, 2nd ed., UofC Press, Berkeley, 1991, p. 33.

[35] Essay cited in n. 14.

[36] ibid., pp. 270-271.

[37] ibid., p. 271.

[38] ibid., p. 375.

[39] "Percipient" is used by J. Kittay in "Descriptive Limits," *Yale French Studies* 61, 1981, pp. 225-43.

[40] See D.P. Fowler's instructive article, "Narrate and Describe: The Problem of Ekphrasis," *Journal of Roman Studies* 81, 1991, pp. 25-35, as well as W. Steiner's chapters on "The Painting-Literature Analogy," and "The Temporal versus the Spatial Arts" in *The Colors of Rhetoric*, Chicago UP, Chicago, 1982.

[41] University of California Press, Los Angeles, 1978, vol.33, no.1, pp. 3-7. Miller's "Ariadne's Thread" appeared in *Critical Inquiry*, Autumn 1976, 3, pp. 56-77.

[42] Barbey, p. 375.

[43] In *The Eye in the Text: Essays on Perception, Mannerist to Modern* , Princeton UP, Princeton, 1982, p. 51.

[44] Barbey, p. 375, italicized in text.

[45] In Jacques Petit's note, p. 1362.

[46] Ovid, p. 155.

[47] ibid., p. 159.

[48] Barbey, p. 374.

[49] ibid.

[50] ibid.

[51] ibid., pp. 374-75.

[52] ibid., p. 376.

[53] ibid., pp. 376-77, italicized in text.

[54] ibid., p. 377.

[55] J. Clair, *op. cit.*, p. 169.

[56] Barbey, p. 377.

[57] ibid., p. 378.

[58] ibid.

[59] ibid., p. 87.

[60] C. Baudelaire, *Oeuvres complètes*, introd. Claude Pichois, Gallimard, coll. de la Pléiade, Paris, I, pp. 85-86.

[61] C. Baudelaire, OC, I, 126.

[62] In *Vocabulaire d'Esthétique*, PUF, Paris, 1990, pp. 362-363.

[63] D.H.Richter, *Fable's End: Completeness and Closure in Rhetorical Fiction,* The University of Chicago Press, Chicago, 1974. Several ideas in this chapter were elaborated in *Romanic Review*, vol. 90, 1999.

Chapter VI

Reversals and Disappearance:
Georges Rodenbach's *L'Ami des miroirs* and *Bruges-la-morte*

A peine me connais-je en ce désordre extrême:
Me rencontrant en lui, je me cherche en moi-même.
Rotrou, *Les Sosies*

1. *L'Ami des miroirs*

When Ovid first depicts Narcissus adoring his own reflection in a pool, Narcissus is a chiastic diptych undisturbed. Narcissus I reads, or worships, his "text," which could be labeled Narcissus II, with unequivocal admiration and desire. That anything should have gone wrong, that he should have found within his "mirror" anything or anyone other than himself would have led to a different kind of conclusion. While Ovid refers to the strangeness of Narcissus's infatuation, late nineteenth-century interpretations of the myth, such as those of Georges Rodenbach and other *fin de siècle* writers, create personae who turn away from society and look inward, as if they were mirrors of themselves. Among them are Oscar Wilde (in *The Picture of Dorian Gray*), Huysmans's des Esseintes (in *A Rebours*), Mendès's Baroness d'Hermélinge (in *Méphistophéla*), or Rachilde's Raoule de Vénérande (in *Monsieur Vénus*), and so many more, including Jean Lorrain.

J. Lorrain (1855-1906), whose work will be examined in Chapter 7, was a writer who formed part of the Symbolist, Decadent movement of literature and art at the end of the 19th-century. His infamous novel, *Monsieur de Phocas*, seems to be partly inspired by Wilde's *The Picture of Dorian Gray*. Lorrain also published a narrative called *Narkiss* (1908), which was a *fin de siècle* adaptation of Ovid's Narcissus myth. In it J. Lorrain calls Narkiss "a mirror's captive."[1] He compares Narkiss to swans that come and go, back and forth, admiring their own reflections in the water. They are called prisoners of their own reflections in the circles of water they create as they swim: "Chacun n'est attentif / Qu'à se considérer soi-même: / C'est comme un autre soi dans l'eau; / L'eau s'est plissée en un halo / Dont il est captif ;/ Comme il s'apparaît blême! / Et dans quel recul! / Il est bien celui qui renonce; / L'eau se fonce… / Et peu à peu dans ce miroir il devient nul."[2] In this text we see circles, reversals, psychological captivity, and finally, disappearance. The swans become "nuls," void. Because Georges Rodenbach was from Bruges, "the Venice of the North," as it was and still is sometimes

called, water and canals figure prominently in his prose, much as they did in
J. Lorrain's poetry and prose.

These thematics appear most clearly in the short story, *L'Ami des
miroirs* (1901), in which Rodenbach elaborates the "strangeness" of
Narcissus's infatuation with mirrors. This maniacal enthrallment leads him to
pathological madness and suicide. The protagonist does himself, as it were,
in, by running headlong into his mirror, believing he will penetrate it. He dies
as a consequence thereof. He is both created (or repeated) and effaced in his
own image.

This short story by Rodenbach, that appeared in a posthumously
published collection of works entitled *Le Rouet des brumes* (1901), was
chosen by P.-G. Castex for his *Anthology of French Fantastic Tales*,[3] and
certain definitions of the fantastic lead one to ponder how Rodenbach's text
participates in the genre itself. The element of the uncanny is denied from the
start, as the events narrated are explained by the insanity that besets "l'ami
des miroirs." Because the visions the protagonist sees inside his mirrors are
clinically categorized as the product of a paranoid and self-destructive
imagination, they could be placed under the Todorovian rubric of "le
fantastique expliqué."[4] Far more important is Rodenbach's use of ambiguity
and proleptic discourse to undercut textual sequentiality and narrative
progression, thus reflecting his characters' paranoia and madness. Rodenbach
brings about, in various ways, the collapse of differences in both his *énoncés*
(*what* is narrated) and in his *énonciations* (*how* the text is narrated).

Structure and narration are inseparable. In *Thinking in Circles*, M.
Douglas says that "a formal literary structure is not the same as thematic
structure" and that "a formal structure is not based on contents; it is a set of
empty frames or containers for the contents."[5] I must demur. This separation
between "empty frames" into which the contents are poured exaggerates the
quest for pattern as well as the interpretation of content. Douglas does say
that "there should be always some fittingness between contents and
structure," but she goes too far when she asks her readers to "think of the
poet having to pour a newly formed idea into bowls and jugs of different
shapes, some of which are at hand in local conventions, and some of which
have to be invented" [6] Form may be studied, as I do in this book, but it
cannot be separated from a work's meaning, as a "bowl or a jug" into which
meaning is poured.

2.   A Twice-Told Tale

L'Ami des miroirs begins with a general statement: "Madness," the
narrator says, "is frequently nothing other than the paroxysm of a sensation
that originally appeared to be purely artistic and subtle."[7] The narrator had a

friend who died dramatically in a sanatorium, we are told in the first paragraph, in a manner that he will soon relate. "*A l'origine*," we read in the second paragraph, in italicized type, this friend loved mirrors, nothing more. End of paragraph. Since the reader now knows that the protagonist dies in the end, it is as if one had just read a résumé of the Narcissus tale. The narrative begins again, and details, step by step, the development of a pathology – of *two* pathologies, rather. The protagonist begins to be afraid of mirrors because they haunt him, they reflect him poorly, they take his life away from him. The narrator suggests to his friend that this is perhaps due to the fact that those mirrors were lying, that we are all ugly because of the *mirror*'s ugliness. "Narcissus," as I will name the protagonist, since he is called nothing other than *mon ami* by the narrator, concludes that the shop-front mirrors in which he sees himself reflected are poor in quality and that he should buy expensive mirrors that are "true." Acquiring a growing taste for exotic looking glasses, he surrounds himself with a collection of the best ones he can find. The word "looking glass" is, in itself, ambiguous. Is the glass looking? Or is it a person looking into the glass? "Narcissus" loves his Louis XV and Louis XVI mirrors, "whose faded golden frames encircled the mirrors as a crown of October leaves surrounds the edge of a well...".[8]

The protagonist becomes content, and encloses himself within his house of mirrors, which might be called his "fun-house." During a visit, the narrator asks him about women: does he not miss following them down the streets, as he sometimes used to do? "Narcissus" replies that each mirror is like a street, and that in each one he sees the image of women whom he does follow, although they never allow him to get near.

Shortly after this conversation, Narcissus I loses his sense of identity. He can no longer recognize himself in his mirror but tips his hat to his own image, as if he were a stranger. When the narrator visits him for the last time, "Narcissus" seems happy again. He is surrounded by a crowd, he says, "where everyone looks like me."[9] Shortly thereafter, we are told, it becomes necessary to hospitalize him for "excentricities that had caused a scandal in his windows."[10] He leaves quietly when he is made to go to the psychiatric ward. He misses his collection of expensive mirrors, but soon grows fond of the one that hangs in his hospital room: in it he sees the images of women who will love him. But his illness grows worse; he sometimes becomes hot, sometimes cold, and begins to think that it probably would feel good to be inside the mirror. Some time later he is found with his head smashed in, bloodied, gasping his final breath. He had lunged into the mirror, says the narrator, "in order to enter it, to be part of the crowd that resembles him – at last!"[11]

In *Entre Lumières et romantisme*, P. Noir, who writes about J. Lorrain, makes an interesting statement about "decadent Narcissus." He states that the interpretation of *fin de siècle* Narcissus denotes the castration complex in that it exhibits fractal dimensions, a decadent malaise, a preoccupation with the body, in pieces, exploded, mutilated, or, as he puts it poetically, a body "qui vole en éclats, s'étoile et s'étiole."[12]

3.   Ambiguity and Disappearance

The idea of effacement, or disappearance, which D. Kelly describes as being the most constant element in Freud's, Todorov's and Derrida's notions of the uncanny,[13] means that the text puts its own pre-established limits into question. In Freud effacement occurs when the repressed and the conscious intermingle; in Todorov it occurs when the outside and inside worlds are mixed (as in the themes of the "je"), or when societal or sexual laws are transgressed (as in the themes of the "tu"); and in Derrida effacement equals dissemination and the undecidable.[14] In her study of Charles Nodier's *Inès de las Sierras*, Kelly shows how all of the categories of opposition in the text collapse or bring about "nondisjunctions" of dualistic differences. While the reader's inability to decide between fiction and reality is an initial state of affairs in Nodier's text, in the end, Kelly states, the ambiguous co-existence of both the canny constative and the uncanny performative discourse effaces the limits between the two.[15]

Not only does disappearance function in Rodenbach's text, but an appropriate metaphor for the structural disposition of effacement in *L'Ami des Miroirs* is the serpent ourobouros. The end of the tale is found in its beginning, and the beginning in the end, a chiastic statement in itself. Much as the words "a looking glass" have a double meaning, the title of Rodenbach's short story, in itself, sets the stage for ambiguity. *L'Ami des Miroirs* can be interpreted as having the emphasis placed either upon the protagonist who becomes enamoured of mirrors, or upon the mirrors themselves of whom the protagonist becomes a friend. The mirrors attain anthropomorphic capabilities and adopt the protagonist as *their* friend: "l'*ami* des miroirs" is, at the same time, "l'ami *des miroirs*." A third possibility points the finger at the narrator, for it is he who refers, throughout, to "mon ami," never once endowing his "friend" (or himself, for that matter) with a name. Like the mirrors he criticizes, it is as if he had vampiristically absorbed his "friend's" identity, his very name, into himself. Even the title of the collection resounds ambiguously: *Le Rouet des brumes* evokes the image of encircling fog, of uncertainty, of that which is neither dark nor light.

After starting his narrative with the general statement about madness and its relationship to its having begun as something that is "artistic" and "subtle," the narrator tells us: "I had a friend who was placed in a sanatorium, where he died dramatically of an illness that I will soon narrate, the origin of which began in a harmless way and by means of remarks that seemed to be those of a poet."[16]

As Roland Barthes asks: "Who speaks?" Who relates things in an artistic, subtle, and dramatic way? Who makes remarks that seem to be "those of a poet"? Is it the protagonist, a rich dilettante who goes berserk, or a supposedly "objective" narrator, like the *persona* Balzac creates in *Facino Cane* who must earn a living by means of his words?

The narrator is using auto-referentiality to call attention to his craft, to writing. He spins a tale that is contained, in fact, in miniaturized form, in the first paragraph: once upon a time the narrator had a friend who went mad. He was sent to a sanatorium where he died an artistic, subtle and dramatic death. All is there, including the narrator's relationship to his "friend." The words "artistic," "subtle," and "poetic" are ambiguous in that they are used as referents to the "friend's" manner of being. But they can also be applied to the persona who narrates, since his friend died in a manner, he says, "that I will soon narrate." The narrator is a teller of tales, of tales in which fiction and "reality" are confounded, chiastically. Since a condensed version of the tale is contained in the first paragraph, the end of the text is thus contained in its beginning. Omega is found within Alpha's mouth. But the narration begins *again* in the second paragraph. In its entirety the paragraph reads: "A l'origine [in the beginning] he had a craving for mirrors, nothing more." *A l'origine*: in the beginning was the word, or the narrative, and in the end the tale begins all over again. Creation and effacement meet when, first, the tale has been told, and second, when *l'ami* joins the crowd where "everyone resembles him": as he saw himself, in life, as part of a crowd, so is he also part of the great crowd of the dead in the end, when his life is terminated in his own image. Rodenbach's protagonist also lives again and again, each time the mirror of the text is contemplated by the reader. Disappearance is the structural disposition of this text just as repetition, according to H. Miller, forms part of the structure of narrative[17].

The stamp of madness, of repetition and disappearance, is placed upon this narrative from start to finish, since it begins with the word "madness" and ends with the adverb *enfin*. "*Enfin*" might well be construed as a pun: divided, "en fin" contains both a preposition and a noun that relate both to death and to the conclusion of the text. In "the end" effacement and dissolution are present, and disjunction between opposing or antithetical entities is obliterated. To say that "*a* equals *non-a*" is madness, but madness is both the subject and the object of this tale.

4.   Narrative and Narrator

The relationship between the narrator and the object of his narration is a symbiotic one. In order to explain, at the start, the fact that his "friend" had become afraid of staying alone in his house, where objects had turned hostile to him, and that he was, therefore, planning to leave town, the narrator says: "Since he was free as well as rich, it was only natural that he could be capricious in his decisions." This seemingly guileless statement betrays a subtext of jealousy on the narrator's part. The remark is double-edged. It reveals the protagonist's wealth, on the one hand, and the narrator's negative judgment, or jealousy, on the other. As a writer, he himself is doubtlessly not rich; he cannot afford to be capricious in *his* decisions. *He* is the chiastic, or mirror image of *his* "friend."

In describing his fear of looking into certain mirrors, "Narcissus," uses the following simile: "It was like water that was going to open up and then close in upon me!"[18] The horizontal axis of water, of pool, well, or pond is the medium contemplated by Narcissus. The correlation between mirrors and water is made several times in *L'Ami des miroirs*, the intertextual referent to Ovidian Narcissus being obvious in the description of the Louis XV and XVI mirrors: "...their faded golden frames encircled the mirrors as a crown of October leaves surrounds the edge of a well...".[19] Not only is classical Narcissus reflected in Rodenbach's text, but the words "faded" and the allusion to "October leaves" surrounding, wreath-like, the edge of a well, denote cooler climes, the termination of the year, and, proleptically, the termination of "the friend's" life.

Both Rodenbach and Barbey, like most Decadent writers, were fond of words like the verb "ternir," "to tarnish," and the adjective "fané," "faded." Barbey's narrator saw the pallid image of the Ravalet lovers in the lusterless, tarnished mirror that he "places" above the fireplace. Rodenbach's heroes, like the "dead city of Bruges," are faded, lacking in freshness. They droop, like lillies after a rainstorm, prefiguring their own death. Rodenbach wrote an accompanying essay to *Bruges-la-morte* that has been translated, recently, as *The Death Throes of Towns*.[20]

To equate, metaphorically, mirrors that have hard surfaces, with water, whose surface is permeable, is a natural thing to do, since both are reflective media. But for the protagonist of *L'Ami des miroirs*, to confound the two and to think that the mirror will close in upon him, or swallow him up, is to eradicate the distinction between the tenor and vehicle of metaphor. Both mirror and water *are* the same in his mind, and the distinction between them disappears. The hard and the soft surfaces melt, ambiguously, into one. We are still reading a nineteenth-century Symbolist text, not a surrealistic play written by Cocteau, such as *Orphée*, where Heurtebise goes in and out of walls, or in looking at the film version of the play, where the mirror becomes a mercurial pool, and yet the Symbolists prefigure the Surrealists in many ways.

The positive, or horizontal axis of water, a medium that is life-giving and creative, is equated in Rodenbach with its opposite, a negative, or vertical axis in which Narcissus believes he will descend and be swallowed up. Mirrors are water; they will, l'ami believes, "close up over him." Water can swallow one, as a dangerous medium, but as a liquid medium it can also entrap, when it freezes. The swans that Rodenbach describes in a récit called "Noces mystiques," are captured when the water in which they are swimming freezes. The Béguines from the convent in Bruges are metaphors of entrapment. When they return from Mass to their lodgings, those places are called "des essors hâtifs de cygnes ayant peur de se prendre dans l'étang qui gèle et d'être captifs de leurs ailes tout à coup soudées aux glaçons…" It is as if the Béguine convent were a carcere, a prison drawn by Piranesi, but in a still and quiet manner, all in white, which is spotted by the black vestments of the nuns. The lake that is found at the center of their habitations is a metaphor of captivity.[21]

The role the narrator plays throughout Rodenbach's text only helps l'ami to confuse the horizontal with the vertical axis. He is only too understanding of his "friend's" plight. When he comments upon his "friend's" initial decision to leave town he says:

> I was not surprised, knowing my friend to be sensitive, knowing, besides, what impressions can be created upon one's return to one's place, within closed rooms, amidst the dust, the musty odor, the confusion, the melancholy one feels for things that seem to have died a bit during one's absence. Oh, the sadness of evenings of jubilation! Evenings of return, after the forgetfulness one experiences while away. It seems as if all of one's sorrows that had remained at home come out to greet us…[22]

What cheerful thoughts, these! What we do not know, since the narrator cleverly avoids telling us, is whether these words were actually *uttered* by the narrator to his "friend." By means of rhetoric addressed in constative language, the narrator subtly evades this question and creates ambiguity. But we may surmise that since he, in fact, uses direct discourse with his "friend" in many places in the text, the lugubrious intonations of the statements quoted above were expressed to, or at least understood by, the one who returns.

Because his friend decides *not* to leave town, and upon a chance encounter claims to feel ill, the narrator wishes to express his "good" intentions by telling his "friend" that he looks amazingly well. The protagonist replies that, on the contrary, all kinds of mirrors prove the opposite:

> I go out. I think I'm well, cured even. But mirrors watch
> me…They live off of their reflections. They lie in wait of
> passers-by…It is perhaps they who steal from us our
> healthy coloring. It's from having given them our living
> color that we have become pale… The health we possessed
> is lost in them like lovely make-up in water…[23]

It is at the end of the nineteenth century that a mirror became what Baudrillard calls the object owned by the rich in which the self-admiration of the bourgeois finds the privilege of multiplying his appearance and playing with his possessions.[24] This critical comment is a statement of what a bourgeois society had come to value: itself. It was not long after the publication of *L'Ami des miroirs*, in 1901, and thanks to the new procedures elaborated by the manufacturing company of Saint-Gobain, that mirrors began to appear everywhere, in opera houses, theaters, casinos, boutiques, department stores, cafés, brasseries, bakeries and wine merchant's shops, not to mention their proliferation in bourgeois apartments, boudoirs, manor houses of the rich, palaces and châteaux. When we think of Paris at the turn of the century, we can immediately recall restaurants and brasseries such as "La Pérouse," "Julien," "Boffinger Bastille," which is now classified as a "monument historique," "Vagenende," "Le Grand Véfour," "La Coupole," which opened in 1900, "La Tour d'Argent," "Maxim's," the "coupole" of what is today called the "Marbeuf," the "Ambassadeurs" in the Hôtel Crillon, and on and on. The City of Lights had become the City of Mirrors as well, and still is so today. Rare is the street in Paris where one cannot see oneself reflected *somewhere*, and this proliferation of "selves," with all it signifies, could not have taken place had it not been for Colbert's political machinations with Venice and Murano in the seventeenth century.

Vampiristic reversal of "friend" and "mirror" in *L'Ami des miroirs*, as well as of "friend" and "narrator" is revealed, since these remarks were made about mirrors' "living off of our reflections." They apply to both narrator and "friend." Instead of returning verisimilitudinous representations of health to the on-looker, the mirrors (and the narrator) become Dracula-like, draining the life-blood from those who look at their reflection therein.

Vampiristic language is used by the narrator, reinforcing what he has heard his "friend" say:

> *Everyone* is ugly in those mirrors. One sees oneself
> deformed, pale, or livid, with bloodless or violet lips.…

> One perceives oneself as being knock-kneed or obese, too
> tall or too fat, as in the concave or convex mirrors of a fair.
> One is always ugly therein. But they lie. And we are ugly
> from their ugliness, and pale from their illness...[25]

The adjectives "deformed," "pale," "livid," "bloodless," "violet," and
"illness" connote death. P. Lejeune's formula, *auto-mortrait*, expresses the
mirror's vampiristic tendencies cleverly.[26] Using mortuary imagery the
narrator simply repeats, or reflects, what "Narcissus" had just said before.

Instead of becoming depressed, "Narcissus" buys a large number of
expensive mirrors and surrounds himself with them. The narrator says that
some of them had turned green with age. They are like the brackish waters of
a rotting lake. They remind one of the lake into which Poe's *House of Usher*
crumbles at the end of that novella: "Some of them had turned a bit green
with the passing of time. One looked into them as if they were sheets of
water." [27] The narrator himself is confounding the positive, life-giving axis,
with the negative, or death-producing brackish color green in order to evoke
immersion or a plunge into the dismal waters of disappearance.

Because "Narcissus" seems happy in his looking-glass labyrinth that
communicates as if the mirrors in his house were streets, and which
consequently reflect the labyrinthine structure of the text itself in which one
reflection leads to another, the narrator tests him by trying to make him
return to what he calls a "reality of the most prosaic sort." He does so by
asking his friend about the opposite sex: "And what about women in this
confinement of yours, you who liked them, following them sometimes, down
the street?" [28] It is "women" that seem to be referred to by the narrator as
"reality of the most prosaic sort"!

5.   Reversals: The Reflected, and the Labyrinth of the "Real"

When "Narcissus" replies that his mirrors are full of women, of all
types of women whom he follows, it is at this moment that a crucial turning-
point in the text occurs: he soon loses consciousness of who he is. As he
passes in front of his mirrors he no longer recognizes himself. Instead of
seeing a reflection, he sees "the physical reality of a human being." A turn-
about has taken place; his self, and the representation of himself in the mirror
exchange places. But this reversal leads immediately to dissemination: "And
due to so many mirrors that are juxtaposed, the solitary silhouette was
multiplied into infinity, as it ricocheted everywhere..." [29]

When the narrator visits his "friend" for the last time, *l'ami* seems
happy, for he is involved in his multiple imagery that seems to reverberate as
if it were a voice within a grotto that contains thousands of echoes.[30]
Intertextual echoes of Echo can be "heard" at this time. It becomes necessary,

soon after, to lock up the narrator's "friend" due to a number of "excentricities" that caused crowds to gather at his windows, thus increasing the lubricious aspects of his actions.[31] Although the reader is never told directly what these excentricities are, one might assume that *l'ami* had been exposing himself to his neighbors. The transgression of societal and sexual laws forms part of the idea of effacement in Todorovian terminology.

6.   Dyadic Dangers in Repetition and Inversion

The dyadic implications of this text follow the reversals noted previously. They remain consistent with both the *énoncés* (what is said) and the *énonciations* (how things are said) when it comes to oppositions and ambiguities. The repressed and the conscious intermingle in the uncanny visions that are both seen as well as desired. While one would expect water to be a feminine principle, and immersion to represent immersion into femininity, the image of water here is nefarious, instead. It becomes equated with death, with the imagery of being devoured, thus becoming a metaphor of the *vagina dentata*. The question the narrator asks about women (a mean, jealous, if not vengeful question, it would seem), brings about a dispersion of the identity of "Narcissus." What l'*ami* had perhaps secretly wished to see was the beautiful image of a male. His hidden or repressed desire was for sameness, that is, for maleness, for the narrator himself. It is almost immediately after the narrator perversely asks his question about women that his "friend" loses his notion of what mirrors are about. Due to the presence of so many mirrors, "the solitary image of the solitary man disperses, ricochets everywhere, constantly creating a new double. They all resemble each other, having become copies of the first one who remains separate from the crowd by who knows what emptiness…".[32] The series of alliterative and sibilant *s, ch,* and *z* sounds that the narrator uses to describe this diffusion of identity is striking. We are reminded of Racine's Orestes, whose madness, whose loss of identity is expressed through sibilant *s*'s. Shortly after asking: "Est-ce Pyrrhus qui meurt? et suis-je Oreste enfin?",[33] Orestes succumbs to total madness and wonders, in that famous line, what demons, what serpents Hermione is dragging behind her as she embraces Pyrrhus: "Pour qui sont ces serpents qui sifflent sur vos têtes?"[34] Significantly, Orestes, too, uses the imagery of being devoured: "L'ingrate mieux que vous saura me déchirer;/ Je lui porte enfin mon coeur à dévorer."[35]

The function of the narrator in *L'Ami des miroirs* is a decisive one. Not only is it he who narrates, but every intervention he makes on his friend's "behalf," provokes a reaction that leads "Narcissus" further and further down toward the abyss of final disappearance. One of the last statements "Narcissus" makes to the narrator before being confined to the psychiatric hospital is: "Look! I'm no longer alone…Friends are such strangers. They are so different from us! I am living amidst a crowd – where everyone resembles me."[36] The word "different" and "similar" are most important at this juncture.

The subtext of this short story is one of desire that is most "subtle" and "artistic." "Narcissus" has, perhaps, come to desire the narrator himself, his own "friend," and is rebuffed by him (or the other way around). His "friend" turns out *not* to be his friend, for he asks pernicious questions and is also an *alter* ego, different from himself. His friend is, in reality, his ennemy, a chiastic mirror image. He loses himself, therefore, in an imaginary world, where there is no alterity between the "I" and the "you." "Narcissus" therefore exposes himself to a crowd of people who assemble at his windows, creating a scandal. He can no longer tell the difference between the outside and the inside worlds, a pathology that will lead to his internment and eventual suicide.

One might surmise that the narrator who had asked the question about women at the start of this mad adventure, was, himself, jealous of his "friend's" previous predilection for the opposite sex: previously, "Narcissus I" had, in "fact," followed women down the streets. The narrator's revenge, therefore, is to lead "Narcissus," step by step, down the path in which he will desire *sameness,* and then frustrate that desire. It is shortly after this that *l'ami* becomes progressively ill. In a feverish state he will reflect physical ambiguity, an objective correlative of psychic ambiguity: one moment he is too hot, the next too cold. It is only within the mirror that it must "feel good," he says. Heat and coolness are intertextually woven into Ovid's description of Narcissus's pool: "Grass grew all around its edge, fed by the water near, and a coppice that would never suffer the sun to warm the spot. Here the youth, worn by the chase and heat, lies down."[37] Rodenbach has *his* Narcissus become both hot and cold: Eros is related to Thanatos. As he states in another of his short stories, *L'Amour et la mort,* that was published in *Le Rouet des brumes,* love and death are interrelated: "If so many lovers wish to die and do, in fact, perish a bit more each day while they are still in love, it means that love and death are related by means of analogies, by means of subterranean corridors that communicate. One leads to the other. One refines and exacerbates the other."[38]

Not only is the narrator vampiristic; he indulges in being retributive as well. Of the inexpensive mirrors in which his "friend" had seen himself initially reflected, the narrator had said that we are ugly from their ugliness, pale from their illness. Because a mirror not only takes, but also gives back, it is as if the narrator had imparted his own "ugliness," his own "illness" to "Narcissus." The narration reflects its own function, since the narrative's *énoncé* is about taking and, chiastically, giving back; it is about writing and speaking and interpreting and influencing. The reader reads the text as a mirror reflects and influences its reader. *L'Ami des miroirs* is self-referential in that the tale reflects writing. In the beginning the narrator refers to the story he is going to narrate. It reflects "specular vocality," since a mirror is compared to voices that resound in a grotto with "a thousand echoes"; and it reflects conversations that are as elaborate as a Louis XVI mirror. To describe his "friend's" subtle ways of speaking, the narrator says: "He was a unique conversationalist..., abundant, albeit precious. His words unfolded into the air with ornamented phrases that frequently ended up in the realm of the unknown."[39] There are precise links between "les mots et les choses" in Rodenbach's tale of two people. The narrator is actually describing his *own* baroque style. Although not abundant, *his* own phrases are "ornamented and end up in the realm of the unknown." Similarity and difference reveal themselves once again: the style of the narrator and that of his subject are similar.

Repetition, inversion, ambiguity, and final disappearance are the order of this text. The end is in the beginning, male and female are confounded, mirrors not only give back but also imbibe images, and the very name, or identity, of the protagonist is "ingested" by a vampiristic narrator who takes the mirrors' side of the matter. He sucks in the identity of the protagonist so as to create a tale of his own. He becomes to his subject as what Echo becomes to Narcissus, a voice crying in the wilderness, an example of "specular vocality."[40]

The narrator creates a narrative of his own, and even though "Narcissus" dies, the narrator lives on to tell his tale, like the narrators in Balzac's *Facino Cane* and Barbey's *Une Page d'histoire*. While effacement or disappearance is signalled in the very process through which Rodenbach has his narrator and his subject intermingle ambiguously, making of this a most modern text in which disjunctions cancel themselves out in a vertiginous interplay of dualistic mimeticisms and alterities, the process itself calls attention to *both* parts of the chiastic equations. Rodenbach could not have had his narrator do this if, in the beginning as well as in the end, the word had not been there to build and sustain labyrinthine images, structures, and meanings that do, in fact, make sense, even as they entrap the protagonist as well as the reader in contradictions and ambiguity.

.

II.   *Bruges-la-Morte*

La Femme, dans son essence première, l'être inconscient,
folle de l'inconnu, du mystère, éprise du mal, sous la forme
de séduction perverse et diabolique.... Les chimères
sombres, terribles, mortelles; chimères de l'espace, des
eaux, du mystère, de l'ombre et du rêve. Au loin, la Ville

Morte, aux passions sommeillantes; Ville du Moyen Age,
âpre et silencieuse, aux passerelles nombreuses, aux ponts
rudimentaires et primitifs, aux ruelles montantes et
serpentantes...

Gustave Moreau[41]

Signe des temps, le chef décollé n'est plus sur un plateau,
mais sur les pages d'un livre.

Jean de Palacio[42]

The extent to which Rodenbach used mirrors as a source of
inspiration is visible not only in his short stories but in his novels as well.
Bruges-la-morte mirrors *L'Ami des Miroirs* in its employment of reversals
and consequent ambiguities.

Dead and dying women appear frequently throughout nineteenth-
century literature and art. The Romantics' tortuous delight in experiencing
what Shelley called, in his poem on the beauty of the Medusa, the
"tempestuous loveliness of terror," continued to be part of the *fin de siècle*'s
creative expression of frenzy, fetishism, and anguish. But to the pleasurable
shudder the Romantics experienced when they depicted severed heads or
dying bodies, the Symbolists added a treacherous type of tranquillity.

Rodenbach's *Bruges-la-Morte* (1892) reveals a number of
problematics relating to Symbolist sensibility: Narcissism in a text's meaning
and structure, mirror reversals in the portrayal of woman as Ophelia/Medusa,
equivocal interpretations of sexuality, chiastic forms and rhetoric. The
enigmatic significance of water and mirrors in this text adds elusive and
mysterious elements to its make-up, creating a paradigmatic study of
reflexivity, of *mise-en-abyme*.

The principal male figure in Rodenbach's novel, Hugues Viane, is a
hair fetishist whose erotic fascination with death places him within the heart
of Symbolist aesthetics. In the beginning of the novel Viane had spent
exactly half as long as he had been happily married, five years, as a widower
living in a town house that he had made into a shrine for his dead wife, who
remains nameless except for the appelation *la morte*. He had turned two
rooms, in particular, into a *fin de siècle* "temple" in which every bibelot,
pillow, screen, curtain, mirror, portrait and drawing had become consummate
icons to be worshipped.[43] The most precious object found in this
"physiognomy of the interior" (a term Walter Benjamin uses to describe
Poe's talent as a "physiognomist" of interior spaces)[44] is a strand of golden-
amber hair that Hugues had cut from his wife's head, as she lay on her death
bed, and had braided into a plait that he kept inside a glass-covered box, or
reliquary. He worshipped it as if it were a sacred object.[45]

When Bachelard points out when he discusses the symbolism of drawers, trunks, closets *et al.,* he says that everyone knows that there is a homology between the geometry of a safe and the psychology of a secret.[46] To go even further, he says of a jewel-box, when it is closed, that it takes its place in the exterior world. When it is opened, treasures are found therein. The outer world disappears, to make place for surprise, for the unknown. The dimension of intimacy has been made public. The fact that Hugues Viane keeps, fetishistically, his wife's braid of hair in a glass jewelry-box makes what is inside visible – and yet it is private. The box becomes a reliquary through which the relic is visible. To open a reliquary, to take its contents out and parade them around the room, as does Jane, at the conclusion of the novel, is to desecrate the braid of hair. Jane desecrates the difference between outer and inner spaces.

As he wanders through the serpentine streets and over the gloomy bridges and canals of Bruges, of Bruges-*la-Morte* (since the city becomes a double of the dead wife), Viane frequently sees her reflected in the water.[47] An encounter with a woman who is a replica of *la morte*, an actress named Jane Scott, changes his life. As he becomes increasingly involved with Jane, Hugues's neighbors gossip, and Barbe, his housekeeper, is told by her confessor that she should leave her master were he to bring Jane to the house.

At the very center of the novel, when Viane takes two of his wife's dresses to Jane because he wishes to see her in them as an *exact* copy of his wife, the resemblances between wife and actress begin to blur in the widower's eyes. Because Jane makes fun of the dresses, her relationship to Viane begins to change; she mocks him, betrays him, and this causes him to become even more obsessed by her. When she comes to Hugues's house on the day of Bruges's grand Procession of the Holy Blood, Barbe, the housekeeper, leaves her employer. Going to the second floor, Jane brazenly opens the casement window, revealing her presence to the devout crowd below. Viane insists that she close it. Pouting, she reclines on the sofa while he watches the Procession's medieval-like pageantry from behind the curtains. The shrine with its reliquary containing the drop of holy blood goes by, and Viane is moved to kneel, in mystical fervor. Mocking him, Jane prepares to leave, but then insists on seeing the two rooms on the ground floor that "communicate with one another."[48] She picks up and handles Hugues's sacred objects, his wife's pictures, trinkets, and fabrics. Taking the hair from its box, she runs around the room, teasing the widower. Viane loses his head ("[il] perdit la tête"), and in a sudden frenzy, he strangles her with the golden braid. Jane dies, and Hugues looks on, in a daze, as, in his mind, both women become as one.[49]

7.   Structural Contractions

Bruges-la-Morte is composed of 15 chapters, two of which, X and XI, were not included in the original manuscript. They were added later to describe how Hugues and Bruges "find" each other again when resemblances between wife and mistress begin to disappear. The novel, then, was originally composed of thirteen chapters.[50]

The work's composition takes the form of a diptych, of a mirror that has been cut in half. Like juxtaposing mirrors in a "psyché," each half faces the other, reversing and reflecting the imagery of the opposite half of the text. The "hinge" of the diptych is located in chapters VI and VII, at the work's core. At the end of chapter VI the narrator says: "Today, by a sudden seemingly miraculous encounter, this sense of resemblance had occurred again, but this time, it did so in in inverted way]."[51] At the conclusion of Chapter VII, when the narrator describes Hugues's beginning disenchantment with his wife's double, he says: "For the first time, the fascination of physical conformity could not suffice. It still worked but *against the grain*." We recognize the title of what is, perhaps, the most well known of Huysmans's novels, *à rebours*.

At the center of the novel the words *d'une façon inverse* and the Huysmansian *à rebours* appear as a deixis of what occurs in the novel's second half: the sacred "virginal" wife, "Ophélie," is reflected as a reversed image, as a Medusa, an actress who had initially hidden, by virtue of her resemblance to "Ophelia," her monstrous nature. P. Joret points out the monstrous nature of Hugues himself by calling him a "Tristan-Barbe bleue."[52]

Ophelia is mentioned twice in Chapter II. Viane finds her reflected in the waters of Bruges, and it seems to him that a whispering voice rises from the water to meet him, "as it rose to meet Ophelia."[53] And "Medusa" is evoked by means of many symbolic allusions. Ophelia and Medusa turn into each other in the end, doubling each other as they become one in Hugues's mind.

The first and last chapters, I and XV, contain many of the same semes, signifiers, and motifs. The first paragraph of the book begins with: "Le jour déclinait, assombrissant les corridors de la grande demeure silencieuse, mettant des écrans de crêpe aux vitres;"[54] the last chapter does not begin with a day's end, but with its beginning: "Comme la journée avait *mal commencé*! On dirait que les projets de joie sont un défi."[55] In the second paragraph of the first chapter, "Hugues Viane se disposa *à sortir*"; in the second paragraph of the last chapter, Hugues hears the door bang when Barbe goes out. *Solitude* is found in this paragraph, just as *solitaire* is found in chapter I. In chapter I the phrase "*rêvassait... perdu dans ses souvenirs*" describes Hugues's principal activity, while "il *songea* à la morte" appears in chapter XV. The word Hugues repeats to himself at the beginning, "Veuf!

Etre veuf! Je suis veuf!," which is signalled as a *mot impair,* is echoed in Hugues's repetition of another monosyllable in the end: "Morte... morte... Bruges-la-Morte..." The phrase is repeated twice, to the tolling rhythm of Bruges's bells, after Jane has been strangled. The expression replicates the singleness of Hugues's situation at the beginning of the novel and underscores the unity of both women, of *la morte* with *la morte* in the "tale" of the ourobouros' mouth.

After Jane arrives, in the last chapter, she goes to the window, her hair "mis *à nu*...attirant l'oeil avec leurs lueurs de cuivre."[56] The wife's "tresse *nue*" appears in chapter I.[57] As Viane recalls his wife's long, wavy hair, he remembers that when it was unpinned, it covered her back. Her hair is compared to that of early Christian paintings of saints, whose hair flows "en frissons calmes."[58] These "frissons calmes," in the end, contrast with the frenetic *crispation* resulting in death. Mary Magdalen has been frequently portrayed, in the history of art, with long, flowing, red hair.

In the beginning of the novel Barbe prepares the house for the feast of the Presentation of the Virgin.[59] In the concluding chapter, the fête, although religious, is quite different: it is the Procession of the *Saint-Sang* that goes by in its reliquary.[60] The "virgin" wife, who is described as "fanée et blanche comme la cire" in chapter I, will be metaphorically evoked in the ruby-like blood at the end.

In chapter I we read the phrase "une seule syllabe, sans *échos;*"[61] in chapter XV we read "déjà on entendait des *échos* de musiques lointaines;"[62] in chapter I we read that *la morte* was as white as wax,[63] and in chapter XV we learn that "Hugues avait allumé lui-même *les cires* sur l'appui des fenêtres;"[64] the windows are repeated in both chapters; Barbe's name appears three times in chapter I and once in XV; in chapter I she is described as an old Flemish servant wearing her white bonnet,[65] and the past of Flanders is evoked in chapter XV, when groups of *candides* pass by who are like a "verger de robes *blanches*; we see the "concile de vierges-enfants autour d'un Agneau pascal, *blanc* comme elles et fait de *neige frisée.*"[66] *La morte*'s portraits are referred to in both chapters. In the latter, Jane picks up one of the portraits on the mantle and says: "Imagine that! Here's one that looks like me...".[67] The same fetishistic signifiers are repeated at beginning and end. "Bibelot," "rideaux," "plis," "écrin transparent, boîte de cristal"[68] are echoed in "bibelots," "chiffonant les étoffes," and "coffret de verre."[69]

While many other repeated semes in the first and final chapters of *Bruges-la-morte* reveal the deliberateness with which Rodenbach tightened the noose around his novel's neck, choking it to its structural limits in a gesture mimetic of the text's diegesis, the ending of both chapters merits recognition. In Flaubertian prose the narrator ends his first chapter by stating that the fine Flemish rain "transit l'âme comme un oiseau dans un filet mouillé, aux mailles interminables!":[70] Claustrophobia and imprisonment prevail. The final chapter also terminates poetically: as Viane listens to the tolling of Bruges's bells that are *lasses* and *lentes*, the narrator compares them to "[de] petites vieilles exténuées qui avaient l'air - est-ce sur la ville, est-ce sur une tombe? - d'effeuiller languissamment des fleurs de fer!"[71] The *f*'s, *l*'s, *s*'s, and *m*'s of the former, the *f*'s, *l*'s, *s*'s, and *m*'s of the latter establish differences within sameness, alterity within the very heart of repetition. Chapters I and XV mirror each other, creating symmetry and returning the text into itself. They also signal metamorphosis, for in its development of symbolic allusions, in its progression from virginity to blood, in its evolution from "frissons calmes" to a "crispation frénétique," the reader detects a most powerful symbolic depiction of a *fin de siècle* sexual climax. The final words of the text then indicate the languor that follows sexual frenzy: words are repeated "avec la cadence des dernières cloches, lasses, lentes." The bells are "exhausted" after having languidly "[effeuillé]... ces fleurs de fer."[72]

The frequency of repeated semes, or of what S. Metzidakis calls, in his book on semiotics, "phrasal and lexical repetitions,"[73] appears in the first and final chapters of *Bruges-la-morte,* revealing, thereby, the deliberateness of Rodenbach's use of repetitive rhetoric. Onomastic resemblances also exist between Via*ne* and Ja*ne*, Hu*gues* and Bru*gues* (Bruges used to be pronounced "Brugues"), of *Rosa*lie, the nun at the Beguine convent who is a relative of Hugues's housekeeper, and the "quai du *Rosa*ire," where Hugues lives. Contrast is found at the heart of Vi/a/ne's name, which is composed of both life, "vie," and a suggested opposite in the negative "ne," bringing to mind the significance of Lafayette's "Ne/mours."

The word *stricture* means both "abnormal contraction of any passage or duct of the body" as well as the "act of enclosing or binding tightly" (*Random House Dictionary*). As Rodenbach imposes structural strictures upon his work, he makes of his text a metafictional narcissistic narrative in which both sexuality and negation of the Other are present. It is "process made visible," to cite a phrase L. Hutcheon uses in *Narcissistic Narrative.*[74]

8.   A Study of Ambiguity: Ophelia/Medusa

In its development of symbolic allusions, in its progression from virginity to blood, and then back to reflective tranquillity, there is ambiguous sexual imagery. Contraction refers not only to the structure of the text, but to the narrative's sexual subtext.

Men and women were frequently indistinguishable in Symbolist art. The influence of the Pre-Raphaelites, of Rossetti, Burne-Jones, Aubrey Beardsley and others, was of utmost significance in Symbolism, and occult, erotic, satanic and mystic motifs permeated Symbolist thematics and style. Félicien Rops's *Pornocrates, The Sacrifice*, Maurice Denis's *Lutte de Jacob avec l'ange*, and *Saintes femmes au tombeau*, the numerous paintings of John the Baptist's and Orpheus's decapitation exhibit these tendencies. The various renderings of woman as a strong, dazzling, and dominating figure engendering temptation (Moreau's *The Sphinx, Salomé, Dalilah*, von Stuck's *Sin*, Armand Point's *Princess and the Unicorn*, and *The Siren*, Khnopff's *L'Art ou Les Caresses* and *The Blood of the Medusa,* to name but a few), go hand in hand with pallid, ethereal, and effete paintings of youth and men. Puvis de Chavannes's *The Sacred Wood*, Delville's *Orpheus*, Khnopff's *The Sphinx* and Minne's *Relic Bearer* call attention to androgyny, to perverse women and delicate men.

The Symbolists were a tightly-knit group, and Rodenbach's friendship with Khnopff, Verhaeren, Samain, and Maeterlinck was well-established. Of Khnopff's women Verhaeren wrote: "With their glacial attraction and medusa-like perversity ... mouths slit as if by a fine horizontal sword-cut, and smooth brows ... [they] are above all the aesthetic expression of his ideas. His art is refined, complicated by mysterious and puzzling meanings elusively filtered by a multiplicity of allusions."[75] In Khnopff's *The Blood of the Medusa* the monster's mysterious eyes reveal her as inaccessible, remote, a woman who is both enthralling and domineering in her animal nature.

Bruges-la-morte's structure is mirror-like, and for this reason the reflections of women's and men's double natures appear on each side of the diptych, confounding the ethereal and base qualities mentioned above. Viane's "virginal" wife, in death, is like a recumbent stone statue, even though it is "evil" Medusa, (in this case, Jane) who traditionally turns men into stone. The wife is described as *gisant*, and her shorn *chevelure* is placed on the piano "désormais muet, simplement *gisante...*".[76] In chapter II Viane visits Notre-Dame, where he likes to go because of its morbid evocations. He describes the inscriptions as being corroded, like stone lips.[77] He admires the figure of Marie de Bourgogne over the tomb (one notes the appelation *Marie*), and he observes her head "sur un coussin, en robe de cuivre (Jane's hair, in the last chapter, glimmers with "des lueurs de cuivre"[78]). The statue is "*toute rigide*," and Viane dreams of the time when he, too, will lie rigidly beside his wife, as does Charles le Téméraire.

Another pertinent reversal is evident when "evil" Jane, who mocks religion, dies as did innocent Ophelia: "Jane ne riait plus; elle avait poussé un petit cri, un soupir, comme le souffle d'une bulle expirée à fleur d'eau."[79] The identification of Ophelia-like imagery with Jane occurs as early as Chapter V: "Quand il prenait dans ses mains la tête de Jane, l'approchait de lui, c'était pour regarder ses yeux, pour y chercher quelque chose qu'il avait vu dans d'autres: une nuance, un reflet, des perles, une flore dont la racine est dans l'âme-et qui y flottaient aussi peut-être."[80] The intertext could well be Millais's depiction of Ophelia, painted as dead, floating in the water, her mouth open and her hair spread about her, intertwined with flowers. As G. Bachelard says, "on pourrait...interpréter *Bruges-la-morte*...comme l'*ophélisation* d'une ville entière."[81]

References to Ophelia and Medusa in the text refer the reader, constantly, to "the other side of the mirror," and one notices, here, the ambiguity of *Barbe*'s name, which signifies the fourth-century martyr as well as a man's beard. It is only in the death of both women that they become united completely in Hugues's mind. So like each other in life, they resemble each other even more so in death due to the pallor of their faces. Viane, we read, "ne les distingua plus l'une de l'autre - unique visage de son amour."[82] Thanatos and Eros finally unite.

When Viane saw Jane Scott for the first time, the narrator uses a Mallarméan formulation in having him think: "Le démon de l'Analogie se jouait de lui!" Jane had the same eyes, hair and voice as his dead wife. In fact, he believes there is no difference between the two women.[83] The rhetoric of "sameness," however, does not remain constant throughout. "Sameness" means static undifferentiation. The narrator uses verb forms that are contrary to fact, such as the conditional, the imperfect (which can indicate supposition), the pluperfect or various tenses of the subjunctive. As in Todorov's definition of the fantastic, supposition, hesitation, conjecture are foregrounded by verbal and lexical means. These usages introduce a slit, a hair-line cut into the tight structure and rhetoric of the text.

In Chapter IV, at the beginning of Hugues's and Jane's liaison, however, desire transcends all difference, and Viane tells himself that the image in the mirror is a living one. "Elan, extase du puits qu'on croyait mort et où s'enchâsse une présence. L'eau n'est plus nue; le miroir vit!" In the sentence that follows, however, the narrator returns to "objectified" discourse and tells the reader that in order to convince himself, Viane would close his eyes half-shut, listen to Jane speak and believe her voice to be *almost* identical to that of his dead wife's.[84] Free indirect discourse returns the reader to Hugues's thoughts, but even there, in the midst of illusion, the conditional, or a comparison, creates a division: "Ce qui *paraissait* fini...allait recommencer. Et il ne tromperait même pas l'Epouse, puisque c'est elle encore qu'il aimerait dans cette effigie et qu'il baiserait sur cette bouche telle que la sienne."[85] A comparison indicates an ambiguous interstice in which two are one and one are two. In his essay on Raymond Roussel, Michel Foucault says that "le langage est cet interstice par lequel l'être et son double sont unis et séparés; il est parent de cette ombre cachée qui fait voir les choses en cachant leur être."[86] Many of Medusa's mythical elements are evoked in *Bruges-la-morte*: dark eyes, piercing looks, similes and metaphors of immobility, backward stances, reversed reflections, recoiling reactions, the act of strangling as a symbol of decapitation. When Viane first sees Jane, "il s'arrêta net, *comme figé;* la personne qui venait *en sens inverse*, avait passé près de lui."[87] The discourse repeats the novel's composition. He puts his hands over his eyes, "comme pour écarter un songe." He turns back ("il rétrograda"), and then follows her.[88] He keeps ogling her, with a look that would have seemed improper "si elle n'avait apparu toute hallucinée." The young woman is described as being impassive, as looking without seeing, much like Khnopff's Medusa. When Viane gets too close to her he recoils. His reactions to her make of him a Perseus/Narcissus: "Il semblait attiré et effrayé à la fois, comme par un puits où l'on cherche à élucider un visage."[89]

In certain instances in the novel the Perseus and Medusa-like allusions are displaced, relocated in other persons or objects. When he first follows Jane, Hugues barely realizes he has arrived at the Grand' Place "où la Tour des Halles ... *se défendait contre la nuit envahissante avec le bouclier d'or de son cadran.*"[90] In his enthrallment at having found Jane, Hugues "ne voyait plus *la ville rigide.*"[91] Even though chapter VIII is dedicated to housekeeper Barbe's visit to the Beguine convent, Medusa's influence seems to permeate the very house of God: "Toutes les coiffes se juxtaposaient, leurs ailes de linge *immobilisées.*"[92] When his relationship to Jane deteriorates, Hugues spends hours walking between his house and hers. At one moment, "à pas rapides, il marchait *dans la direction opposée.*"[93] Hugues is unable to stay home, where memories multiply around him "*comme une fixité d'yeux.*"[94] At one time Jane's teeth seem "*faites pour des proies.*"[95] When Barbe is told Jane is coming to the house, "[elle] sentit *tout son sang se figer.*"[96]

To recall, briefly, the myth, Perseus was sent to decapitate snake-haired Medusa because he had boasted to Polydectes that he could do so. Aided by Hermes and Athena, he was told not to look at Medusa directly when he tried to slay her because her eyes had the capacity of turning men into stone. But by looking at her reflection in his shield, Perseus was able to decapitate her and avoid the fate of all others whom she had petrified. Perseus eventually delivered Medusa's head to Athena, who henceforth wore it on her aegis.[97]

Medusa has been identified, throughout the ages, with seeing, with hypnotizing her victims so as to turn them to stone. She fascinates, attracts, terrifies, kills. The verb "méduser" has been translated as "to stupefy, to paralyze, to turn to stone" (*Cassell's*). But Medusa also represents sexual ambiguity and bimorphism, hence the fascinaton of the Decadent movements with her in France, Belgium, and England .

In the beginning, Medusa was a pure incarnation of evil. According to early references, in words and in visual representations (eighth and seventh centuries B.C.E.), her look was intolerable to man. She revealed masculine traits, such as having a beard or thick eyebrows. By the sixth century she becomes more feminine and seductive. She becomes both Beauty – *and* the Beast. But it is always through her eyes that she fascinates. Because she appeared even in religious art, she was called "the holy patron of artists." [98]

The long-lived aversion to shagginess and to hirsute types forms part of Medusa's horror and attraction. She represents both order and reason, she is the guardian of what can and cannot be seen (see Merleau-Ponty's *Le Visible et l'invisible*), as well as a representation of chaos and madness. In German, the verb "to look" suggests "to reflect, to recall, to meditate, to change one's mind." The verb also suggests a return, a turning back, a *déjà vu*, a "re-gard," a convulsive and deadly repetition. Turning back: one can evoke Noah's sons, Shem and Japheth, who, after hearing Ham's report of Noah's drunkenness and nakedness, walked backward, carrying a cloak, to cover their father. They walked backwards so as not to see his nakedness.[99] Lot's wife looked back, and she was turned into a pillar of salt.[100] In both reports evil, infringed taboos, and transgression take place. Looking (or *not* looking) at a father's nakedness occurs in the first report, and looking back at the destruction of Sodom and Gomorrah "petrifies" Lot's wife. Orpheus, too, was forbidden to look back at his beloved Eurydice, losing her, as a consequence of his gaze. By not confronting Medusa's piercing and petrifying eyes, Perseus was able to protect himself from destruction. And yet Perseus himself committed incest in order to liberate Andromeda.

Medusa's iconography is lengthy and complex. I will mention, only briefly, Athena Parthenos, who wore Medusa's head on her shield. Athena was a goddess with pale sea-green eyes. The color *glauque,* as mentioned before, or gray-green, is a color that fascinated French and Belgian writers and artists. Medieval and Renaissance representations abound in icons of Medusa-like creatures. In many, if not most, eyes are hyperbolically displayed. One interpretation of this phenomenon states that sight relates to being aware, to watching out for danger. Eyes are not only called the vector of poison,[101] but monsters also devour or destroy those who are not on their guard.

A strange complexity is involved in the examples "sighted," from Noah to Lot's wife, to Perseus, not to mention Giotto's "Envy," whose eyes have been pierced by an arrow. Parmigianino's convex "mirror" ("comment n'y pas voir l'exact équivalent du *gorgonéion,* écu protecteur sur lequel se reflète, *al vero,* l'image du jeune peintre qui, par la gloire éclatante de son art, peut désormais s'égaler aux dieux?" asks J. Clair.[102] One recalls

Caravaggio's shield, or Rubens's "Head of the Medusa," where the artist depicts the blood flowing from her head as engendering spiders, scorpions, salamanders, and all kinds of noxious beasts. Both form part of the myth: curiosity about chaos, as well as looking for as well as not paying attention to danger.

The human and the bestial are also closely related in Medusa's myth. Her iconography, during the French Revolution, was significant. Thousands went to watch the beheadings of kings and fellow citizens. These occasions provided feasts for the eyes, feasts that would "unhinge" those who had deprived the people of bread, or, as the apocryphal saying goes, of "brioches." Women began to wear red ribbons around their necks, to signify they had lost a family member to "la Veuve."

Salomé became Woman the Powerful in nineteenth and early twentieth-century literature and art. She was represented by Füssli, Beardsley, List, Burne-Jones, Lévy-Dhurmer, A. Martini, G. Moreau, Klimt, O. Redon, D. Rops, Von Stuck, Klinger, d'Annunzio, Hoffsmanstall, de Chirico, and later on one "sights" Medusa in Manet, Balthus, Breton, Magritte, Duchamp, Ernst, Masson, Motherwell, and even Pollock (who was jokingly called "Jack the Dripper.")[103]

In the final chapter of *Bruges-la-morte* there is a multiplication of references to serpents. As the Procession approaches, "la musique *des serpents* et des ophicléides monta plus grave," and shortly after, "[Jane] tournait *les yeux sur lui, hérissée.*" This repeats the final phrase of chapter I, when the narrator describes the stinging rain of Bruges "[qui] tisse de l'eau, faufile l'air, *hérisse* d'aiguilles les canaux planes."[104] Hugues's strangling Jane with the snake-like braid of hair is a final symbol of decapitation. The decapitated head, Medusa's, Orpheus's, John the Baptist's, and the heads, busts, and torsos of many others are repeated subjects in Symbolist art.[105]

In *Bruges-la-morte* beautiful hair connects Jane Scott to Medusa. In Ovid's *Metamorphoses* Perseus is asked why only one of the Gorgon sisters has serpents for hair. Perseus replies that before having been ravished by Neptune in Minerva's temple, Medusa was the loveliest of the three sisters: "She was once most lovely in form," he says, "and the jealous hope of many suitors. Of all her attributes, her hair was the most beautiful." After she was ravished by Neptune, Jove's daughter, shocked by what she had witnessed, punished Medusa for her carelessness by changing her locks into hideous snakes.[106]

Almost identical words are used to describe the eyes and hair of both women in the novel: *la morte*'s "yeux de prunelle dilatée et noire dans de la nacre"[107] are repeated in Jane's "yeux de prunelle dilatée et sombre dans la nacre."[108] The wife's hair was "d'un jaune ambre,"[109] and Jane's hair is "d'un or semblable, couleur d'ambre et de cocon, d'un jaune fluide et textuel."[110]

9.   Fetishism

The color of both women's hair brings to mind Lucien Lévy-Dhurmer's golden haired *Eve*, Rossetti's auburn and red-headed women, including *Lilith*, *Venus Verticordia*, *La Ghirlandata*, and many other paintings of women with striking manes in late nineteenth-century painting. This is clearly the stuff of Symbolist fetishism. Freud says that fetishism occurs when the normal sexual object is replaced by another that bears some relation to it, but is entirely unsuited to serve the normal sexual aim. Feet and hair, he says, are examples of this pathology, and he likens the objects to fetishes in which savages believe their gods to be embodied.[111] Freud's view of "savages" smacks of notions that modern anthropologists have long since tried to correct, but his stating that the fetish attains religious, if not "transcendent" status, i.e., that the fetish is a displacement of the object of worship into some thing other than itself is applicable to Hugues Viane's veneration of his dead wife's hair. Jane herself becomes a fetish, since she replaces *la morte*. "Silent devotions in front of objects associated with his wife," says P. Mosley, "are as blatantly erotic as they are subtly religious."[112] In 1886 R. von Krafft-Ebbing stated that fetishism is most commonly found in *religious* and *erotic* spheres.[113]

If one applies Freudian terms to metaphor, this makes metaphor seem pathological when the signified is cut off from its signifier. Even though he thinks of it as "cette chevelure qui était encore Elle," Viane's sacred object becomes a "tresse interrompue," a "chaîne brisée."[114] The fact that the wife has no name in the text means that she has been cut off from any personally identifiable syntagm. Nothing seems to be left of her but her lock of hair, an imagined visage in a mirror, and other curios that had belonged to her.

Mallarmé chose "Hérodiade," the mother's name, rather than that of her daughter, the dancer "Salomé," as the heroine of his poem. Mallarmé's suppression of both dance and name was done in the interest of achieving a reflective stillness that recalls the pallor of Pre-Raphaelite beauty.[115] Rodenbach's well-documented friendship with Mallarmé[116] was undoubtedly an important factor in the former's depictions of *la morte*, of Jane Scott as well as of the swans that are particularly numerous in Bruges. Rodenbach's swans are imprisoned in the icy waters of a lake that exists still today in the "village"/convent of the Béguine nuns. Doubtlessly inspired by Mallarmé, whiteness is one of the main "colors" for which Rodenbach had a predilection. In his prose-poems entitled *Musée de Béguines*, Rodenbach uses white throughout. And referring to his own descriptions, he calls them "des natures mortes."[117]

Hérodiade's "transcendent sphere," in Mallarmé's poem, as opposed to her participation in the domain of historicity, causes her to remain apart, retaining power through non-action. If she attracts, it is not through movement but through manipulation of the mind.[118] Decapitation in Symbolist art and literature attains a new meaning in such terms. The head, the sphere of thought and of manipulation of and by the mind has been detached from a meaningless and historicized body. And yet, in the development of the theme itself, A. Pym points out that most writers and painters showed a lack of sympathy for John the Baptist's virtue, and chose, instead, to depict the beheading "as an irrational end to an irrational revolutionary."[119] 1789 was closer to them than were the Gospels, Pym notes, and John's head came to represent, as did the immobility of Salomé's aesthetic dance, "a transcendent value without correlative."[120]

A decapitated head does not usually emit words. One must omit Orpheus from this statement because he was, after all, the son of Calliope, the Muse of epic poetry, and after the Bacchantes had cut off his head, it floated down the river on his lyre, singing. A decapitated head is the perfect Symbolist object due to its quietude, its stillness, its aesthetic invulnerability, emitting no sound. Silence and severance are related: a severed head is voiceless. Jean Lorrain, for instance, ends his novella *Sonyeuse* with an act of decapitation, and this predilection looms in the background of what would later become a commonplace in Surrealist representation. One has only to peruse a text on Surrealist art to become aware of a plethora of hands, feet, breasts, eyes, lips *et al.*, that are disconnected from a body proper. The Surrealist passion for mutilation and dismemberment has Symbolist antecedents: they lead to "La Femme Sans Tête."

That Viane tries to derive his virility, his manhood, his own selfhood from what he has cut off seems to be the case. He depends upon a circle of braided hair to feel that he is "held together." He worships that which will "petrify" him, save him from Bruges's watery realms, make him erect as a man. His admiration of the stone figures in Notre-Dame is a symbolic example of desire. His peregrinations through the labyrinth of the city with its canals, which are feminized by being identified with his wife, cause him to think about the city's cathedrals: "Les hautes tours dans leurs frocs de pierre partout allongent leur ombre."[121] That phallic towers should be dressed in "stone frocks" is an ambiguous intermingling of imagery that leads to the final dramatic scene of the text.

10.   "Off With Her Head," Said the Queen to Alice

The description of Viane's "decapitation" of "Medusa" is unequivocally sexual. The entire paragraph deserves to be quoted:

> Alors Hugues s'affola; une flamme lui chanta aux oreilles; du sang brûla ses yeux; un vertige lui courut dans la tête, une soudaine frénésie, une crispation du bout des doigts, une envie de saisir, d'étreindre quelque chose, de casser des fleurs, une sensation et une force d'étau aux mains - il avait saisi la chevelure que Jane tenait toujours enroulée à son cou; il voulut la reprendre! Et farouche, hagard, il tira, serra autour du cou la tresse qui, tendue, était roide comme un câble.

What is foregrounded in this passage is not only violent male sexuality, but ambiguity. Hugues *seems* to be demonstrating virility by pursuing snake-haired "Medusa." Although he *seems* to be wishing to castrate her in order to re-possess her virile strength, the text states, metaphorically, that it is *he* who "loses his head." When Jane takes the lock of hair, "l'amenant vers son [propre] visage et sa bouche comme un serpent charmé, l'enroulant à son cou, boa d'un oiseau d'or...," Hugues screams: "Rends-moi! rends-moi!"[122] His choking Jane with the hair makes the stricture *his*, makes the "contraction" of sexuality *his*. It is *he* who will use the hair, which is metamorphosed symbolically into pubic hair, to "enclose tightly," to "constrict," as in female orgasm, Jane's neck. It is *he* who experiences "une envie de saisir, d'étreindre quelque chose"; it is *he* who, "farouche," "serra autour du cou la tresse." The subtext is declaring that what Vi/a/ne fights for, kills for, in fact, is his own femininity. The mirror reversal is complete in this example of Symbolist androgyny. Narcissus, who was loved by both males and females in Ovid and in so many texts throughout the history of texts, is sexually dual in Rodenbach as well.

11.   Chiastic Rhetoric: Dead Bruges/Bruges-the-Dead

The narrator uses chiasmus, at the end of Chapter II, to depict the identifications that exist between Viane, his wife, and the city: "Bruges était sa morte. Et sa morte était Bruges."[123] The chiastic trope is both a micro- and a macro-structure. Chiastic rhetoric points to the comforting aspects of symmetry, on the one hand, and to the terrifying aspects of mirror-imagery, on the other, revealing that the future might be nothing other than a duplication of the past. Linear progression is seemingly abolished in chiastic rhetoric, making it seem as if there were forces in the background of action that are beyond one's control. At the same time, chiasmus reveals a pattern in which cyclical time abolishes historical, diachronic, "progressive" time. M.

Nänny calls attention to what he calls "non-progressive stasis" in chiasmus.[124] We recall Valmont's trying to eradicate diachronicity by sending the same letter over and over again to Mme de Tourvel. And we also recall M. Krieger's analysis, in Keats's "Ode to a Grecian Urn," of "timeless time." There is a certain assurance, a certain comfort in the realization that time is stable, that there *is* a rhythm to the universe, be it described in terms of balance, reciprocity, or Manichean opposition. But chiasmus also unveils a truth that is disquieting, which is that one is possibly nothing other than a cog in a machine, a reflection in a glass. One is merely deluded into thinking that there is alterity within sameness. Hugues Viane begins to think the following when Jane becomes different from *la morte*: "Quel pouvoir indéfinissable que celui de la ressemblance! Elle correspond aux deux besoins contradictoires de la nature humaine: l'habitude et la nouveauté."[125] Hugues had come to know *l'habitude* by having lived ten years with a woman whom he had loved. And yet, says the narrator of the novel, "l'homme se lasse à posséder le même bien. On ne jouit du bonheur, comme de la santé, que par contraste."[126] Is it the narrator, one cannot help asking, who delves into the creation of perversity due to his own sense of boredom?

In his study of the chiasmus in Unamuno's work, Thomas Mermall shows that one aspect of chiasmus is "the interpenetration of opposites."[127] This is true of one of Rodenbach's chiasmus, since, schematically, the macro-structure "Ophelia-Medusa—Medusa-Ophelia" reveals just that sort of interpenetraton. In the "Bruges était sa morte. Et sa morte était Bruges," a struggle is latent in the heart of a seemingly simple reversal. Viane cannot remain still in his search for his dead wife: he must find her in Bruges because Bruges is identified with her. Viane is deluded, however, in thinking that the woman he sees and follows in the city is an exact replica of his wife. Jane will also tragically find that out. There is "instability of meaning and identity"[128] in Rodenbach's trope, much as there is reciprocity in the oppositions of his text.

A paradox found in *Bruges-la-morte*'s mirror-structure is that, like John the Baptist's decapitated head, which does not utter words but signifies, nonetheless, the author/narrator has the "static" novel signify through words. As Ophelia, who talked her way into a watery grave, and whose "voix chuchotante" is twice "heard" in Chapter II, the reader is "petrified" by the strength of the text. Medusa the "Silent" signifies, even when deprived of the power of speech, since in the myth her head continues to exert power even after it had been severed. Perseus uses it to turn Atlas into a mountain; and when Perseus sets it down on a bed of sea-weed to rescue Andromeda, it turns sea-matter into a coral-reef.

Like Ophelia and Medusa, *Bruges-la-morte* is both a void and a voice. While talking its way, ultimately, into silence, the novel "signifies" in the relationship the reader entertains with the text. Viane's liturgical repetition of "Bruges-la-morte," "Bruges-la-morte," in the end, recalls the novel's title, in remembrance of itself. And yet, a hair-line breach is sliced between each of Viane's repetitions. As Barthes once remarked, "le propre d'une Topique, c'est d'être un peu vide."[129] A mouth repeating mechanically the title of the novel the reader has just read cannot but be "a bit empty." It remains eminently *scriptible* because it manifests a zero degree of writing in the symbol of a head that has been deprived of contemplative thought - but "speaks," nonetheless.

12.   Mises-en-Abyme — Bruges-la-Morte

Lucien Dällenbach distinguishes three types of *mises-en-abyme*. The first he calls "*simple duplication* (a sequence which is connected by similarity to the work that encloses it)"; the second is "*infinite duplication* (a sequence which is connected by similarity to the work that encloses it and which itself includes a sequence that...etc.)"; and the third is "*aporetic duplication* (a sequence that is supposed to enclose the work that encloses it)."[130] In *Bruges-la-morte* all of these are present. Mirrors as objects are used as semes, similes, metonymies and metaphors that reflect many aspects of the novel within the novel. In chapter I, the windows of Hugues's house "donnaient sur le quai du Rosaire, au long duquel s'alignait sa maison, *mirée dans l'eau;*"[131] Viane's relationship to his wife is compared to "[des] quais parallèles d'un canal qui mêle *leurs deux reflets,*"[132] as he thinks of polishing the mirrors in his rooms, Hugues thinks of his wife's reflection in them: "Et dans les miroirs, il semblait qu'avec prudence il fallût en frôler d'éponges et de linges la surface claire pour ne pas effacer son visage dormant au fond."[133] As a symbolic pond of Narcissus, Hugues's mirror forever holds within it the image of the beautiful figure. The reflection of Jane Scott, who is both *la morte*'s and Bruges's double, appears when Hugues looks at the mirror and thinks about her image's being superimposed upon his wife's. This occurs when Jane looks at herself and powders her face in that same mirror. When Viane walks around Bruges, he crosses the Quai Vert, the *Quai du Miroir*, and moves off toward the Pont du Moulin, disappearing into sad, poplar-fringed suburbs.[134]

A mirror, like Medusa, is a treacherous thing. To this day, on the outside of Bruges's houses, mirrors are affixed to the windows. They are called *espions*. These are oblique mirrors "où s'encadrent des profils *équivoques* de rues; *pièges miroitants qui capturent*, à leur insu, tout le manège des passants, leurs gestes, leurs sourires, la pensée d'une seule minute dans *leurs yeux* - et répercute tout cela dans l'intérieur des maisons où *quelqu'un guette*."[135] These "spies" reflect the novel as a whole: (a) they are ambiguous or "equivocal"; (b) they are Medusa-like in that they capture fleeting thoughts depicted in people's eyes; (c) they project all that goes on outside into the houses' interiors; and (d) the monster syndrome is reinforced because "someone lies in wait." Lacan cites Merleau-Ponty in a discussion of *Le Visible et l'invisible*. [136] He then adds what could have been a seventeenth-century parlour guessing game in terms of the object to which it was being referred: "Je ne vois que d'un point, mais, dans mon existence, je suis regardé de partout." [137]

Portraits and drawings of *la morte* are also *mises-en-abyme* that are scattered everywhere in Hugues's contiguous rooms. They are on the mantle, on pedestal tables, on walls, depicting his wife at different stages of her life. It is the portrait on the mantle that Jane picks up, in chapter XV, remarking upon its resemblance to herself. The "cheminée, guéridons et murs" in chapter I are repeated in reversed order in chapter XV, achieving, thus, a subtle mirror-imagery of the "mirror imagery" of Jane's looking at her "mirror" in the portrait. The semantic *mise-en-abyme* repeats the diegetic *mise-en-abyme*, achieving "infinite duplication."

Using a formulaic verity, G. Bachelard states that "a house can be read." He also says that one can "read a room" just as one "reads a house," given that both house and room are psychological diagrams that guide writers of novels and poems in their analyses of intimacy.[138] One thinks of Balzac's "readings" of cities, such as Venice, of houses, rooms, of his "physiognomy" of interiors, such as the minute descriptions of la pension Vauquer in *Le Père Goriot*. They are *mises en abyme* of the personae's souls.

The fetishistic elements that one sees in Hugues Viane's house are reflections of the city that can be "read," by him and his narrator's readers, as they amble about with him in labyrinthian bridges and water-ways. The Narcissistic elements of water have described explicitly – and the objects in a house have, after Balzac, been explicitly analyzed for their psychological referents. Bachelard has a beautiful formula that describes the process of reading spaces: "La maison vécue n'est pas une boîte inerte. L'espace habité transcende l'espace géométrique."[139] Or again: "Toute grande image simple est révélatrice d'un état d'âme."[140]

Rodenbach creates two sequences of *mises-en-abyme* in the novel, one in the realm of music, one in art. After having followed Jane through the streets, Viane loses sight of her when she enters a theatre. On the verge of leaving, he discovers her on stage, where Meyerbeer's opera, *Robert le diable*, is playing. She appears immediately after the ballerinas who are enacting condemned nuns are found in the graveyard. Awakened from death, they form a long procession, and as Helena/Jane is raised from the dead, she throws off her shroud and gown. She is a double personage from the start, since she wears the mask of an actress. When Viane sees Jane, he can only think that it is his wife.[141] Before the opera begins, Hugues looks around, and it is no accident that the word "jumelles," meaning both "opera-glasses," and "twins," is used to describe peoples' reactions when they see him, reflexively: "D'autant plus qu'on avait remarqué sa présence et qu'on s'en étonna en une insistance de jumelles qu'il ne fut pas sans apercevoir."[142] Those who look and he who is observed are both aware of each other.

Another microcosm within the novel's macrocosm is placed between the operatic and the ekphrastic *mises-en-abyme*. The Beguine convent that Barbe visits on feast days, and where she learns about her employer's affair, is called "une petite ville à part dans l'autre ville."[143] One is reminded of Nemours, when he steals Mme de Clèves's portrait in miniature. He steals what he would like to possess "in reality." Her represented or ekphrastic being is a microcosm of the person that she, in fact, "is." The large is found in the miniature; the small is symbolic of the Princesse's whole being. The macrocosm is in the microcosm.

The swans that swim in the lake and canals of Bruges sometimes fear having their wings frozen in the waters during the icy-cold winters. In one of his prose poems, "Les Dentelles de Bruges," the author describes one of the Virgin's processions in which he equates, or compares, the nun's procession to that of swans, which are also white. He describes the swans as they float in the canals, on two sides of the little bridge that leads to the Béguinage. He says: "...les chastes cygnes procession[nent] à leur tour."[144] The ornithological world is a small replica of the larger, human and symbolic procession of "the virgins."

Immediately after making the statement about the Beguine convent's being a small village inside a larger one, the narrator refers to the nuns' weaving, mentioning the "fils inextricables des bobines."[145] In *Musée de Béguines*, Rodenbach refers, many times, to the lace that the nuns weave. Most references to weaving (from Penelope on in the history of literature), are reflexive references to textuality. In chapter V, when Viane undoes Jane's hair, the narrator says: "[il] en inondait ses épaules, les assortissait mentalement à un écheveau absent, comme s'il fallait les filer ensemble."[146] The reference is polysemic: it occurs directly after Hugues takes Jane's head in his hands (Medusa), seeking in her eyes a flora whose roots are floating in her soul (Ophelia); he spreads her hair out over her shoulders, separating the strands as if he were going to weave them together. By this we are referred back to *la morte*'s hair "qui, déployés, en couvraient tout le dos."[147] We seem to witness the activities of the novelist/narrator/protagonist/ implied reader/readers who weave the various strands of narrative together in different ways, forming and experiencing, together, a text.

The ekphrastic *mise-en-abyme* Rodenbach develops is Memling's reliquary. This work is located in Bruges's former hospital of Saint John (now the Memling Museum), founded in the twelfth century. Because it owes its name to its patron saint, St. John the Evangelist (from the beginning it was called 'domus beati Johannis,' or the house of St. John), the other John, namely, the Baptist, also became associated with it. As H. Lobelle-Calluwe says, both, or their attributes alone, the lamb (for the Baptist) and the chalice (for the Evangelist) appear on all kinds of objects as well as on the hospital's coat-of-arms.[148]

Among the most renowned painting in the Hospital chapel is Memling's altarpiece of St. John the Baptist and St. John the Evangelist (1479). In its middle panel this painting shows the Evangelist holding a chalice with the poisonous snake inside (an allusion to the fact that an attempt was made to poison him), and the Baptist, who is recognized by his camel-haired robe and the lamb at his side. The left-hand panel depicts the head of the Baptist on a plate being held by a young woman (undoubtedly Salomé). His body is stretched out on the ground, decapitated. That this altarpiece should appear on the high altar of the chapel, while the St. Ursula Shrine that Rodenbach describes was given a place of honour in the *same* chapel in 1489, and that both are there to this day is significant because neither the decapitated head of the Baptist nor of Medusa is mentioned in the novel, making of them intertextual references that must be "spied out," like Bruges's *espions*, by the novel's readers (or spies).

In "Crépuscules au parloir," one of his prose poems in *Musée de Béguines*, Rodenbach has the narrator describe the Béguines as they speak, in hushed tones, of their fears and superstitions. The question of mirrors that are broken comes up, and sister Godelive relates her fears. She says that as a child, in her parents' house, each time a mirror was broken it was a symbol of death. Because each mirror has a soul, she explains, a ransom is demanded if a mirror is broken, and someone in the household must die in order to "pay" the ransom. When the mirror is broken, she continues, each small piece contains a thousand reflections – each is the subdivided image of the whole. Much as the narrator in Barbey's *Une Page d'histoire* "saw," in the mirror, images of the incestuous lovers of Tourlaville, Rodenbach's Sister Godelive says: "Rien ne s'y perd. Les anciens visages de ceux qui s'y sont mirés y persévèrent. Les morts survivent au fond...."

While *Bruges-la-morte*'s narrator makes no mention of the Memling altarpiece, St. Ursula's reliquary is described minutely. The narrator calls the chapel a "sanctuaire d'art où rayonne la célèbre châsse de sainte Ursule, telle qu'une petite chapelle gothique en or, déroulant, de chaque côté, sur trois panneaux, l'histoire des onze mille Vierges."[149] That the reliquary copies the chapel in which it is found makes of it a *mise-en-abyme* of the first order. That Rodenbach's narrator has it be like Viane's reliquary effectuates a double *mise-en-abyme*.

The ekphrasis accentuates martyrdom, death, massacre, blood, wounds that resemble petals, blood that does not drip but flows, "petal-like," from the Virgins' breasts. The Virgins are themselves reflected on the soldiers' armour: "Les soldats sont sur le rivage. Ils ont déjà commencé *le massacre*; Ursule et ses compagnes ont débarqué. [The reader recalls Bruges's canals and watery realms.] Le sang coule, mais si *rose! Les blessures sont des pétales.* Le sang ne s'égoutte pas; il *s'effeuille* des poitrines. Les Vierges sont ... tranquilles, *mirant leur courage dans les armures des soldats, qui luisent en miroirs.*"[150] In Memling's time, so many paintings reveal reflective armour that Rodenbach wished to create a text that was ekphrastically reflective.

The "literal" mirrors in the text reflect the reversed diegesis at the end of *Bruges-la-morte* in which it is not "Perseus," the hero, who looks into the reflection in his shield, but the Virgins who observe themselves in the soldiers' armour. Viane is reversed and feminized, and the bells of Bruges are equated with a masculine principle: their sounds are compared to iron flowers, a "petrified" matter.[151] The reversals and ambiguities presented throughout the text, from metaphoric to diegetic, from structural to psychological, from rhetorical to narratological lead to the fact that in the end, it is "Silent" Medusa who gets the last laugh.

*   *   *

In the concluding years of the nineteenth century, the Decadents took the Narcissus myth to extremes. In chapter VII the young boy in Jean Lorrain's *Le Crapaud* exhibits the continuation of Lacan's "mirror stage" in a most dramatic if not clinical way. Having known what it was to like to experience the ludic phase as he drinks the water from a refreshing pool, the boy goes on to discover therein a horrible toad that is blind, bleeding, dying. The rest of Lorrain's prose fiction sustains this type of vision.

Jean Lorrain's work invites psychoanalytic explanations, especially since his father was absent from his life and work ("Le *Non* du Père"). The mother's invasiveness, to the point of her taking her son's name after his death, cannot but have led Lorrain to the breach Lacan describes. That breach is created when the "seer" becomes aware of the "the seen," when the *Innenwelt* ("inner life") and the *Umwelt* ("the world around us") are recognized as different as well as the same. Hypocondria, aggression, castration fears - all are expressed chiastically in Lorrain's prose. These tendencies were "mapped out" psychologically, years later, by Freud himself, and by his positive/negative successor and critic, Jacques Lacan.

Notes

[1] *Narkiss* is found in the collection of short récits entitled *Princesses d'ivoire et d'ivresse* , Séguier, "Bibliothèque décadente" éd. J. de Palacio, Paris, p. 90.

[2] ibid., p. 233.

[3] P.-G. Castex, *Anthologie du conte fantastique français* (Paris: José Corti, 1963) 313-318. Page references to *L'Ami des Miroirs* are made, throughout, to the Castex volume because it is more accessible than is *Le Rouet des brumes*, Société d'Editions littéraires et artistiques, Librairie Paul Ollendorff, Paris, 1901, pp. 27-35. Several ideas in this chapter, in particular those relating to *L'Ami des Miroirs* and *Bruges-la-morte* appeared, in different forms, in *Modern Language Studies*, xix:3, summer 1989, as well as in *Georges Rodenbach: Critical Essays,* ed. Philip Mosley, Fairleigh Dickinson Univ. Press, 1996.

[4] Castex, in fact, gives a clinical explanation when he says, in a brief introduction to Rodenbach's short story, that the author of the text, compared to Edgar Allan Poe's *William Wilson*, "does not give the impression, as does the American writer, of participating in the folly of his character: he simply observes him and describes, clinically, with minute slowness, the successive stages of his pathetic decline." Castex first confuses author with narrator, then fails to see the role the narrator plays in the successive stages of his "friend's" mental deterioration. The same conclusion as that of Castex is reached by two other critics. In "La Folie spéculaire," P. Pelckmans says: "Throughout the short story [the narrator] adopts the tone of a clinical physician which has him remain a stranger to the adventure he relates," *Cahiers internationaux de symbolisme*, 1981, pp. 42-44. In "Le Monde imaginaire de Georges Rodenbach," Hiroo Toyama says: "Throughout the narration of this short story, the author is nothing other than a dispassionate observer of this conduct: he describes his charater as being mentally deranged," *Etudes de langue et littérature française,* 42, March 1983, p. 59. I disagree with all three interpretations.

[5] op.cit., p.102.

[6] ibid.

[7] *Anthologie*, p. 313.

[8] ibid., p. 315.

[9] ibid., p. 317.

[10] ibid., p. 318.

[11] ibid.

[12] The subtitle of this book is "Etudes réunies et présentées par P. Auraix-Jonchière avec la collaboration de C. Volpilhac-Auger, Presses Universitaires Blaise Pascal, Clermont-Ferrand. Noir's article is on pp. 275-298.

[13] In "The Ghost of Meaning: Language in the Fantastic" *SubStance* 35, 1982, pp. 46-55.

[14] ibid., p. 46.

[15] ibid., p. 53.

[16] *Anthologie*, p. 313.

[17] See Miller's first chapter, entitled "Two Forms of Repetition" in *Fiction and Repetition*, Harvard UP, Cambridge, 1982, pp. 1-21.

[18] *Anthologie*, p. 313.

[19] ibid., p. 315.

[20] W.S. Bookwell, Finland, 2005, transl. Mike Mitchell & Will Stone, introd. A. Hollinghurst.

[21] G. Rodenbach, *Musée de Béguines* , Séguier, Paris, 1997, p. 53.

[22] *Anthologie*, p. 314.

[23] ibid.

[24] Baudrillard, *Système,* p. 27.

[25] *Anthologie*, p. 315.

[26] P. Lejeune, *Moi aussi*, Seuil, Paris, 1986.

[27] *Anthologie*, p. 316.

[28] ibid.

[29] ibid., p. 315.

[30] ibid., p. 317.

[31] ibid., p. 318.

[32] ibid., p. 317.

[33] *Andromaque*, V, l. 1568.

[34] ibid., l. 1638

[35] ibid., l. 1643-44.

[36] *Anthologie*, p. 317.

[37] Ovid, p. 153.

[38] See Rodenbach, *Le Rouet des Brumes*, 17, n.1.

[39] *Anthologie*, p. 315.

[40] See E. Pellizer, p. 113.

[41] Included by R. de Montesquiou in *Altesses sérénissimes*, Librairie Félix Juven, Paris, 1907, pp. 1-64. The essay was written by Gustave Moreau on November 1897, and was included in the first chapter, "Le Lapidaire," of Montesquiou's book. It celebrates the occasion of Moreau's having given about eight thousand paintings and drawings to the Ville de Paris, and is a commentary made by Moreau on his own *Chimères: Décameron satanique*.

The particular imagery and tone of the essay could easily apply to *Bruges-la-morte*, the author of which, Montesquiou, in his typically malicious and witty way, referred to as "le Brugeois gentilhomme."

[42] Jean de Palacio wrote the "Présentation" to Jean Lorrain's *Princesses d'ivoire et d'ivresse*, p. 14.

[43] See E. Apter, "Cabinet Secrets: Fetishism, Prostitution, and the Fin de Siècle Interior," *Assemblage* 9, 1989, pp. 7-19.

[44] Apter says: "With its heavy, dark red drapes festooned with golden tassles, Huysman's neurasthenic hero is clearly inspired as a decorator by the ideal house that Poe, in his "Philosophy of Furniture," put forth as an antidote to the crass, nouveau-riche apartment that was encroaching, in his day, on the domain of aristocratic taste. The first "physiognomist of the interior," according to Walter Benjamin, Poe stamped his domestic space with the inimitable stylistic flourishes of his literary haunted houses, but, more importantly for our discussion, he equipped it with the trappings of hidden surveillance," p. 9.

[45] G. Rodenbach, *Bruges-la-morte*, Actes Sud/Labor, Bruxelles, 1986, p. 22.

[46] In *La Poétique de l'espace* , PUF, Paris, 1957, p. 86.

[47] *Bruges-la-morte*, p. 26.

[48] ibid., p. 102.

[49] ibid., p. 105.

[50] See "Principes de la présente édition," written by C. Berg in the Actes/Sud edition, pp. 134-135.

[51] ibid., p. 51.

[52] P. Joret, "Au delà d'un masque. Une lecture isotopique d'un poème de Georges Rodenbach," *Linguistica Antverpiensia*, 18-19, 1984-85, pp. 59-73.

[53] *Bruges-la-morte*, p. 26.

[54] ibid., p. 19.

[55] ibid., p. 99.

[56] ibid., p. 100.

[57] ibid., p. 22.

[58] ibid., p. 20.

[59] ibid., p. 21.

[60] ibid., p. 102.

[61] ibid., p. 19.

[62] ibid., p. 99.

[63] ibid., p. 20.

[64] ibid., p. 99.

[65] ibid., p. 22.

[66] ibid., pp. 101-102.

[67] ibid., p. 103.

[68] ibid., pp. 21-22.

[69] See Apter, pp. 8-9.

[70] *Bruges-la-morte*, p. 23.

[71] ibid., p. 106.

[72] ibid.

[73] In *Repetition and Semiotics: Interpreting Prose Poems,* Summa Publications, Inc., Birmingham, 1986, pp. 72, 79.

[74] See *Narcissistic Narrative: The Metafictional Paradox*, Methuen, New York, 1984.

[75] Cited by R. Goldwater, *Symbolism*, Harper & Row, New York, 1979, p. 209.

[76] *Bruges-la-morte*, p. 22.

[77] ibid., p. 27.

[78] ibid., p. 28.

[79] ibid., p. 105.

[80] ibid., p. 43.

[81] See G. Bachelard, *L'Eau et les rêves, essai sur l'imagination de la matière*, José Corti, Paris, 1942, p. 121.

[82] *Bruges-la-morte*, p. 105.

[83] ibid., p. 39.

[84] ibid., p. 40.

[85] ibid., p. 41.

[86] See M. Foucault, in *Raymond Roussel*, Gallimard, Paris, 1963, p. 154.

[87] *Bruges-la-morte*, p. 28.

[88] ibid., p. 29.

[89] ibid., p. 28.

[90] ibid., pp. 33-34.

[91] ibid., p. 47.

[92] ibid., p. 61.

[93] ibid., p. 71.

[94] ibid., p. 73.

[95] ibid., p. 86.

[96] ibid., p. 95.

[97] See *Classical Mythology*, ed. M. Morford and R. Lenardon, Longman, New York, 1977, chap. 19: "Perseus and the Legends of Argos" pp. 341-352.

[98] J. Clair, *Méduse: Contribution à une anthropologie des arts du visuel*, Gallimard, Paris, 1989, pp. 234-235.

[99] Genesis 9, p. 23.

[100] ibid., 19, p. 26.

[101] J. Clair, p. 83.

[102] ibid., p. 109.

[103] ibid., p. 11.

[104] ibid., p. 22.

[105] See D. Kosinski's excellent book, *Orpheus in Nineteenth-Century Symbolism,* UMI Research Press, Ann Arbor, 1989, p. 184.

[106] Ovid, IV, p. 235.

[107] *Bruges-la-morte,* p. 20.

[108] ibid., p. 29.

[109] ibid., p. 20.

[110] ibid., p. 29.

[111] See S. Freud, *Three Essays on the Theory of Sexuality*, trans. and ed. J.Strachey, Basic Books, New York, 1962, p. 19.

[112] In "The Soul's Interior Spectacle: Rodenbach and *Bruges-la-morte*," *Strathclyde Modern Language Studies* 9, 1989, pp. 25-40.

[113] R. von Kraft-Ebbing, *Psychopathia Sexualis: A Medico-Forensic Study*, trans. From the Latin by H. Wedeck, introd. E. van den Haag, G.P. Putnam's Sons, New York, 1965, p. 36.

[114] *Bruges-la-morte,* p. 22.

[115] ibid., p. 316.

[116] See *L'Amitié de Stéphane Mallarmé et de Georges Rodenbach*, préface de H. Mondor, introd. et notes F. Ruchon, P. Cailler, Genève , 1949. In this volume there is a reproduction of a portrait, by Vanaise, of Anna Rodenbach, G. Rodenbach's wife. The painting depicts Anna from the back, with her head in profile. Her long golden hair cascades to mid-torso.

[117] *Musée de Béguines*, précédé de *Rodenbach, le poète des villes mortes*, par G.-G. Lemaire, Séguier, Paris, 1997.

[118] A. Pym, "The Importance of Salomé: Approaches to a Fin de Siècle Theme," *French Forum* 14, Sept. 1989, p. 316.

[119] ibid., p. 320.

[120] ibid., p. 321.

[121] *Bruges-la-morte,* p. 45.

[122] ibid., p. 104.

[123] ibid., p. 26.

[124] See M. Nänny, "Iconocity in Literature," *Word and Image* 2, 3, July-Sept. 1986, pp. 199-208.

[125] *Bruges-la-morte* , p. 49.

[126] ibid.

[127] Mermall, p. 248.

[128] ibid.

[129] In *Fragments d'un discours amoureux*, Seuil, Paris, 1977, p. 9.

[130] Dällenbach, *op. cit.*, p. 35.

[131] *Bruges-la-morte*, p. 19.

[132] ibid.

[133] ibid., p. 21.

[134] ibid., p. 26.

[135] ibid., p. 46.

[136] Gallimard, Paris, 1964.

[137] See Thévoz's *Le Miroir infidèle*, Ed. de Minuit, Paris, 1996, p. 9.

[138] *Poétique de l'espace*, p. 51

[139] ibid., p. 58.

[140] *Bruges-la-morte*, p. 79.

[141] A manuscript variant states: "C'était *sainte Rosalie* descendue de la pierre de son sépulcre, c'était vraiment la morte ressuscitée," p. 37. Does this mean that Rodenbach had initially given Hugues's wife the name "Rosalie" before replacing it with *la morte*? In any event, one can only be sure that one of the sisters of the Beguine convent was named after saint Rosalie in Meyerbeer's opera, even though the reference is only evident in a manuscript variant.

[142] ibid., p. 35.

[143] The Beguine convent, in Bruges, is, even now, "a small village" that is placed unto itself, apart, inside the larger city. It is what Bachelard calls attention to in *La Poétique de l'espace,* PUF, Paris, 1957, a microcosm that is "correlative" to the macrocosm, p. 157. As he analyzes "la miniature" (chapter VII), Bachelard thinks of Baudelaire, who, while commenting upon some of Goya's lithographs, uses the expression "vastes tableaux en miniature," p. 159. Baudelaire also used the following expression as a commentary upon some of Marc Baud's enamel paintings, "il sait faire grand dans le petit," p. 159.

[144] ibid., pp. 36-37.

[145] ibid., p. 63.

[146] ibid., p. 43.

[147] ibid., p. 20.

[148] See *MemlingMuseum[sic]: Bruges*, ed. V. Vermeersch and J.-M. Duvosquel, Ludion S.A., Cultura Nostra, Brussels, 1987, p. 9.

[149] ibid., p. 79.

[150] ibid., p. 80.

[151] ibid., p. 106.

Chapter VII

Man Mirrors Toad, or Vice-Versa:
Decadent Narcissism in Jean Lorrain's Oeuvre

C'est dans de l'atroce et du monstrueux
que j'ai toujours cherché à combler
l'irréparable vide qui est en moi.
Robert de Montesquiou[1]

1. The Myth - In a Different Mode

Like mirrors that deceive, no myth is innocent. As I have shown in the previous chapter, myths represented by Symbolist and Decadent novelists, poets, playwrights and artists, such as Georges Rodenbach and the circle of artists surrounding him, were especially characterized by their equivocal nature. The "beauty of the Medusa" is only one way of expressing it. Jean Lorrain's oeuvre, similar to that of other *fin de siècle* writers such as Villiers de l'Isle-Adam, Rachilde, Octave Mirbeau, Marcel Schwob, Rémy de Gourmont, Henri de Régnier, Tristan Corbière, is attracting new readership. This is perhaps the case due to the ambivalence exhibited in the Decadents' interpretations of myths. They prefigure numerous theoretical twentieth-century opposition of extremes, and imply certain socio-historical tendencies that are operative these days in literature, cinema, art, music, and dance. They also prefigure the paradoxes surrounding the writings of the end of the twentieth century, be they in sexual, social, or political spheres.

Jean Lorrain, a *fin de siècle* journalist, poet, novelist, dandy, and man of letters, represents, from the beginning to the end of his career, a taste for decorative and the plastic arts, in particular in the works of *Art Nouveau*. He loved not only the art of this epoch but its music as well. W. McLendon calls attention to the paradoxes that existed in Lorrain's tastes, those that embraced movement (as in dance) as well as their opposite, that is, hieratic poses that represented stilled time and immobility.[2] The painter Gustave Moreau was Lorrain's mentor, and the sheer decorative weight shown in some of his paintings impressed Lorrain. One example is in the costume Salomé wore as she pointed, staring fixedly at the head of John the Baptist as it floated in the air, dripping blood, in the painting called *L'Apparition.* Her costumes display the richness of exotic stones that look as if they could have weighed her down. These costumes, says McLendon, must have influenced the much sought-after couturier Fortuny, who would become popular, some time later, on both sides of the Atlantic. Instead of using an expression such as "the beauty of the Medusa," McLendon describes the popularity of deadly stillness as "the beauty of inertia."

Lorrain himself expresses his own fascination with Moreau, whom he called the "Master Sorcerer," by writing articles on the deathly pale mythic creatures Moreau painted. Lorrain was most intrigued by "ces sveltes Salomés, ruisselantes de pierreries, et des Muses porteuses de chefs décapités d'Orphée et des Hélènes aux robes maillées d'or vif, au front diadémé de gemmes, s'érigeant, un lis d'or à la main, pareille, elles-mêmes, à de grands lis fleuris sur une fumier saignant de héros massacrés."[3] Lorrain emphasizes their silence, their pallor, their immobility, the *femme fatale* aspect of these women. One could say that the beauty of their appearance was a justification of the painter's as well as his disciple's misogyny. The beauty of these fatal creatures represents the "beauty" of death, of destruction, of castration, and of vampirism. Lorrain even chose a picture of the Muses carrying the head of Orpheus as a frontispiece of his first book, *Le Sang des dieux*. One might ask whether this is misogyny or fear of castration. But then one could also ask whether the Cheshire cat is a benevolent or a malevolent creature: Alice had seen a cat without a grin, but a grin without a cat posed certain problems for her, as she created a chiasmus that led her to think that Wonderland was the most curious place she had ever seen.

In Lorrain's *Le Crapaud*, published in 1895, three years after Rodenbach's *Bruges-la-morte* (1892) appeared in print, Lorrain did not use Narcissus overtly, as he did in his short story *Narkiss*, but he did utilize it as a frightful sexual subtext in the second tale of a trilogy of narratives entitled "Enfance." These appear at the beginning of a collection of writings, *Sensations et souvenirs* (1895).[4] Structurally imbricated between the dithyrambic *Cloches de Pâques* and a tale, *Nuit de Veille*, in which a son keeps vigil over his mother who is near death, *Le Crapaud* attains a perversely initiatory tone, making of it a representation of the discovery of birth mirroring death, on the one hand, and of the fear of woman and castration, on the other.

Le Crapaud is narrated by an adult who looks back upon an experience that occurred to him when he was ten years old. He cannot recall it without becoming, he says, nauseated by fright and disgust.[5] Emotional and physical displeasure are foregrounded by references to the heart, the lips, the sense of taste. It is the mouth that tells a tale, so the act of narration is valorized from the outset. Because eyes will accrue significance therein, the narrator's and the reader's roles are accentuated as decoders of the mythical messages within the text.

The ten-year-old boy in *Le Crapaud* spent his summer vacations on the immense property that belonged to one of his uncles. Filled with trees, dark shadows, and drenched with dormant waters that had been artificially confined in numerous pools, the grounds enveloped a former convent that had been transformed into a country house. The religious had been laicized. It was called Valmont. The name, of course, says the narrator, refers to his own rediscovery of it in "the worst, the most cruel, and the most dangerous book written in the eighteenth century."[6] Readers know the title the narrator does not mention: *Les Liaisons dangereuses*. Like myths, the intra-text is not innocent. It is also referential. In his biography of Lorrain, P. Jullian refers to his subject as an "enfant solitaire, amassant des images...de l'eau avant tout [Lorrain est un aquatique], les plus belles captées dans cette abbaye de Valmont appartenant à des cousins...".[7]

The narrator describes his solitude, stating that he experienced no desire to play with his cousins. As did Ovid's version of Narcissus, he had "an instinctive fear of the boys' noisy games and the girls' already coquettish teasings."[8] His pleasures were solitary ones. While others were having their siestas, the boy would go on what the narrator calls "des pérégrinations *sournoises*."[9] He would study "creatures that do not know they're being observed,"[10] bringing voyeuristic thematics into the narrative. Later in the text, the child will become a voyeur "observed," reversing, chiastically, the relationship between seer and seen.

Both sensual and culpable vocabulary is utilized to describe the waters of Valmont. Bachelard's studies of water, or of "elemental reverie," as J. Pierrot calls it in *The Decadent Imagination*,[11] come to mind when the narrator notes: "C'était une volonté déjà étrange, étant donné mon âge, à céder à la fascination de l'eau. L'eau qui m'a toujours attiré, séduit, pris, charmé, et qui m'ensorcèle encore...".[12] One of his principal pleasures, which he qualifies as being guilty, "refined by forbidden proscriptions," was to escape from house after lunch, run to his favourite pool, where he would arrive, hot and perspiring. There he would gulp down the water that was glacial and blue.[13] The sensual frenzy of his drinking is stressed in this passage by onomatopeia, alliteration, and poetic repetition of the narcissistic "je." The passage then concludes with: "It was a frenetic type of sensual pleasure, tripled by my being aware of my disobedience, and by the disdain that I had for others..."[14] Solitary pleasures are filled with guilt for the narrator.

When Ovid's Narcissus was punished for having spurned the lovesick boy who desperately desired him, and who had prayed: "So may he himself love, and not gain the thing he loves," so will the spring - or *source*, become the source of punishment in *Le Crapaud*. One day, after having satisfied his "gourmand sensuality" by lying next to the pool and actually immersing his face in the voluptuous water, he notices a hideous creature on the flagstones, an enormously large, viscous, bleeding toad - observing him.

The boy had drunk from his favorite pool, and, suddenly, at the very edge of that pool, he sees a monster. At first he thinks the creature is watching him: "c'étaient deux yeux ronds à paupières membraneuses horriblement fixées sur les miens, et la forme était flasque, comme affaissée et rentrée en elle-même, quelque chose de noirâtre et de mou dont la seule idée du contact m'énervait."[15] After seeming to stare fixedly, the toad moves towards the boy. "Narcissus" and his decadent counterpart are juxtaposed.

In his description of the man Jean Lorrain, E. Jaloux focuses on his eyes: "Ils étaient glauques, à fleur de tête, à demi capotés par d'énormes paupières qui ne s'ouvraient pas comme les autres paupières, mais retombaient sur le coin de l'oeil... Il gardait l'air d'un homme qui se sait toujours regardé."[16] The man becomes a mirror of the text, just as the toad mirrors the boy in his obsessive observation.

The idea that he had drunk from the source where the monster lived and crawled fills the boy with dread. He is replete with the taste of dead flesh, with the odour of rotting water. In a climax to the horrific experience, the boy becomes aware that, instead of observing him, the toad "avait les deux prunelles crevées, les paupières sanguinolentes et qu'il s'était refugié dans cette source, supplicié et pantelant, pour y mourir."

In Lorrain's *fin de siècle* version of Narcissus, we sight a representation that mirrors not only one text but many (Ovid's, Conon's, Pliny's, Pausanias's, Guillaume de Lorris's, etc.): "A discourse...simply repeats, in a different mode, another discourse," said Edward Said.[17] This mirror-text partakes of mirroring from its inception, but "in a different mode." It is this "different mode" that Jean Lorrain creates in *Le Crapaud,* even as he participates in the "sameness" of the myth that preceded him.

The function of Narcissus in *Le Crapaud* is allusive, metaphorical. He becomes a seme, a sequence of "I's" (as well as of e-y-e-s), a boy, running, repeatedly, to his "preferred pool," repeating the reader's eyes as they read or reread the text: "*je* relevais *mes* manches jusqu'aux coudes pour y plonger *mes* deux mains frémissantes, *j*'y puisais à pleine poignées, *je m*'en emplissais la bouche et le gosier avec des glouglous jouisseurs, j'y pointais *ma* langue comme dans de la glace, et *je* sentais descendre en *moi* un froid aigu et pénétrant et pourtant doux comme une saveur."[18] One cannot miss sighting the usage of the first person in this text.

2.   Myth and Maternity

Lorrain's Narcissus, at this point in the text, is a prelapsarian Narcissus, a Narcissus before the Fall, a Narcissus before birth, before the initiatory experience of birth, and therefore, of knowledge. While the mirror quality is evoked in the vision of the toad as well as in a description of pools in autumn, the season of the "Fall" (i.e., of *cadere, of de-cadere,* or decadence), the water the boy sensually imbibes is the water of *la source*, the source of life. It is the matrix par excellence, and the pleasure-taking embryo is part and parcel of it, filling his mouth with "des glouglous jouisseurs."

Lorrain's Narcissus is in love with water - to the point of saying, before his discovery of the toad, that he loved it, possessed it as voluptuously as a mistress.[19] Aspects of the myth coincide with the role J. Lorrain's mother played in his life. As J. Berman points out, Ovid's Narcissus "originates from a sexual crime. His fatal attraction seems to be a repetition of his mother's near drowning. Entranced by his reflection in the body of water, Narcissus may be gazing at the maternal body.... The incest taboo awakens fear of stern punishment. Echo already bears witness to the frightful punishment meted out by the gods...."[20]

Even as we assert that literature is an ordered [and sometimes not so ordered] fictive construct of language,[21] one cannot ignore the role J. Lorrain's mother played in his life. She was the only constant and ever-observing female presence watching over him. Most of the others were male. At the age of 31, Lorrain wrote her: "Ma chère et bien-aimée maman, *ma seule passion*, toi seule que *j'aime vrai*, car j'aime peu de ma nature...si nous devons être séparés un jour par la mort...et si l'un de nous doit survivre à l'autre, au moins aurons-nous la consolation de *nous être adorés l'un pour l'autre*, car *je t'aime tant* qu'il y a des soirs où j'ai des larmes plein les yeux, rien que de te savoir loin de moi."[22] It is as if the boy in *Le Crapaud* were speaking of his "source préférée," his source "passionément aimée," "voluptueusement possédée." Jullian says that the umbilical cord was never really cut, and that all of Lorrain's childishness and capricious nature were a result of his having remained a child, in his mother's eyes, all of his life.[23]

Although we read maternity as an ever-present element in *Le Crapaud*, the word "mother" is mentioned only once, when the adult narrator recalls the word "mère."[24] In Ovid, the water-nymph Liriope, Narcissus's mother, had conceived her child when she was raped in the stream by the river-god Cephisus. The narrator, in Ovid, also alludes to the fact that the child was so beautiful that he could be loved even then. Ovid tells us: "When her time came the beauteous nymph brought forth a child, who already, at that time, was able to be loved by a nymph and named him Narcissus."[25] "To love" - "to be loved by" - the double in the Narcissus narration is constantly present. The double comes into being in Jean Lorrain, as well, from the child's initiatory discovery of the *source* to the discovery of mutilation.

In M. Besnard-Coursodon's psychological analysis of Maupassant's work, she points to *le piège* as the central theme and dominant structure of his oeuvre: "One has been placed in a trap...and when one tries to get out, the trap tightens up, and kills."[26] Commenting upon this, A. Fonyi reads Maupassant's *Sur l'eau* as a trap that is the fear of birth itself, which is nothing other than the fear of death. Fonyi interprets as a "fear of being born" the instance in which the fisherman in *Sur l'eau* imagines himself as "me débattant au milieu des herbes et des roseaux que je ne pourrais éviter...." He says that "il me semblait que je me sentirais tiré par les pieds tout au fond de cette eau noire."[27] An analogous reading to Fonyi's, to that which seems like an interpretation of a breach birth, could apply to the description of the toad in *Le Crapaud*. The toad is a hideous creature that represents the mother, the mother's trap, even as the child struggles to gain independence in the process of birth itself. A breach birth is a chiastic version of a "regular" birth. It is the same thing, upside up.

In the phrase "sous l'ombre dentelée des fougères" one detects "les roseaux du pubis maternel." The beginning of birth might be found in the expression that describes the toad's movement: "Sous l'ombre dentelée des fougères, l'amas gélatineux et brun s'étira vers moi." Might not this description be viewed as the very process of birth? And the text is an experience of initiation, much as is birth – and rebirth.

It is a litotes to say that Woman fared ill in the literature of decadence. Powerful she was - but she evoked danger - the siren singing in order to bring Man to destruction. One recalls the ever-present music on the mother's piano in *Le Crapaud*. The siren is both attractive and repulsive. The child will adore the womb, wishing always to return to it. One finds the motifs of repetition as well as of culpability in the boy's constant escapes to his beloved *source*, but the womb can be as frightening as a text in its representation of loss of innocence and knowledge of death.

The narrator's description of the toad as if it were almost a pregnant object is particularly striking: "Un ventre d'un blanc laiteux traînait entre ses pattes, ballonné et énorme, tel un abcès prêt à crever; il remuait douloureux à chaque effort en avant de la bête, et l'ignoble pesanteur de son arrière-train écoeurait."[28] This is no beautiful Madonna in waiting - but a highly expressive vision of a being bursting with fecundity, or, in this case, with fetidness. The creature, who is like a pregnant woman with a big belly "prêt à crever" is both "ready to burst" and ready to die. Mythic if not magical properties are not denied it. It becomes a "crapaud magicien, tout au moins centenaire, demi-gnome, demi-bête de sabbat, comme il en est parlé dans des contes, un de ces crapauds qui veillent, couronnés d'or massif, sur les trésors des ruines, une fleur de belladone à la patte gauche et se nourrissant de sang humain."[29] Mutual or reflexive nourishment, in the myth, has the mother feeding the child in the waters of the pool, and mutually feeding upon it – "nourishing itself with human blood." Because the "fleur de belladone" is a poisonous flower, it reminds us that both mother and son are floral signifiers in the myth. *Leiriopé*, Narcissus's mother, recalls a flower, since *leirion* means "lily."[30] And the narcissus was considered, in antiquity, to be a cold and humid flower.[31]

When time came for Jean Lorrain to choose a pseudonym (his registered name was Paul Duval), his mother, Mme Duval, helped him find one - even though "Mme Du-Val" has resonances that easily place the name within the water-drenched valleys of "*Val*-mont." One recalls not only Laclos's *Val*mont, but Marguerite de *Val*ois and Marguerite de Ra*val*et in Barbey's tale of incest and of decadence at the end of the sixteenth century. During their life together, Mme Duval adopted, more and more frequently, her son's own pseudonym, and at the time of his death she would henceforth sign her name "Duval-Lorrain." Onomastically, she continued to feed on her son's identity even after his death - as he had been nourished by her blood before his birth.

As he lay dying, Jean Lorrain, who was in and out of a delirious state, spent the third night before his death, 27 June 1906, improvising and singing "La Ballade du Bohémien." Part of it goes like this:

> Prisst! Frisst! Visage noirci
> Crapaud prisonnier
> Dans de l'eau de pluie
> Gelée
> Et venin durci
> Qu'une main de nonnain essuie...
> De suie
> Les cheveux du mort sentent le roussi. [32]

In one of the short stories that Lorrain includes in his *Princesses d'Ivoire et d'ivresse*,[33] entitled "La Princesse Neigefleur,"[34] which is, to some extent, a rewriting of Snow White," or Snow Flower, he has his narrator show how Queen Imogine takes the back leg of a magical frog and throws it into the fire, in a rage. She had just been told by her mirror, once again, that "Neigefleur" was "the fairest of them all." When the frog hits the flames, he is described as going "frisst, grisst et prisst" before he evaporates like a dry leaf.[35] Lorrain himself will chant at least two of these onomatopoeic sounds on his death-bed, "Prisst!" and "Frisst!" The hideous toad described in *Le Crapaud* thus becomes the real writer himself, viewed in the mirror of his text.

Lorrain spent his final hours in his mother's arms, saying: "Maman, on va encore m'ouvrir le ventre."[36] He had lost part of his intestines in a previous operation, and the doctors had tried to revive hope by promising to operate again. The toad, in this instance, is a hideous pregnant subtext of J. Lorrain himself, with "un ventre d'un blanc laiteux, traînant entre ses pattes, ballonné et énorme, tel un abcès prêt à crever." The beast becomes a hideous mother-figure, pregnant with rotting matter.

The culmination of *Le Crapaud*, like that of *Oedipus Rex*, reveals both blindness and in-sight - in the text. The descriptions of the blind toad's bleeding eyelids, of this "agony of mutilation in this clear water tasting of blood," contain powerfully expressed intra- and intertextual innuendos. This decadent Narcissus seeing his image in the pool does not find the *imago* of a beautiful boy - but its opposite. The nineteenth-century mirror has reversed the image. He finds a hideous creature which represents what he, in fact, is: a monster filled with incestuous guilt, on the one hand, and a despiser of Woman, of the womb, on the other. The clear water that "tastes of blood" expresses this ambiguity – as in a breach birth.

3.   Eyes: Freud and Fetishes

Strewn throughout Lorrain's narratives, poems and plays is a phantasmagorical fetish - or spectacle - that has to do with eyes. The entire framed narrative, *M. de Phocas*,[37] is a quest on the part of the eponymous hero to find a "glaucous transparency," of which he is enamoured, in the eyes of a human: "Cette lueur, je la cherche en vain dans les prunelles et dans les pierres, mais aucun humain ne la possède. Parfois, je la trouve dans l'orbite vide d'un oeil de statue ou sous les paupières peintes d'un portrait, mais ce n'est qu'un leurre."[38]

Not only is it the colour of eyes by which M. de Phocas is obsessed (always a blue-green, or a variety of *glauque*), like those of Athena, but of fixedness, of ferocity, of ecstasy, as one finds in what Dorothy Kosinski calls "the gaze,"[39] of the androgynous beings depicted by Fernand Khnopff. Monstrous-like echoes of *Le Crapaud* can be heard in the intra- and intertextual instance in which M. de Phocas, seeking to appease his passion by attending mass, can only repeat to himself verses written by Rémy de Gourmont:

> Que tes yeux soient bénis, car ils sont homicides,
> Ils sont pleins de fantômes, et l'ironie des chrysalides
> Y dort comme l'eau fanée qui dort au fond de grottes vertes,
> On voit dormir des bêtes parmi des anémones bleues, vertes.[40]

In *Réclamation posthume* the narrator explains to his friend that he himself had painted the eyes of a decapitated head made out of plaster that he exhibits: "Je lui eus appris, tel enfant pris en faute, que le barbare coloriage de ce plâtre, le vert glauque des aveugles prunelles...était mon oeuvre de peintre."[41] Jean Lorrain actually kept in his possession such a grotesque "chef de décolée," not to mention his immense collection of ceramic as well as living frogs and toads. In "La Princesse au Sabbat,"[42]Princess Ilsée loves nothing but mirrors, flowers, eyes, and toads. She loves her subjects' eyes because she can admire herself in them. In other words, she loves nothing but her own image. In one of the pools that decorate her land, she has two enormous gargoyles made of greenish-coloured bronze placed at each side. They represent toads that spurt out glacial water into the pool. She also fills her palace with toads and frogs. After she participates in a witch's sabbath, however, she wakes up from it and can no longer find any reflected image in any of her mirrors. All of her frogs had also been broken or destroyed. The paradox of movement and stillness is singularly exotic in Moreau, Gallé, and Mucha. McLendon lists a rather extraordinary series of paradoxical motifs that appear in the production made by these artists. Here are just a few that he cites: chauves-souris/libellules; crapauds/iris diaphanes; champignons phalliques/têtes diadémées ou aureolées; cheveux noirs tortueux à la Méduse/tresses blondes à la Mélisande; gazes coulants à la Loïe Fuller/tentacules végétaux prolifiques, etc. These oppositions form part of *Art Nouveau* poetics in structural, narrative, sociological and esthetic terms. Lorrain himself collected paper-weights, brass lamps in the form of lubricious women or vegetative matter such as mushrooms or sea-weed. He dedicated his tale called *Narkiss* to his friend Lalique, the famous art nouveau jeweller and creator of lamps and jewellery made of bronze and glass, and in crystal.

The relationship between eyes and castration that Freud analyzes in his study of the *unheimlich*, and, in particular, in Hoffmann's *The Sand-Man*, can be detected through the filigree of the works of Jean Lorrain. As we saw in chapter VI, in regard to Rodenbach and the subject of fetishism, Freud convincingly argues that the element of the uncanny does not result from what Jentsch stresses in Hoffmann, that is, the uncertainty readers feel when they wonder whether a figure in a text is a human being or an automaton (such as the human-like doll Olympia in *The Sand-Man*), but from a fear of losing something that is as essential as one's eyes. Jean Lorrain knew the tales of Hoffmann. He has one of the friends of the narrator in *M. de Phocas* compare Freneuse to a character in one of "les contes d'Hoffmann."[43]

The Sand-Man is the recurrent figure in Hoffmann's narrative who, in the beginning, is said to throw sand into the eyes of children who will not go to sleep. The maid elaborates on the story by relating to young Nathanael that when the Sand-Man throws sand in children's eyes, "the eyes jump out of their heads all bleeding. Then he puts the eyes in a sack and carries them off to the moon to feed his children. They sit up there in their nest, and their beaks are hooked like owls' beaks, and they use them to peck up naughty boys' and girls' eyes with."[44] Nathanael identifies the Sand-Man with the lawyer Coppelius, a fearful person who visits Nathanael's father at night. The boy hides in the study, and when the two men busy themselves at the hearth, the boy believes he hears Coppelius call out "Here with your eyes!" and the boy screams in fear and horror. Coppelius seizes him and, just as he is ready to drop red-hot grains of coals into his eyes, the boy's father begs Coppelius to save Nathanael from that terrible fate. Every instance in the text entails some horror that has to do with losing one's eyes. Freud's principal conclusion is that "it is the threat of being castrated...which excites a peculiarly violent and obscure emotion, and...this emotion is what first gives the idea of losing other organs its intense colouring."[45]

Jean Lorrain's toad not only has "bleeding eyelids"[46] that remind us of eyes that have been burnt by coal, but that last decadently poetic phrase of the text, "Oh! ce crapaud aveugle, cette agonie de bête *mutilée* dans cette eau claire *au goût de sang!*" foregrounds blindness that seems to be a result of mutilation. Like Oedipus, the boy will reflect upon what he has seen. The relationship between eyes and their absence is obvious when M. de Phocas admires the eyes (or lack thereof) of the statue of Antinoüs, the figure who is an emblem of homosexual love, or of the absence of love between two *different* sexes. "Il n'y a de vraiment beaux que les visages des statues...Et puis quelle intensité de regard dans *leurs yeux vides!*"[47] Elsewhere M. de Phocas repeats Charles Vellay when he says that Narcissus's eyes are like a yawning chasm: "La folie des yeux, c'est l'attirance du gouffre."[48] The abyss motif stands as a representation of the void, or, otherwise stated, of the attraction to death. In the apostrophe to this chapter, R. de Montesquiou, who was one of the models of Proust's M. de Charlus, states that he had always tried to fill "l'irréparable vide qui est en moi."

From Baudelaire's "homme d'Ovide," who represents the void in a socially dynamic situation at the time of his writing "Le Cygne," we arrive at a time in which society was attracted by "le gouffre." Blindness and in-sight are thematic constants from Tiresias to Narcissus, from Oedipus to Alice, from thematics of seeing in *La Princesse de Clèves* to the conclusion of *Les Liaisons dangereuses*, from the mistaking of one person for the other in Rodenbach's work to "the madness of eyes" in J. Lorrain.

4.   Chiastic Rhetoric and the Void

The motif of absent eyes appears in one of Lorrain's most famous fantastic tales, *Les Trous du masque*, a tale that was reproduced in Castex's anthology of fantastic short stories.[49] In this narrative, the protagonist is taken to a chateau where all the men (there are only men present, the reader is made to believe), are wearing velvet hoods, silk stockings, and patent-leather shoes, identifying themselves as a society of homosexuals. The protagonist, who has been given a green velvet hood to wear, becomes more and more terrified as the night wears on, and suddenly, standing before a mirror, he tears off his hood and discovers that there is nothing underneath. A chiastic phrase embodies the sameness of the mirror image the protagonist sees when looking at a hooded figure whose hood has been pulled off: "le *capuchon* de velours vert était *vide, vide* le *capuchon* des autres masques..."[50]

The impossibility of being able to "see *nothing*" (which is an oxymoron), if one is looking at oneself, is never discussed, but the chiastic phrase used to describe the experience says a great deal. One does not need to be an expert in Freudian theory to pierce through the psychological significance of this chiasmus. When the *capuchon* (a symbolic condom, perhaps? - they *had* been invented by a man named Condom in the eighteenth century...) is taken off, there is no thing underneath. The chiastic phrase, "capuchon-vide—vide-capuchon" has the seme *capuchon* enclosing the *vide* that is "framed," or "surrounded," by nothingness inside. By means of the repetitive *v*, the fear of nothingness is underlined by being placed at the centre. Alliteration stresses the point even more: "le capuchon de *v*elours *v*ert était *v*ide." One could go to semantic extremes at this point and point out that a *v* stands, traditionally, for female sexuality, and that a *v* in reverse, that is, ^ , represents the phallus. In this case, however, it represents a non-phallus, or the inversion of a phallus. And four *v*s in a row (*v*elours-*v*ert-*v*ide-*v*ide) cannot be ignored.

It would be difficult to find a more explicit representation of the fear of castration than the one represented in a tale found in *Contes d'un buveur d'éther* entitled *Une Nuit trouble*. The narrator, Edouard, had been invited to a party at a friend's house in the country to celebrate the friend's recent marriage. Edouard spends the night in a room far removed from the others. His hosts had forgotten to light the fire in the chimney, so they had installed a heater (a *chouberski*—the Russian word adds to the exoticism of the place) to warm the room. Edouard is awakened by a strange noise in the chimney, "comme un large effarement d'ailes,"[51] and as he lifts the hood of the fireplace, he discovers "un être accroupi dans l'ombre [qui] reculait en ouvrant démesurément un hideux bec à goître, un bec membraneux de chimérique cormoran."[52] The bird, like the toad in *Le Crapaud*, has a huge belly: "hideuse et fantomatique avec son ventre énorme et comme bouffi de graisse, elle sautelait maintenant dans le foyer, piétinant, ça et là, sur de longues cuisses grêles et grenues aux pattes palmées, comme celles d'un canard, et, avec des cris d'enfant peureux, elle se rencognait dans les angles où ses grandes ailes de chauve-souris s'entrechoquaient avec un bruit de choses flasques."[53] Edouard attacks the beast mercilessly with the fire tongs. Bloodied, the monster hides in the corner, "la membrane hideuse qui lui servait de paupière retombée sur son oeil terne[;] j'étais moi-même à bout de force et, je laissais tomber les pincettes sanglantes."[54] Edouard, with his bloody *pincettes*, seems like a violent and sadistic doctor brandishing forceps.

After thinking he has pushed the bird back into the chimney, Edouard lowers the fireplace hood and goes back to sleep. He will be awakened a second time by *two* monstrous birds "à bec de cormoran, à ventres flasques et renflés de vampire...dardant sur moi leur oeil à paupière membraneuse. Searching for the fire tongs in the dark room, he leans over, and when he does so his hand "s'abattait sur quelque chose d'humide et de mou qui vivait, sur un frôlement de vampire, un rampement de spectre qui m'assénait un formidable coup de bec et, du tranchant de sa corne, me détachait presque le pouce de la main." As he expresses it, "la bête que je croyais morte s'était, à moitié mourante, trouvée à ma portée et venait de se venger en me mutilant." His hosts, who had been celebrating their marriage, one cannot fail to note, explain Edouard's "nightmare" months later, when they have the chimney cleaned. They had found the skeleton of three baby owls who must have been suffocated, they say, due to the heater's fumes.

In this narrative we find, once again, beasts of prey that mutilate as does the Sand-Man, in Hoffmann's tale. The birds have huge bellies like that of the "pregnant" toad, membranous eyelids (like the toad's and like Lorrain's), and they move, or "dart" toward the protagonist. His thumb, a phallic replacement, which is almost entirely cut off by the pointed bird's beak, is to *Une Nuit trouble* what eyes are to *Le Crapaud*, or what *le vide* is to *Les Trous du Masque*.

The oeuvre of Jean Lorrain, and *Le Crapaud* in particular, bring to the fore several elements evident in *fin de siècle* eroticism, among which are tension that exists between pleasurable revelling in and then hating the waters of the womb, as well as narcissistic contemplation of the self as a fascinating but disgusting oedipal object. The boy experiences fear of punishment that could be interpreted as nothing other than a fear of mutilation. He recognizes in the toad aspects of the self that are a result of a loss of innocence. As in Ovid's tale of Narcissus, *Le Crapaud* is a representation of initiation. At the conclusion of the tale, the narrator and the reader, decoders of mirror messages in *Le Crapaud*, are tempted to say: "'Oh, I see,' said the blind man."

5.   The Toad: C'est Moi

As Baudelaire, Barbey, and Mallarmé were haunted by swans and swan imagery, many Decadent writers were haunted by batrachians as a species, and by toads, in particular. In Tristan Corbière's *Les Amours jaunes* (1873), "Le Crapaud" is a strong, impressive, and lugubrious poem in which the poet identifies with the warty creature he hears croak. It is no coincidence that "the swan's song" is heard shortly before the swan dies, and that

Corbière's toad "sings" shortly before it crawls under its cold rock, to die. It is interesting that "to croak," in popular English, is a double entendre. It is the toad's "swan song," in that it signifies the hideous sound emitted regularly by the batrachian, as well as a verb meaning "to die."

Lorrain's toad is like Corbière's in that both are identified by the writers as themselves. As Lorrain's short story focuses on the hideous creature's bleeding eyes and putrid belly, Corbière's poem does not fail to evoke the animal's eyes. But in the negative: "Horreur/...Il chante.— Horreur!/ Horreur pourquoi?/ Vois-tu pas son oeil de lumière.../ Non: il s'en va, froid, sous sa pierre." As the writer, Lorrain identifies the toad's belly with his own, at the end of his life. The poet in Corbière's sonnet makes the correlation clear in the poem itself. In the last line he states: "Bonsoir – ce crapaud c'est moi."

Webster's *Dictionary* tells us that "toads...are usually terrestrial except in the breeding season, when they are aquatic"[55] Lorrain's toad equates death with sexuality, in that the creature with the huge infected belly comes to the water during breeding season, only to die. The young boy contemplating it looks at the image of what the literal writer will become at the end of his life. Corbière's toad makes its reflective appearance in a sonnet whose structure is 3-3-4-4, a reversal of the traditional 4-4-3-3 armature. The mirror image will lead to the poetic persona's identification with the dying creature in the last line. Having created the Narcissus myth as a vibrant intertext (in the first line of the second tercet we read "...Un chant; *comme un écho,* tout vif"), the discovery, or the result of the quest occurs in mid-sonnet, as if it were a hinge. The poet, who had heard "un chant" twice, once in the first line of the poem, and the second time in the second tercet, invites the reader to come along ("Viens, c'est là, dans l'ombre") to discover the provenance of the "song." The quest is rewarded in the first line of the first quatrain: "—Un crapaud!" And the close identification between toad and poet is a deixis, pointing to a creature that reminds one a bit of Baudelaire's "Albatros": "Vois-le, poète tondu, sans aile, / Rossignol de la boue... - Horreur! – /... Il chante. – " Not only is the creature shorn, having no wings with which to fly ("sans aile"), but worse, it is also sarcastically called a "rossignol," a nightingale, that most poetic of all birds, whose history in literature has filled the pages of many a book. Corbière's "nightingale, however, is a toad that "sings"; it is a nightingale whose home is in the mud, whose eye has no brilliance or light. "Non, il s'en va, froid, sous sa pierre," we read in the line next to the last, which makes the correlation between the toad and the poet, who bids us "good night": "Bonsoir – ce crapaud-là c'est moi."

*   *   *   *

In the literature of Symbolism and Decadence, the categories of ambiguity, transition, fluidity (Symbolism would privilege water as its medium), and the techniques of "double-digit" narrators and structures take precedence over what had been called "realist" methods and practices. The ideas constituting the "one in the other" would flow, eventually, into the stream of thoughts, games, manifestos, and productions of the Surrealists.

Having known all of the artists and writers of the Surrealist "movement," but having refused the title of "Surrealist" for himself, André Pieyre de Mandiargues's affective and aesthetic heart was with them, and his own creations would be forever imprinted with the surrealist notion of "passage" of "one to the other," of "one in the other." The distinctions between dreaming and waking, between being conscious and unconscious, between the real and the unreal, between personhood and nature, between the self and the ego were all obliterated in the theoretical bases of the Surrealists. The beliefs in rites of passage, even of literal passages from one place to another, of metaphorical passages from one element to another, the second being already contained within the first, as in chiasmus, were privileged, instead. So were rituals that exalted the liberation believed to be found in the Surrealists' refusal to make distinctions between sacred and profane, transgression and law. In *La Motocyclette*, Mandiargues exalts such rituals - the most important of all being that of writing itself. The movement we follow goes from Narcissus to Dionysus, the latter being present, as I show in the first chapter of this book, in the structural make-up of Ovid's *Metamorphoses*.

Notes

[1] Quoted by P. Jullian, *Jean Lorrain ou le Satiricon 1900*, Fayard, Paris, 1974, p. 263.

[2] W. McLendon, *Jean Lorrain: Impresario de l'Art Nouveau*, Orbis Litterarum, Paris, 1984, 39, pp. 54-64.

[3] J. Lorrain, "Gustave Moreau," in *Portraits littéraires et mondains*, Baudinière, Paris, 1926, p. 33.

[4] J. Lorrain, *Sensations et Souvenirs*, Bibliothèque-Charpentier, Paris, 1895.

[5] ibid., 9.

[6] ibid., 10.

[7] Jullian, p. 22.

[8] *Sensations*, p. 10.

[9] Unless otherwise noted, italics have been added throughout.

[10] *Sensations*, 12.

[11] J. Pierrot, *The Decadent Imagination, 1880-1900*, Chicago UP, Chicago, 1981, pp. 207-237.

[12] *Sensations*, p. 12.

[13] P. Jullian, *op. cit.*, p. 284.

[14] *Sensations,* p. 14.

[15] ibid.

[16] Quoted by Jullian, p. 284.

[17] In *Boundary* 2, p. 14. See also Said's chapter "On Repetition" in *The World, the Text, and the Critic*, Harvard UP, Cambridge, 1983, pp. 111-125.

[18] *Sensations*, p. 13.

[19] ibid., p. 14.

[20] J. Berman, *Narcissism and the Novel* , N.Y.U. UP, New York, 1990, p. 6.

[21] See L. Hutcheon, *Narcissistic Narrative: The Metafictional Paradox*, Methuen, New York, 1984, p. 18.

[22] Quoted by Jullian, p. 195.

[23] ibid., p. 17.

[24] *Sensations*, p. 10.

[25] Ovid, pp. 148-149

[26] In A. Fonyi's ed.of Guy de Maupassant, *Le Horla et autres contes d'angoisse*, Flammarion, Paris, 1984, p. 20.

[27] ibid., p. 20.

[28] *Sensations*, p. 15.

[29] ibid.

[30] P. Hadot, "Le Mythe de Narcisse et son interprétation par Plotin," 82, n.1. In *Narcissus: Nouvelle Revue de Psychanalyse* , printemps 1976, p. 13.

[31] ibid, p. 82.

[32] Quoted by Jullian, p. 294.

[33] Séguier, Paris, 1993, Présentation Jean de Palacio.

[34]. ibid., p. 321-331.

[35] ibid., p. 322.

[36] Quoted by Jullian, p. 295.

[37] J. Lorrain, *M. de Phocas*, Le Livre Club du Libraire, Paris, 1966.

[38] ibid., p. 27.

[39] In "The Gaze of Fernand Khnopff," *Source*, XI/3-4, 1992, pp. 1-10.

[40] *M. de Phocas*, p. 38.

[41] *Réclamation postume*, p. 122.

[42] *La Princesse au sabbat*, pp. 51-60.

[43] S. Freud, *Collected Papers*, trans. J. Rivière, Basic Books Inc., New York, 1959, p. 379.

[44] ibid., p. 15.

[45] ibid., p. 384.

[46] *Sensations*, p. 15.

[47] *M. de Phocas*, p. 32.

[48] ibid., p. 42.

[49] *Anthologie du conte fantastique français,* José Corti, Paris, 1963, pp. 279-288.

[50] ibid., p. 149.

[51] *Contes d'un buveur...,* "Une nuit trouble," p. 115-288.

[52] ibid., p. 116.

[53] ibid., p. 117.

[54] ibid.

[55] Second Edition, William Collins publishers, 1979.

Chapter VIII

The Wheel of Fortune as Mirror:
André Pieyre de Mandiargues's *La Motocyclette*

Comme la plus haute sphère dans le ciel tourne,
Qui de son cercle embrasse de moindres cercles
Et dont l'action fait graviter les sphères
Qui dans leur cours la suivent à la trace;
Ainsi la roue majeure fait tourner avec elle
Les roues mineures et les met en branle;
Et tout comme dans les cieux, à l'intérieur tournent
Des mouvements contraires et des roues dans des roues.
Girolami Preti (cited by Georges Poulet)

Many of the rituals that appear consistently throughout André Pieyre de Mandiargues's prose fiction, as well as in much of Surrealist literature, make use of geometric figures that have mythic, archetypal, and hermetic origins. In *La Motocyclette* (1963), a novel that was later made into a film starring Alain Delon, straight lines and circular figures prevail, creating macro-chiastic and interlocking structures that have symbolic connotations. Rebecca Nul "consumes" a straight line as she hurtles forward into space on the powerful black Harley-Davidson she had received as a gift from her lover, Daniel Lionart; circles surround eight equally long spokes of each of the motorcycle's wheels whose spinnings carry Rebecca ever closer to her rendez-vous with death, and her rest-stops bring back memories of initiatory sexual rituals that had taken place within circular spaces. The final "rest stop" will be her encounter with a giant head depicting Dionysus.

1.   Narrative Stops and Starts
The straight lines and circular figures reflect, contain, and unleash structural, reflective and mythical concerns. The straight line of Rebecca's progress from her home in eastern France to her destination in Heidelberg contains the repetitive course of the narrative's structure as well as the novel's concern with starts and stops, with beginnings and endings, with cut-offs and detours. The whirling circular figures visible on the spinning wheels reflect the symbolic properties, both mythic and occult, that are at work in Mandiargues's fiction. Those turning wheels of *La Motocyclette* are symbolic of the Wheel of Fortune, and various clocks, discs, semaphores,

and clearings the reader encounters in the book have structurally repetitive, archetypal, and esoteric connotations.[1]

Rebecca's trip begins at Haguenau, in Alsace, and ends just before the exit for Heidelberg, where she is heading in order to meet her lover, Daniel. Because she had not worn her watch (making her trip a venture through time as well as into timelessness), and because she is afraid of arriving too early at her lover's dwelling, she stops to rest at three different locations before making her fourth, and fatal, stop. These halts become important points of structural punctuation, since they provide the occasions for the flashbacks that make the process of diegesis imagistic and integrative in their bringing past and present together in the text. These stops, in turn, slip into the symbolic workings of the circular Wheel of Fortune that turns, as relentlessly as do the motorcycles' tires, thrusting the protagonist into collision with death.

During her first stop, Rebecca begins to review the itinerary of a trip she had taken twelve days previously. She is repeating that trip, this time, and as each event and location is encountered, it is contrasted and compared with events and locations she remembers from her first trip. Variations in details become symbolic in their repetitions and reversals. When Rebecca pulls off the road, the first time, she parks her vehicle and stretches out on a bench in a gesture and situation that will mirror her final "resting place." As she lies on the bench she remembers the culmination of her previous journey: it had concluded in a sun-drenched sexual ritual that took place in the exact centre of the terrace of Daniel's chalet, and the circular terrace was engraved, at its centre, with a mosaic eye."[2]

On her way to and during her second stop, on the German side of the Rhine, Rebecca recalls a ski weekend four months before, during which she had met Daniel and had participated, passively and willingly, in his ending of her virginity. She also remembers the first time Daniel had taken her into the woods on his red motorcycle in order to perform sexual rites with her in the centre of a narrow clearing in the snow, not long before her marriage to Raymond Nul, the dull school-teacher to whom she was already engaged (his name says it all). At the centre of the circle she had become an "X" figure: "il lui avait mis les bras en croix et avait refermé chacune des mains, non dégantées, sur un morceau de branche, en serrant assez fort et assez longuement pour qu'elle sût bien qu'elle devait se tenir là sans lâcher prise."[3] Throughout the ritual she continued to remain a figure "X,"[4] making of the iconography an "X" surrounded by a circle. Mandiargues's prose fiction reveals an obsessive interest in the "X" figure.

The third rest-stop Rebecca makes before the final one is especially suggestive. While her fortune can be said to have been "sealed" from the moment she accepted the motorcycle as a wedding gift from Daniel –

"Hadn't she consented, in advance, to her destiny?"[5] - the events that course through her mind and the chosen setting for this pause relate to details visible in the Arcanum X of the Tarot (which is entitled the *Rota Fortunae*), as well as to circumstances that feature in certain rites of initiation. When Rebecca sees the spot where she pulls off the road, she does not stay in the ordinary place that is littered with cans and refuse, banal emblems of banal humanity. She slowly guides her motorcycle, instead, into the woods, and finds a privileged location, "un endroit vaste, vide, et vierge (on dirait) qui est une clairière."[6] This circular space, a clearing in the middle of which a previous ritual is recalled by Rebecca, is a space that we now see for a third time.

To arrive at the clearing, Rebecca has to bend down over the handlebars of her Harley-Davidson in order to pass under the branches of a hazel tree that brush against the black wool of her cowl. She sees the clearing "ainsi que par ouverture d'une porte cochère ou lever d'un rideau de scène."[7] The raising of a curtain onto a sacred terrain, as if it were a stage, is frequently one of the clues to the beginning of Mandiargues's initiation rituals. They not only bear the imprint of his own symbolic eroticism, but also contain elective affinities with many symbols described by M. Eliade in his *Rites and Symbols of Initiation*, by Sir J. Frazer in *The Golden Bough*, by E.R. Goodenough in *Jewish Symbols in the Graeco-Roman Period, et al.* These reflective rituals, which are primarily rituals of birth and rebirth, cause basic changes to occur in individuals' perceptions of themselves and of the world. They are meant to bring about a conversion or an alteration and heightened apprehension of a person's situation in the cosmos. The recognition by the reader of these affinities enriches the reading of any Mandiargues text.

2. Initiatory Rituals

Many rites of initiation occur within a circular ring of earth that depicts the *imago mundi* or the mirror-image of the primordial world as it was when in direct contact with the divine. Readers of *The Golden Bough* have long been made aware that the symbolism of the sacred tree is richly diversified and complex. It is essential to many initiatory rites. The circular *imago mundi* thrusts up from its centre the *axis mundi*, the tree that, in its processes of perpetual regeneration, is representative of the cosmos.[8] The tree is also a link between the finite and the infinite. When Rebecca had been taken to a hotel by Daniel, after the ritual in the snow, she had thought of him as an oak tree: "Tout arbre est une sorte de prêtre, se dit-elle...et elle pensa qu'en lui se trouvaient réunis incomparablement l'aspect du chêne et la figure du druide."[9] Other upsurging figures surrounded by circles also appear in the novel. At one point Rebecca sees "une potence enrubannée [qui] se dressait sur une petite place;"[10] at another she sees "[des] arbres entourés d'un banc circulaire." [11]

The hazel tree under which Rebecca passes is an ancient symbol of fertility, whose branches were used to make wands for seekers of gold in the Middle Ages.[12] The hazel tree was also used in Swabia (the region in which Rebecca is travelling) to make blazing discs that were tossed into the air during Lenten festivals. They were shaped into thin round pieces, a few inches in diameter, their edges notched to imitate the rays of the sun or the stars.[13] Not long before her death, Rebecca passes three trucks, each of which bears "une roue dentée peinte en rouge vif, comme un symbole solaire incisé dans un bloc de granit et que l'archéologue a colorié d'un jus garance pour le faire ressortir."[14]

When Rebecca parks her motorcycle, the third time, she does so against a birch tree that stands near the middle of the clearing. The birch tree figures, more than almost any other tree, in ancient rituals held in the centre of symbolic circles. Rebecca flings herself on the ground "comme elle se jetterait sur un lit de fortune."[15] She thinks of the word "fortune" and the word creates images in her mind of the "îles dites fortunées." The island, like the clearing, is a primordial sacred space, since it is a "monde en réduction, une image du cosmos, complète et parfaite, parce qu'elle présente une valeur sacrale concentrée."[16] The microcosm mirrors the macrocosm. The image of Alice, caught in a miniaturized, or "concentrated," room that is too small for her, comes to mind. The oblique rays of the sun shine through to Rebecca's privileged circle and illumine the symbolic small flowers on the ground. The flowers she notices especially are green and white Solomon's seals that are "comme des étendards du Prophète brandis pour le départ en guerre de hordes de derviches, et leurs jolies clochettes ne font pas oublier le signe mystérieux qu'ils contiennent." Other flowers that adorn the clearing are primroses and "quelques pieds-de-veau, de cette sorte d'arum que l'on nomme aussi manteau de la Vierge."

3. Arcane Specularity

At Rebecca's last rest-stop, she remembers a rendez-vous with Daniel one month before at "Le Bain des Roses," a bath-house in Strasbourg. The ritual there had involved his tying her hands and feet to an arched pipe above the bed so that she had formed an "X" figure inside the demi-parabola. She is told by Daniel to imagine the "X" figure as being upside-down, closing the circle thereby, and doubling the "X" figure itself: "il aurait fallu supposer une autre demi-parabole symétrique où son double eût été lié pareillement mais la tête en bas, suspendu par les pieds, supporté par les noeuds des poignets."[17] The symbolic "X" or "Chi" figure is reflected in a mirror. Facing her, the mirror reflected her miniaturized image, and "she realized that she was not ugly." The litotes Mandiargues uses reminds one of the Narcissus figure who looks in the water and finds himself ravishingly beautiful. The reflection, "curieusement, en outre, la petitesse de son image, si proche d'elle la portait à se voir réduite aux proportions d'une femme pygmée, et Daniel lui paraissait trois ou quatre fois plus grand qu'elle, ce qui lui donnait de la majesté de surcroît." The image of the double is repeated when she remembered that he was a bit older than twice her own age.[18] Daniel had gently struck her body with a bouquet of roses before making love to her. She had become a microcosm of humanity, embodying the forces of passion writ small, finding pride in the symbolic figure and ritual. She had lifted her head proudly as she contemplated her image in the mirror. She had even winked at her reflection.[19]

Mandiargues is fond of miniaturization, not only because of his love of baroque literature, but because it recalls one of the basic doctrines of the occult tradition, "the belief that man is a microcosm, or 'little world,' a miniature replica of the greater world outside him. It follows that whatever exists in man exists also in the greater world."[20] It was also thought that one small alchemical glass cylinder was capable of containing elements that have universal significance. Symbols are similar reductions and concentrations of meaning, as are short stories, or the cards in a Tarot deck. Miniaturization appears in several of Mandiargues's short stories, notably in *Clorinde, Les Pierreuses, Le Diamant,* and *Le Pain rouge.*

Mandiargues's love of baroque sensibility and literature is specifically related to his perception of the macrocosm in the microcosm. In *Les Métamorphoses du cercle*, G. Poulet says the following of the baroque poets' predilections:

> Les écrivains de l'âge baroque ne laissent pas d'être fascinés par cette ressemblance entre l'infiniment grand et l'infiniment petit. Comme le macrocosme est figuré par le microcosme...ainsi la sphère immense de l'univers se retrouve, amenuisée mais curieusement semblable, dans les objets qu'agence la science de l'homme pour reproduire en petit l'espace cosmique ou le temps solaire. Astrobales [sic], mappemondes, planisphères et horloges sont des univers abrégés, des globes où le cosmos est ramené au minuscule.[21]

Mandiargues had a predilection for the writings of Italian and French baroque poets. What Poulet says in the quote above could not better express several aspects of their work that appealed so strongly to Mandiargues.

A few moments before thinking of the "îles fortunées," Rebecca had thought to herself that the Germans would be scandalized if they saw her lead her two-wheeled vehicle into nature.[22] They would not understand this straying from the mundane path. The semes *roue* and *fortune* are closely allied within the contextual framework of the scene. It is up to the reader to sight this alliance and foretell its implications by "straying," as does Rebecca, "from the mundane path." The Xs in Mandiargues's micro-structure repeat his belief and interest in the mirroring actions of the macro-structures of the universe.

4.   The Tarot Card X

The Tarot card X is called the *Rota Fortunae*. It depicts a sphinx armed with a sword, seated upon a platform, under which is a wheel with eight spokes. On the hub of the wheel is the six-pointed star of Solomon, known as Solomon's seal. The tenth Arcanum of the Tarot belongs to the sixth sign of the zodiac, the sign of the Virgin. Its place in the zodiacal sphere causes it to be related to the hexagram of Solomon. On the wheel itself there are two inscriptions: one is the Great Tetragram composed of the Hebrew letters that stand for "Yahweh" (Y H W H) and the other bears the letters of the word ROTA. The letters are mingled, each one being placed at the extremity of each of the eight spokes. Symbols of the four elements, earth, air, fire, and water, are also located at the terminal points of the horizontal and perpendicular spokes. In each corner of the card are four traditional winged images from Ezekiel and the Book of Revelation: the man, the lion, the ox, and the eagle.[23]

The narrator describes Rebecca's motorcycle as being placed near the centre of the clearing, thus locating the wheels in the centre of the circle. The narrator describes the Solomon's seal flowers that contain "a mysterious sign" and the flowers called "Virgin's mantle" in the clearing that is described as "virginal." In yet another version of the Arcanum X, roses are depicted at the foot of the Wheel of Fortune. In her clearing Rebecca finds primroses, as she had found roses in the bath-house.

One of the many symbols contained in the sign of Solomon is that of the four elements, earth, air, fire, and water, and their qualities, "humidity, dryness, heat, and cold." It is also "a synthesis of opposites, and the expression of cosmic unity".[24] The four principal events with Daniel that Rebecca recalls during her rest-stops are emblematic of these qualities: on the sun-filled terrace (fire), in the cold dry air of the hotel in the mountains (air), on the ground in the snow (earth), and at the Bain des Roses (water). Each location where she reminisces provides a repetitive *mise-en-scène* for these "elemental" memories.

When Rebecca leaves the clearing she crushes a few Solomon's seals under her motorcycle's wheels.[25] This is a misadventure, a signifier of her own destiny, since she too will soon be crushed, like the flowers that bear the seal of Solomon.

The Tarot sphinx armed with a sword falls into natural association with the innumerable military references that appear in the novel. The sword-brandishing sphinx on the platform represented in the Tarot card is like the tanks that Rebecca sees at various times during her last trip: "Capots ouverts, les tourelles des chars présentent des têtes de militaires et parfois le buste aussi; les tracteurs et des camions à plateforme montrent tout entiers des individus de la même espèce."[26] A military jeep, parked by the side of the road, will later become the cause of Rebecca's death. Mandiargues despised the military, and never lost an opportunity to denigrate it.

Various animals are also visible on the Tarot Arcanum X, namely a serpent, a crocodile, and a dog.[27] While the dog represents Goodness, the crocodile and the serpent represent the opposite. The serpent appears in *La Motocyclette* in the form of a ring worn by the customs officer on the border between France and Germany. Rebecca believes the ring to be a pederast's "engagement" ring, and if that is the case, she believes, it is a symbol of death.

Both Greek and Latin myths of the Wheel of Fortune (centred in Nemesis and Fortuna, respectively) had an element in common: both held wheels in their hands. As the Wheel ascended it signified life and good luck; its descent indicated death and bad fortune.[28] These wheels were originally representative of the solar year. This is suggested by Fortuna's name, *vortumna*, "she who turns the year around."[29] Twelve days pass between Rebecca's first and second journeys, a span of time that recalls the solar year in miniaturized form. During her first journey, the wheel of Fortune was in its ascending course, while during the second journey, the trajectory towards the lover is punctuated by halts and evil omens that suggest that the Wheel is on its downward course. The image of a circle surrounding a central core that is constantly evoked by Mandiargues also repeats the planetary symbol for the Sun: 0

As a symbol of the solar year, the Wheel of Fortune signals the rhythms of nature and the repetitious changes of seasons in opposite cycles: summer and winter, desiccation and regeneration; birth and death; death and resurrection. When Rebecca's thoughts repeat themselves, like the signs on the road, she makes the comparison with existence itself: "Les mêmes [pensées] reviennent, ou les mêmes images, comme les signeaux toujours les mêmes sur une route pas plus variée que l'existence."[30] During the first trip the sun had been shining; during the second, the sky is gray. While Rebecca had known the time of day during her first trip, during the second trip time becomes void. She had promised herself to look at the time in the café, but in retrospect, she can remember only the baroque details of the clock: "Tant de précision dans l'accessoire ne sert qu'à encadrer le vide de l'essentiel, qui demeure un rond blanc." [31] Her movement is from Being into Nothingness. Her name, which had been *Res* before her marriage, became *Nul*, and that onomastic seme announces her future as well. Like Barbey d'Aurevilly, Mandiargues was obsessed with onomastics.

The closer Rebecca comes to the face of Death, the more accelerated and intense become the indications of repetitions. She passes one truck with a solar sign inscribed on its back panel; then a second; then a third. The solar signs turn, in her mind, convulsively: "Et ces soleils dentés se mettent à tourner vertigineusement dans sa conscience, comme elle imagine que tournent un peu au-dessous de son sexe les pignons du moteur à plein régime."[32] A "pignon," or sprocket-wheel, is "la plus petite des roues dentées d'un couple d'engrenages cylindriques ou coniques" (*Petit Larousse*). The wheels within the wheels evoke Ezekiel's vision, of course. But they also evoke the baroque poets so dear to Mandiargues. Marino says: "La grande roue du Tout est dans un petit Rond."[33] The sexual connotations are obvious.

The narrator warns the reader, from the very beginning of Rebecca's journey, that road signs are portentous: "Un peu avant la fin du boulevard, un panneau bleu signale une double bifurcation, et la figure qu'il présente est si serpentine et si embrouillée que les routiers auxquels il s'adresse feront bien de s'arrêter sans doute et de réfléchir avant de l'interpréter, s'ils n'ont pas une disposition spéciale à comprendre les épures."[34] As road signs must be observed (or sighted) carefully by travellers for meanings, so must readers (i.e., "des routiers") observe signs for their deeper meanings and reflect upon them, as they are reflected within them.

The statement cited above places the text into what L. Hutcheon, in *Narcissistic Narrative*, calls an "overtly" self-conscious text, over against what she names a "covert" form: "Overtly narcissistic texts reveal their self-awareness in explicit thematizations or allegorizations of their diegetic or linguistic identity within the texts themselves. In the covert form, this process is internalized, actualized; such a text is self-reflective but not necessarily self-conscious."[35] Hutcheon makes this statement in what she calls her "ironic" reading of Ovid's Narcissus myth.

While the narrator of *La Motocyclette* recommends a "disposition spéciale" when it comes to reading the text, the reader may even then be led in the wrong direction. One might be tempted to interpret the double bifurcation as the planetary symbol for Leo: (Daniel "Lion"-art). But the fact that the figure is complicated and serpentine more clearly evokes the caduceus, the winged staff of Mercury, or two serpents around a central rod.

The sign of Mercury "possède un double aspect symbolique: l'un bénéfique, l'autre maléfique, dont le caducée présente, si l'on veut, l'antagonisme et l'équilibre."[36] The unification of opposing forces is one of the bases of formulations in the alchemical *opus*, and, as a writer who was interested in, involved with, and contributed to the theories of Surrealism, alchemy fascinated Mandiargues.

The most evident correlation made between circular signs and the Wheel of Destiny appears when Rebecca approaches Karlsruhe. She sees "[des] disques et [des] anneaux [qui tournent] continuellement et concentriquement sur de grands cadrans suspendus au-dessus des carrefours.... Ce mouvement circulaire produisait une sorte de vertige à première vue qui paralysait le novice ou le fascinait au lieu d'aider à la manoeuvre..." Rebecca interprets her own fascination as a "novice" in the following manner: "Si les cadrans lui en imposaient tant, sans doute, c'est que par leur bizarre analogie avec celui de la roulette et ceux des horloges astronomiques ils étaient liés de quelque façon au mécanisme du destin." In braving Destiny, then, she forges ahead, only narrowly avoiding an accident at this juncture.[37]

5. "X" Marks the Spot

If the *mise en scène* of Rebecca's third rest-stop is associated with the Arcanum X of the Tarot, it is not surprising that the geometric figure X should be a constitutive factor in the ritual she recalls while in that setting, which is that of having become, in "reality" and in imagination, a doubled "Chi" inside her reflection in the mirror.

The figure X, or the St. Andrew's cross that Rebecca forms within the oval recurs systematically in Mandiargues's work. Its significance is polysemic. Like the X figure of the lion-man, which is the Sun, ravishing Sarah Mose in *Le Diamant*, Daniel Lionart is here the symbol of the fiery orb. The figure itself is also associated with the Pythagorean Tetraktis, with the ancient problem of the "squaring of the circle," with Leonardo da Vinci's and other Renaissance artists' figures of Vitruvian Man, with the Mandala, with emblematic icons of androgyny, "à condition de couper l'image un peu plus bas que le nombril, on eût pu songer au supplice d'un adolescent de l'autre sexe,"[38] and with chiastic rhetoric and structure.

Rebecca's figure also "turns into" the spokes inside the wheel of Fortune as she becomes one with her fate. Her fate is not only "sealed" in the emblem; she literally *becomes* the wheel, with her arms and legs outstretched. As she imagines a duplicate of herself, turned upside down and suspended by her feet, Rebecca becomes the analogue of the sign of misfortune in Tarot symbolism, which occurs whenever a card is uncovered upside down. She is also emblematic of the wheel in motion, for as the spokes turn, they thrust her headlong into death.[39]

The X figure that Rebecca forms is enclosed within an imaginary oval. The egg shape is one of the most ancient symbols in all iconography, and it is a prominent feature of Mandiargues's *Marbre*, "Le Théâtre de la Mort" (Part III). In that text a "monument ovoïde" leads up to the circular building in the centre of which an old woman named Dona Lavinia is brought to die. Her death is a ritual observed only by the men of a place aptly called Locorotondo. In this tale Mandiargues was inspired by the shapes of the *trulli* in and around Alberobello in the Apulia region of Italy, a region he knew and loved and wrote about in various works, in his *Belvedères* in particular. The egg is the symbol of birth, of the world, of woman, of eternity. It is regeneration and immortality. It features prominently in Etruscan grave paintings and sarcophagi, since it is the symbol of life and resurrection. As M. Eliade says, it is "a cliché image of totality."[40]

The image of a naked woman inside an elliptical wreath corresponds, also, to the last of the trumps of the Tarot, XXI, which is called *Corona Magica*, or *The World*. Its sign is 0, the Sun. Outside the elliptical wreath, which, in some Tarot decks, is formed by the snake ourobouros, the four creatures of Ezekiel, the man, the lion, the eagle, and the ox, are depicted, as in the Arcanum X.[41] Some writers connect the wreath with the cosmic egg. The ellipse, says R. Cavendish, can also be identified as "the mystic centre, the still hub of things, the timeless unity, the lost paradise, Jerusalem the golden, which by ancient tradition stands at the centre of the world and is the earthly counterpart of the shining City of Heaven."[42] In some versions, the woman at the centre of the ellipse is a hermaphrodite, mingling the two sexes as an image of the restoration of divine unity, and representing humanity as male and female at the same time.[43] Rebecca's androgynous body is frequently described in *La Motocyclette*, but it is particularly rich in symbolic properties when she sees herself reflected in the mirror inside the ellipsoid configuration. The hermetic details of the scene at "Le Bain des Roses" are multiple, but the human figure inside the "egg" is the most striking of the various emblems.

When Rebecca leaves the clearing, she sees a female blackbird fly out from a thicket, and thinks of the eggs that must be in the nest. It is ironic that, because Rebecca does not stop to raid the nest and hold the eggs in her hand, as an Etruscan symbol of life, "Rebecca...a mieux à faire qu'à songer en plein jour un pillage de couvée,"[44] she will arrive at the cut-off for Heidelberg at the split-second the beer truck adorned with a circular head of Bacchus pulls out in front of her to pass a car that is going around a parked military jeep. As she is being literally devoured by the monstrous, grinning mouth, which recalls one of the monsters of Bomarzo, about which

Mandiargues has also written, in *Les Monstres de Bomarzo*, her last thoughts are: "The universe is dionysiac."[45] While Daniel Lionart had initiated her into the forces of life and sexuality, Fortuna causes Rebecca to be initiated into the forces of death. But because Rebecca also identifies Daniel with the head of Bacchus at the end, both life and death are brought together in a Dionysian fashion.[46]

6.   The Novel's Chiastic Schemata

La Motocyclette is composed of four grand moments that are initiatory in character. Each takes place within a magic circle, and together they signify Rebecca's rite of passage from girlhood to womanhood, from naïveté to knowledge of sexuality, from intellectual innocence to awareness of the destructive and regenerative forces in the cosmos. The novel's structure, symbolized by a doubled or repeated trajectory in which the straight line of the highway on which Rebecca travels accommodates, in its diegesis, the full dimensions of these rites of passage. Initiation occurs only through a symbolic descent into the underworld, through the experience of pain and death. The myth of being devoured by a monster, of spending time in the belly of a whale, of descending into the chthonic recesses and tellurian labyrinths of Mother Earth, all signify that death must be known before the hero can be born anew.[47] For Rebecca, this descent is symbolized by an "excessively smiling face that was ready to gulp her down."[48] A moment before the end, Rebecca thinks of herself as a "fetus floating on the course of a stream that is conflating with a river," much like the experience of the young boy in J.Lorrain's *Le Crapaud*, although the ending of the two tales is different. The "return to the womb" takes Rebecca back to the beginning, and prepares her climactic apotheosis. A minute later, when "the two wheels of the Harley were on the exact line of the great route that goes from south to north,"[49] she accelerates, moving upwards on the map towards rebirth, or enlightenment.

The straight lines converge with circular figures of the Wheel of Fortune as Rebecca moves towards her ultimate rendezvous with Destiny. Diagrammed, the four-part punctuation provided by the rest-stops compares, chiastically, with Rebecca's first journey:

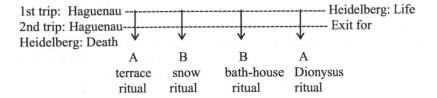

```
1st trip:  Haguenau --|----------------|-----------------|------- Heidelberg: Life
2nd trip: Haguenau--|--------------|--------------|-------------|------- Exit for
Heidelberg: Death        ↓             ↓             ↓             ↓
                         A             B             B             A
                      terrace         snow        bath-house    Dionysus
                       ritual        ritual        ritual        ritual
```

Soon after she leaves the clearing, Rebecca thinks: "Il est toujours plaisant, après une pose [sic] de retrouver les lignes peintes sur la chaussée comme des rails guidant les roues sur un embranchement." These lines are painted lines that lead the motorcycle's wheels towards a goal, and this ultimate goal is illumination: "Know thyself," said the Delphic oracle. "When he comes to know himself..." said Tiresias to Liriope about her son, Narcissus, as Tiresias answered the mother's question about her son's having a long and successful life. The narrator of *La Motocyclette* says: "Elle n'est pas dans les liens, elle n'attend pas, elle va, mais c'est vers une illumination de la sorte qu'à une allure assez prodigieuse pour un être humain (même pourvu de roues) elle se dirige."[50] The straight lines are not only interrupted, in the second trajectory, so as to recall "X" symbols and rites performed within circles during the first trajectory, but they also lead towards a climactic encounter with a circular divinity. What Rebecca discovers, ultimately, is expressed in the last words of the novel. The monstrous circular head of Dionysus in which life and death are conjoined is "perhaps the true visage of the universe." [51]

As Rebecca's motorcycle wheels move the narrative forward on a straight highway that goes from France to Germany, for a second time, Mandiargues does much more than trace a double itinerary; he charges simple geometric figures, in the form of the Greek letter *Chi*, with a universe of meaning.

*   *   *   *

We have seen many injured or decapitated heads throughout this book: Alice's Cheshire Cat's smiling head, Mme de Merteuil's pock-marked face as the punishment for her misdeeds, the blind man's visage in *Facino Cane*, the chopping off of the incestuous couple's heads in *Une Page d'histoire*, the fetichistic head that was owned and looked at by Jean Lorrain as he wrote *Le Crapaud*, the strangling of Jane with the previous's wife's braided hair in *Bruges-la-morte*, and "Narcissus's" running, head first, into the mirror in Rodenbach's *L'Ami des miroirs*. Finally, Rebecca's being literally "devoured" by the smiling head of Dionysus in *La Motocyclette* finishes the cycle of violence that prevails in the chronological sequence of the novels and short stories studied in this book.

La Motocyclette was published in 1963, at a time when Algeria was in turmoil and Vietnam had not yet exploded, but would do so soon. The political turmoil that prevailed is revealed in the innumerable depictions of tanks, trucks, and military vehicles that Rebecca sees on the road. As her powerful Harley thrusts her swiftly forward, she can see the tanks with their hoods open. She sees the gun turrets, revealing the heads, and entire torsos of soldiers driving them. She sees tractors and trucks, their platforms revealing individuals "of the same sort."[52] Mandiargues's glorification of Rebecca's mythic sexuality and archetypically significant rituals equalled his hatred of military might. The sand "thrown into the gears" of her magnificent motorcycle's wheels by a fateful confrontation with a parked military jeep along the highway, creates chaos, turmoil, death. Symmetry, structurally chiastic or imbricated, does not prevail in this novel, despite the neat repetitions of places and events. Asymmetry is, indeed, "the true visage of the universe."

How apt Mandiargues's imagery is, at the beginning of the twenty-first century. Mandiargues himself died before he could see this beginning, but he would not have been, in the least bit, surprised. He would have continued writing about X figures and rites and rituals of initiation, and reflecting upon the state of humankind, both in life and in death.

Notes

[1] Most studies that deal with rituals and symbols bring out, by analogy, the richness of Mandiargues's geometric figures. R. Guénon's *Symboles fondamentaux de la science sacrée* (Paris: Gallimard, 1962) is useful as a study of the circle, the wheel, the swastika, etc. Many ideas in this chapter appeared in my article "The *Rota Fortuna* in Pieyre de Mandiargues's *La Motocyclette, The French Review*, vol. liii, no. 3, 1980." See also J. Lowrie on "René Guenon and the Esoteric Thought of Andre Pieyre de Mandiargues," *The French Review*, vol. lviii, no. 3, February 1985. S. Campanini's dissertation, "Metaphysical Eroticism in the Prose Fiction of Pieyre de Mandiargues," Illinois, 1975, is valuable as an analysis of alchemy, of color symbolism, and of Jungian typologies in Mandiargues's work. Campanini's article, "Alchemy in Pieyre de Mandiargues' 'Le Diamant,'" *French Review* 50, 4, March 1977: pp. 602-609, is also helpful. D. Bond's *The Fiction of André Pieyre de Mandiargues*, Syracuse UP, Syracuse, 1982, is an incisive and comprehensive study of Mandiargues's work. In his *Foreword* to that book, Mandiargues himself said: "I do not think I am mistaken when I say that I experienced that flattering emotion as I observed, chapter by chapter, page by page, word by word, my reflection, and the reflection of my writing, taking shape in the ample mirror of David J. Bond's sensitive and meticulous book," vii.

[2] André Pieyre de Mandiargues, *La Motocyclette*, Gallimard, Paris, 1963, p. 74. All other references to *La Motocyclette* appear in this edition.

[3] ibid., p. 149.

[4] ibid., p. 150.

[5] ibid., p. 38.

[6] ibid., p. 181.

[7] ibid.

[8] M. Eliade, *Rites and Symbols of Initiation*, Harper & Row, New York, 1965, p. 6.

[9] *La Motocyclette*, p. 156.

[10] ibid., p. 44.

[11] ibid., p. 45.

[12] J.Chevalier and A.Gheerbrant, *Dictionnaire des symboles*, Seghers, Paris, 1974, II, p. 104. Henceforth referred to as *Dictionnaire* in the text.

[13] Sir J. Frazer, ed. T.Gaster, *The New Golden Bough,* New American Library, New York, 1964, p. 700.

[14] *La Motocyclette*, p. 178.

[15] ibid., p. 181.

[16] *Dictionnaire*, III, p. 51.

[17] *La Motocyclette* , p. 189.

[18] ibid., p. 190.

[19] ibid.

[20] R. Cavendish, *The Tarot*, Harper & Row, New York, 1975, p. 47.

[21] In *Métamorphoses du cercle* , Plon, Paris, 1951, pp. 24-25.

[22] *La Motocyclette* , p. 180.

[23] The Tarot imagery referred to is based on the A.E. Waite deck that was established in 1910. This deck "is the standard and the best-liked modern Tarot," Cavendish, p. 37. The Solomon's seal imprint on the hub of the Wheel of Fortune is found in the Waite deck that is reproduced in *The Tarot*, by M. Sadhu, Wilshire Book Co., California, 1973. For a chapter on "Origins, Meaning, and Uses of the Cards," see A. Douglas's *The Tarot*, Penguin, Middlesex, 1972.

[24] *Dictionnaire*, IV, p. 159. See also G. Scholem's "The Curious History of the Six-Pointed Star," *Commentary* 8, 949, pp. 243-51.

[25] *La Motocyclette*, p. 193.

[26] ibid., p. 80.

[27] Sadhu, 191, and *Dictionnaire,* IV, p. 125.   One version of Solomon's seal is supposed to have been a ring belonging to King Solomon that contained four jewels in the shape of a whale, an eagle, a lion, and a serpent. These were to give the king power over all dominions, over spirits, animals, wind, and water, *Encyclopia Britannica*, William Benton, Chicago, 1973, XX, p. 877.

[28] R. Graves, *The Greek Myths*, Penguin, Aylesbury, 1975, I, p. 125.

[29] Graves, I, p. 126. See Cavendish: "[The wheel] is a very old symbol of the sun, either by itself or as part of the sun's chariot," p. 101.

[30] *La Motocyclette,* p. 200.

[31] ibid., p. 170.

[32] ibid., p. 179.

[33] Quoted by Poulet, p. 27.

[34] *La Motocyclette.*

[35] Hutcheon, p. 7.

[36] *Dictionnaire,* I, pp. 244-48.

[37] *La Motocyclette ,* pp. 54-55.

[38] ibid., p. 189.

[39] In her dissertation, Part I, chap.5, S. Campanini reminds the reader that X is also the mathematical symbol for multiplication or reproduction.

[40] *Dictionnaire,* III, p. 302.

[41] At one point Daniel compares Rebecca to a companion of angels, p. 190. His intimate knowledge of Swedenborg makes this reference apposite. The other three figures are also present in the novel: Daniel Lionart is the lion; Rebecca's motorcycle is the "taureau." She says: "Jusqu'où m'emporteras-tu taureau noir?" p. 18. And the eagle is imprinted on the coins that Rebecca finds in her glove compartment, scattered among some legal papers, p. 121.

[42] Cavendish, p. 142.

[43] ibid.

[44] *La Motocyclette,* p. 195.

[45] ibid., p. 212.

[46] Just before Rebecca crashes into the truck, she sees it as a "mur qui se précipiterait à près de 130 kilomètres à l'heure," p. 212. It is surely no accident that the number 13 should appear in a multiple form just at the moment of Rebecca's death: the Tarot Arcanum XIII is entitled *Mors.* It is also no accident that Rebecca is 19 years old, 1+9=10, or X in Tarot numerology. In a strangely ironic fashion, it also happens that Mandiargues himself died on a Friday 13th.

[47] M. Eliade, pp. 61-64. See also his *Mythes, rêves et mystères,* Gallimard, Paris, 1957, chaps. 8-9, for an analysis of "being gulped down by a monster."

[48] *La Motocyclette,* p. 212.

[49] ibid., p. 177.

[50] ibid., p. 207.

[51] ibid.,p. 213.

[52] ibid.,p. 80.

Chapter IX

Kaleidoscopic Reflections in Guise of a Conclusion:
Close, Maupassant, Douglas, and Borges

> Par le mot par commence donc ce texte
> Dont la première ligne dit la vérité
> Mais ce tain sous l'une et l'autre
> Peut-il être toléré?
> Cher lecteur déjà tu juges
> Là de nos difficultés ...
>
> (APRES sept ans de malheurs
> Elle brisa son miroir.)
> Francis Ponge: FABLE

1.   Frank Close and *Lucifer's Legacy*

In the physicist F. Close's book, *Lucifer's Legacy: The Meaning of Asymmetry*, which could be subtitled "Le Démon de l'Analogie se jouait de lui," [1] the author describes an experience he had upon visiting the Tuileries Gardens in Paris.[2] On each side of the path, he noted that the statues and fountains repeated each other. A surprise jolted Close, however, when he came across a broken statue of Lucifer. The statue's head had been severed and was lying on the ground. The statue on the other side was intact, inspiring the physicist to use this as the principal metaphor for his book on asymmetry, or on the lack of balance that reigns in the universe.

Physicists believe, according to Close, that at the moment of creation, the moment that led to the competing forces that we experience today, such as gravity, electromagnetism, and nuclear forces, was not a moment lacking in tension. The universe is replete with broken symmetries. Perfect symmetry does not exist, Close asserts. Had the balance of forces been exact "in the beginning," those forces would have destroyed each other and we would not exist. As the *New York Times* reviewer of Close's book (6 August 2000), G. Johnson, put it, "the universe is imbued with hints of a corrupted primal geometry, riddled with broken symmetries."

This theory, fact, or metaphor serves *Sightings* well. Chiastic and imbricated micro- and macro-structures give, at first, the impression of being aligned as well as were, allegedly, the fountains and statues of the Tuileries gardens, before Lucifer's decapitation. But as I have pointed out throughout this book, "sand is thrown into the gears of the machine," over and over again, into the "gears" of the "mechanisms" that show what art does – and says as it does it. Lucifer's head is broken and lies on the ground. That statue does not replicate the one on the other side.

Although seemingly perfect for each other after M. de Clèves's death, Mme de Clèves and Nemours will not form the ideal couple in what the French call "a happy end." This ending was and sometimes still is unacceptable to some readers. Mme de Merteuil breaks the symmetry of *Les Liaisons dangereuses* with a scribbled note, a superb anacoluthon that plays the role of an ellipsis, scribbled at the end of one of Valmont's missives: "Hé bien! La guerre." The well-designed frame of Balzac's *Facino Cane* leads the reader to expect the narrator to accompany Cane back to Venice in order to retrieve the gold Facino had found, and to repeat, complete, and duplicate, thereby, the narrative's frame in the "picture." But the blind old man dies of a catarrh. The ugly word "catarrh" was chosen deliberately by Balzac as the jolting last word of his tale. He ends with a bang.

In Barbey d'Aurevilly's *Une Page d'histoire*, a poetics of incest is created which, on the surface, seems to bring two into one by positioning back together a brother and a sister who had already shared the same space in their mother's womb before each was born. They would also share a passionate love for each other as adolescents and adults. The short story contains interpretive statements that fall within, as well as deny the purview of symmetry. *Une Page d'histoire* not only foregrounds the use of rhetoric when it comes to the creation of texts (making them symmetrical, that is, repetitive, or mirror-like), but its narrator negates the very usage of rhetoric, and the protagonists, in the end, are decapitated.

The Decadents, like Rodenbach and Jean Lorrain, break their mirrors into thousands of pieces, as did "Narcissus II" in *l'Ami des miroirs*, and as did Hugues Viane when he used the symmetry of the plaited braid of hair that had belonged to his wife to choke "Ophelia/Jane" in the end. The braided "chain" is defiled, the systematic use of symmetries is broken in *Bruges-la-morte*, and despite what Viane thinks after his brutal act, that the two women are now one, they are, in fact, none, in the end. Viane decapitates, metaphorically, Jane, with the braided lock of hair of his dead wife.

Although the Surrealists, many of whom were close friends of Pieyre de Mandiargues, tried to abolish "la différence," Mandiargues himself, in *La Motocyclette*, has the second trajectory of Rebecca's journey contradict its repetitive nature by Rebecca's crashing into the smiling head of Dionysus on the truck that suddenly veers in front of her speeding motorcycle. The age-old division whereby the universe, if not art and persons, are perceived as being either Apollonian or Dionysian is contested by those who would prefer to inhabit a universe in which parallelisms exist, where theories would always be "neat," where the complimentary word that mathematicians use to describe a theorem satisfies. But what I loosely call literary "chaos theory" contradicts such desires, and Rebecca is symbolically "devoured" by the head of Dionysus.

Let us return to Alice as paradigm. W. Empson, among others, pointed out what a high proportion of jokes, word plays, and metaphors in the Alice books foreground eating (a life activity) and its opposite, disappearance and death. The Alice books are amusing – but they are also grim. Even as Alice, "who always took a great interest in questions of eating and drinking"[3] is continually eating little cakes, drinking from a bottle that says "drink me," nibbling on pieces of mushroom that make her small or large, depending on which side of the mushroom she nibbles, or having a spot of tea at "A Mad Tea Party," her adventures are filled with random and inexplicable violence. Hugh Haughton pointed out that "the Wonderland garden is no childhood Eden, but a life-and-death croquet match presided over by a homicidal Queen shouting 'off with their heads' every second minute. Faced with all this random violence and competitiveness, Alice cannot keep from noting that "they're dreadfully fond of beheading people here." She goes on to think that "the great wonder is there's anyone left alive." To place Alice in historical contexts other than her own, one could almost believe that she was present at the taking of the Bastille, that she witnessed all the horrors of 1793, or is now in Iraq, in the twenty-first century, where beheadings are almost a daily occurrence.

Amusing as they are, some of the incidents in the *Alice* books seem dominated by madness, a madness, for instance, in which the head alone of a Cheshire cat grins, as it floats in the air, revealing a smiling senselessness that many readers accept and find amusing. Yet I have known children who refuse to have any of the *Alice* books read to them. Alice herself might have been tempted to wear a red ribbon around her neck, as did survivors of the French Revolution, to indicate that they had lost family members and friends to the guillotine. As a critique of its time, the Alice books are a mirror of the modern world in which violence interrupts a chessboard's or a game of cards' symmetry in the verbally chiastic world of Wonderland. If not beheaded, innocent people still hear a hideous Queen's screeching "off with her head!"

Alice and Narcissus as paradigms: the former reflects, as Haughton puts it, Alice's consciousness "as she struggles to make sense of a world through the looking-glass that is more unstable, changeable and radically nonsensical than her author could acknowledge elsewhere,"[4] and the latter, Narcissus, is an androgynous young man who could never admit into his world any other but himself. Discomforting as are these narratives, they actually lead to the Delphic oracle's injunction to "know thyself," that can only be achieved through the process of reflection, intellectual reflection, and to the appreciation of the voice (be it only an echo) and the flower of literary art that remain, once the chaos has abated, to some degree. Literature, and I include myths within that category, is not created to comfort us or lull us into a pleasurable sleep, even though it is while napping that Alice makes her discoveries of bodiless Cheshire cat heads, screeching Queens and Mad Hatters who never take off their hats. Works of art are made to jolt readers, viewers, or sight-seers, into questioning themselves and the values espoused by the world in which they live. Part of the beauty of memorable myths and works of art is not only the manner in which they are "constructed," but also the manner in which they never stop making us question ourselves and our world. We read and sight them, and live what Jean Rousset calls "une vie par délégation," a life by and through The Other. Fiction and history: each shows as well as shores up the other.

No matter how many scholars have studied its ramifications, the Narcissus myth still makes us ponder, still questions the mirror image that defies us to "know ourselves." Narcissus says "I am he" when he finally "sights" himself in his reflected image.

Even though I have concentrated mostly on prose fiction in this book, the persona in Tristan Corbière's poem, "Le Crapaud" (1873), applies to *Sightings*.[5] Much as J. Lorrain's young boy does, in *Le Crapaud*, or the real writer, J. Lorrain, did, at the end of his life, when he composed, the third night before his death, "La Ballade du Bohémien," there is identification between boy, man, writer, and toad. Corbière, the poet, will have his persona say: "Bonsoir – ce crapaud-là c'est moi." The difference between Narcissus and the toad is that Narcissus is beautiful, while the persona in Corbière's reversed sonnet (its structure is 3-3 — 4-4 instead of the traditional French sonnet disposition, which is 4-4 — 3-3), sees the hideous toad as hideous – and himself, consequently, as well. But both are similar in that each discovers, in Tiresias's dictum, "who he is."

2.   A Road Not Taken: Maupassant's *Bel-Ami*

Mirrors function in a multiplicity of ways, be they used as rhetorical strategies, single phrases that reflect the overall structure of a novel, an epic, references to physical objects of reflection and/or references to reflective material culture, psychological, spiritual, and political examples of modes of thinking and analyzing, or armatures for an entire work of prose fiction. And they do so chiastically or in imbricated ways. Texts in which "literal" mirrors do appear, but have no deep structure to reveal, such as Maupassant's *Bel-Ami* (1885), were not chosen for close analysis in *Sightings*. That is not to say that the mirrors' role in *Bel-Ami* is lacking in significance, but a brief look will show where they do appear in that novel and why they were not chosen for sighting. Counter-examples, however, of not-so-conclusive "Conclusions" are found in the works of J. L. Borges. He uses the very word "mirror" or "mirrors" frequently in his work, and these usages foreground literature itself as well as the deep structure found in Borges's undercutting his own prose fictions through and throughout his work. It is as if every one of his tales ended (or did not "end") as does Balzac's *Facino Cane*, with a jolt, with the use of the word "catarrh."

Literal mirrors do make an appearance eight times in *Bel-Ami*. One is immediately tempted to cry out "Eureka!" and look for chiastic elements therein. The first mention is the most interesting. A poor young dandy, Georges Duroy, seeking to work for the owner of the newspaper, *La Vie Française* (is this title symbolic?), goes to visit the editor, Forestier, in his own house. As he goes up the stairs, "with beating heart and anxious spirit," fearful of looking and being ridiculous, he perceives a well-dressed young man looking at him. Both find themselves so close that Duroy backs away before realizing that the man he sees is himself: "It was he, reflected in a large pedestal mirror that created, on the landing, a lengthy perspective of the gallery." His response is a pleasant one, because he finds himself looking better than he had thought.[6] This is the opposite reaction to that of Louis XIV, when he thought that the man he saw in the mirror had raised his sword, in order to attack him. He was so chagrined at having shown fear that he had the mirror removed.

After Forestier's death, Georges will marry Mme Forestier, and he will look at himself in each of the mirrors placed at each of the landings of the Forestier house. Every time he sees himself he admires himself, thus "mirroring" his ascent in the social world he has joined without having merited the financial and social climb.

The other mirrors in *Bel-Ami* are unexceptional, such as the small mirror in which Georges sees himself reflected when he shaves: in the first instance he thinks of writing his father, and in the second, while he shaves before his duel, he thinks he might be seeing himself for the last time. A more interesting instance is his seeing his reflection in the mirror that had been placed above the fireplace of the pied-à-terre he had rented for his trysts: as he straightens his hair and adjusts his tie, he notices Mme de Marelle, one of his mistresses, reflected in it. She stands behind him. One might interpret that instance as his rising in the social spectrum of Paris due to the various women who fall in love with him and give him their social and financial support.

The only time a reference one might call Narcissus-like in the novel is when Georges and Suzanne Walter, Mme Walter's daughter, whom he will marry after having had an affair with her mother, look into the goldfish pond in the green-house and observe their own reflections, "reversed in the water."[7] The significance of this allusion is, perhaps, that the daughter has taken the mother's place.

The mirrors in *Bel-Ami* are placed throughout the work at discrete distances one from the other. They represent stepping-stones in the social ascension of Georges *Duroy* – to the point of his becoming Georges *Du Roy* in the end. Maupassant's is a novel in the realist mode, one that bears the mark of Zola and of the Ecole de Médan. It is a bitter, ironic, and even sarcastic look at the social structure of Paris at the end of the nineteenth century. One stepping-stone leads to another, and the reader realizes that the young social-climber has no talent of his own other than that of seducing important men's wives and daughters in order to take the men's places. Even as he walks out of the Madeleine in the end, triumphantly, with his new bride, Suzanne Walter, at his side, he sees one of his former mistresses, Mme de Marelle, and remembers seeing her adjust her curly hair in the mirror of their pied-à-terre. Her hair was always unkempt when she got out of bed. George's gaze then follows the course from the steps of the Madeleine to the Place de la Concorde and onward to the Chambre des Députés: "…it seemed to him that he would make one leap from the portico of the Madeleine to the portico of the Palais-Bourbon." All he can think of is himself: "He saw no one. He thought only of himself." Egotistic narcissism is the only interpretation one can give to George's "ascent." Structurally the novel simply moves from one stepping-stone to another in a straightforward sequence of unfolding events as they mark the self-important ascent that Maupassant is mocking.

3.   M. Douglas's *Thinking in Circles*
The brilliant anthropologist, Professor Dame Mary Douglas, died on 16 May 2007, the same year her book, *Thinking in Circles*, was published by Yale University Press. In the London *Times obituary,* May 18, 2007, a statement made about her husband, James Douglas, fits her to a T: "he was widely respected for his intellect and ability to transcend disciplinary borders." Dame M. Douglas was, perhaps, the most widely read anthropologist of her generation. She was persistent in finding systems and symmetry in customs and cultures that were not at all obvious to untrained ears, and she learned Hebrew late in life in order to read the Hebrew Bible in the original. She was determined to find patterns in ancient texts, in Biblical books that most scholars had denied as possessing any order, such as the book of *Numbers*. The fact that she could *not* find a ring pattern in *Leviticus* contributed to her general theory of "ring structures" that she *did* find in ancient texts. When she was invited to give one of the Gifford Lectures at the Divinity school in Edinburgh, she became a friend of G. Audel, her host, and with her typical sense of humour she called him "an indefatigable pattern spotter," an expression that could be applied to herself.

In *Thinking in Circles* she analyses the Biblical book of *Numbers*, *Tristram Shandy*, the *Iliad*, and concludes with "*Jakobson's Conundrum.*" In her *Preface*, she mentions J. Myres, who was also looking for patterns in literature. Myres's use of "pedimental" writing was useful for Douglas, since her own theory of circles or rings coincides with it. "Pedimental" means writing that goes up to a central point, makes a turn, then comes down step by step on the other side, like wide-angled pediments on doorways. Douglas says that "pedimental" is another name for a chiasmus. "It is usually applied to shorter pieces of writing," says Douglas, "whereas I am using "ring composition" for much larger texts."[8]

In her chapters on "Ancient Rings Worldwide," and on "How to Construct and Recognize a Ring," Douglas defines the criteria she uses to describe a ring composition. She calls it "a framing device" that has the beginning join with the ending of a literary text, thus closing the ring and endowing the work with unity. "It is basically the chiastic structure," she says on p.2, "ABBA, or ABCBA, a form that pervades the Bible and other famous archaic texts." Douglas also mentions the "impressive *Chiasmus Bibliography*, a book that deals, primarily, with publications on the use of chiasmus in *The Old Testament*, the *New Testament*, the *Book of Mormon*, and *Other Literatures*. The books and articles listed last were written on Sallust, Caesar, Tacitus, Justinus, Catullus, etc.[9] Welch lists fifteen criteria by which a chiasmus can be used to measure its strength in a given written work. Douglas found that seven criteria were enough to identify or define ring patterns in long texts. She says that a ring pattern demands that at least these seven criteria be found in order for a work to qualify as having a "ring circle." A summary follows:

1.*Exposition or Prologue*: The exposition sets the stage, sometimes time and place of what will happen. It prepares the reader for the centre of the work.

2.*Split into two halves*: If the end is going to join the beginning of the work, at some point it will need to start returning to the start – one is outgoing, and the other returning. In a long text it is essential to signal and have the reader recognize the mid-point.

3.*Parallel sections*: After the mid-section, each section needs to be matched by parallelisms.

4.*Indicators to mark individual sections*: Some indicators are needed to indicate consecutive units of structure, such as key words that are repeated, specific signals that indicate beginnings and endings of sections. Homer did this, Douglas says, by alternating days and nights.

5.*Central loading*: The turning point of a ring is the middle term: AB/C/BA. A clue that the middle has been reached is the repetition of word clusters found at the beginning.

6.*Rings within rings*: A large work, such as the *Iliad* may contain rings within rings.

7.*Closure at two levels*: By repeating the beginning, the ending signals completion. Verbal as well as thematic repetition are signals to the reader that the ring is replete.

In this brief summary of what Douglas states as criteria that must be present, in order for a work to be recognized as a ring pattern, there are a few problems for the literary critic. In her *Preface*, she recognizes one of these problems herself. "Friends ask me," she says," what does it matter? Why is it important to know the construction? This leads to another point: in a ring composition the meaning is located in the middle."[10] She seems to answer this by stating that a formal literary structure is not based on contents. "It is," she says, "a set of empty frames – or bowls and jugs into which the poet pours his ideas." Since many poetic structures depend on the social happenings for which a poem is to be created and recited, (initiatory rites, military events, funerals, sermons), Douglas states that this is right down anthropologists' alleys. The reason? It locates the work in the social events that call for it.[11]

In order for her own book to begin and end with similar "bowls" into which she "pours" her meaning, Douglas uses R. Jakobson's notions at the beginning of her book as well as the middle and end as she writes about parallelism's being inherent in the relationship that exists between grammar, language, and the brain. At the end of her book she states that what Jakobson says is true (that writing in parallels comes to everyone naturally), but she still wonders why ring composition went out of style in the fourth and fifth centuries, and why it has become difficult for people to recognize ring structures. She answers her own question, as a good anthropologist would do, by stating that postmodernism eschews formality and structure due to social and historical reasons. These days, she says, there are cultural biases against certainty.

Douglas calls on B. H. Smith to describe "a decentred reality," claiming that in 20th-century arts there is a bias toward anti-closure. Douglas answers what she calls Jakobson's conundrum by referring to cultural and social changes. Since Douglas states that a ring structure demands that one look at the centre of a work in order to see the shift, the place where the text loops back over itself and begins the "descent," it is interesting to look at the centre of her own book to see whether she tries to mirror herself in that pattern. Her book has eleven chapters, the last being "The Latch: Jakobson's Conundrum," which can be taken as an echo to her *Preface*. In the middle we find chapter 5 being called "The Central Place: *Numbers*," and chapter 6 is a structural analysis called: "Modern, Not-Quite Rings." In chapter 7, she analyzes "*Tristram Shandy*: Testing for Ring Shape," and even though she finds the structure of this most complex novel to have something of a "ring shape," she adds the words "almost," or ""not- quite rings" to analyze Stern's novel. She then moves on to her analysis of the *Iliad* , to show what a "real" ring shape is.

In *Sightings*, I have tried to show that from the seventeenth to the twentieth centuries, chiastic structure prevails in the works I chose to examine, but where I disagree with Douglas is that the existence of chiastic structures stopped being found after the fourth century. My affirmation is that an organized "machine" must exist in order for sand to be "thrown into its gears" as far back (or as early) as the seventeenth century. In the works I chose to analyze, both symmetry and asymmetry can be sighted as in strangely reflecting mirrors. A brief look at Borges (even though he wrote in Spanish and not English or French) will show how sand can be thrown, perhaps by the fistfuls, to impede a structure from "closing."

4.　　All the World's a Book: J. L. Borges

Borges writes most keenly as well as playfully about all literature and all writers when he examines one real or invented oeuvre, or one real or invented author. He discusses the novel *April March* in his tale entitled *A Survey of the Works of Herbert Quain.*[12] The implied author who is examining Quain's tale *April March* recalls having heard Quain say: "I have reclaimed for this novel…the essential features of every game: the symmetry, the arbitrary laws, the tedium."[13] It is noted that everything in Quain's *April March* is reversed, starting with the title itself, and that with regard to such a structure, "it may be appropriate to say…what Schopenhauer said about Kant's twelve categories: 'He sacrifices everything to his rage for symmetry."[14]

In mentioning Quain's "heroic two-act comedy," which sounds as if it were an oxymoron that is entitled *The Secret Mirror*, it is as if the implied author takes back, as he does frequently, everything he had said about *April March*. He mentions Quain's "rage for symmetry," and states that it simply falls apart. It fails. Is shattered. But I would note that the symmetry must first be affirmed, must "be there," like the mirror in the conclusion of *L'Ami des miroirs*, in order for the principal character to rush headlong into it and smash not only his head but the mirror as well. Both are torn asunder. Splintered into fragments. The protagonist does himself "in" with his own symbolic decapitation.

The plot of Quain's two-act play is composed as a parallel plot, but in the second act, "everything is slightly menacing…put off, or frustrated."

The final commentaries of *A Survey* are reserved for Quain's "last work," called *Statements*, in which the *statement* is made that in each of the eight stories contained therein each promises "a good plot, which is then intentionally frustrated by the author." Eight texts: there is a "rage for symmetry" in that number. One notes that the implied author is reflecting Borges's own habit of using mirror imagery, vocabulary, and structure. He is imitating in a backward or opposing vein his own appreciation of "the illusory depths of...mirrors" (a quotation taken from *Tlön, Uqbar, Orbis, Tertius*).[15] He uses titles that refer to or reflect subjects that are mirrored in his own work.

In *The Approach to Al-Mu'tasmin,* the tale is as carefully structured, reflective, and as diverse as is a kaleidoscope. [16] The reader is told that the author of *The Approach* had been written by the Bombay attorney, Mir Bahadur Ali. The first brief paragraph contains the names of seven writers and artists. In the second paragraph, two editions of the work are mentioned. One appeared in 1932 in Bombay, and a second edition in 1834, and was "titled *The Conversation with the Man Called Al Mu'tasim.*" The reader notes the slight variation existing between the original title and the second one, that was "coyly subtitled *A Game with Shifting Mirrors.*"[17] The title of Borges's tale is the same as that "of the first edition (1932)," but it is "the second edition, of 1934" that the implied author examines and discusses, since he was unable, he says, "to come upon the first." The kaleidoscope is, indeed, in motion, with its fragments of multicoloured glass reflecting, at every turn, in its angular mirrors, infinite combinations of images in rapid and changing succession. This is, indeed, a "game with shifting mirrors," "coyly" ready to change perspectives at every turn.

One is never told the name of the "visible protagonist" of Bahadur's novel simply because it is never revealed. We follow him through religious conflicts, riots, street battles, processions, and killings. We come to the phrase "he crosses two railroad tracks, or twice crosses the same track." [18] The structure of this sentence is rhetorically complex (a-b-c—b-a-c), leaving us to wonder, also, whether this is not a clever take-off of the picaresque novel.

Borges's usage of quotation marks, of citing texts within his own text, is a kaleidoscopic game in itself. A. Compagnon, in his *La Seconde main*, studies the use of intertextuality, which is included in the use of quotation marks, and I have dealt with this question in my study of *Les Liaisons dangereuses.* Shortly after the protagonist of *A Game of Shifting Mirrors* "crosses two railroad tracks, or twice crosses the same track," we read: "A 'lean and evil mob of moon-coloured hounds' emerges from the black rosebushes." Why is a "lean and evil mob of moon-coloured hounds" in quotation marks? The usage is a semiotic signal of Borges's creating verisimilitude. Borges, like Laclos, wishes to confound his reader by mixing "reality" with "fiction," by surprising the reader when he has his implied author describe the protagonist of this complex tale's climbing an iron ladder, some rungs of which are missing. [19] On the one hand, Maupassant's Georges, in *Bel-Ami,* never misses a step when he climbs his social ladder. No rung is ever missing. On the other hand, Borges, "coyly" has his reader discover, at the end of that most complex and varied chapter, that all the details "bring the reader to the end of the second chapter of the book."[20] Since the following paragraph begins with a reference to the "remaining nineteen chapters…one deduces that the book has twenty-one chapters, even though one initially assumes that it must have twenty, because the phrase "that brings the reader to the end, not of the first, but of the second chapter of the book" sneakily makes one assume that "second" actually means "first."

After stating that it is impossible to trace the adventures of the protagonist of the subtitled text, *A Game of Shifting Mirrors*, the implied author presents, twice, a summary of the complex plot, or, as he calls it, of "Bahadur's heavily freighted novel." After searching, for years (all fiction is a quest within a labyrinth in Borges's authorial world), the protagonist "comes to a gallery 'at the end of which there is a doorway and a tawdry curtain of many beads, and behind that, a glowing light.'" A voice bids the student enter. And in a veritable *Wizard of Oz* non-ending, in which the reader does not hear anyone say: "I am Oz, the great and the terrible," Borges's student draws the curtain and steps into the room. "At that point," we are told, "the novel ends," and the reader's expectations remain unfulfilled. The conclusion of the novel under consideration is "de-concluded." [21] So, the reader wonders, how is Borges going to have his implied author conclude *his* tale? He has him end with a long and elaborate footnote that is included in the text about *other* texts, one of which is an acknowledgement of his debt to "Richard Burton's *1001 Nights*, Vol. X, and to the Margaret Smith study entitled *The Persian Mystic, Attar* (1932)."

Perhaps it is because "1001" is a chiasmus that the implied author will use a verbal chiasmus in the final paragraph of his footnote with which he ends the tale. In comparing Bahadur's novel to *1001 Nights*, he says that "other ambiguous similarities may signal the identity of the *seeker* and the *sought*; they may also signal that the *sought* has already influenced the *seeker*." "Seeker-sought—sought-seeker": literature, Borges seems to be saying, is a grand chiasmus leading to surprise endings. This is implied in a supposed quotation from Plotinus: "Everything in the intelligible heavens is everywhere. Any thing is all things. The sun is all stars, and each star is all stars and the sun."[22] When the curtain is pulled back and the student is invited to enter, "the novel ends." Closure is neither one of the characteristics of a Borguesian labyrinth – nor of a Library. The final sentence states: "Another chapter suggests that Al-Mu'tasim is the 'Hindu' that the law student *thinks* he murdered" (underlining added). There is no certainty, no conclusion here: mirrors reflect, kaleidoscopically, other possibilities, other structures in their ever-changing patterns of coloured fragments.

The title Borges gives to this entire collection of eight tales (1941), is *The Garden of Forking Paths*. Of the tales therein, the last one is entitled *The Garden of Forking Paths*. Borges prefigures that title in the conclusion of the next-to-last tale, the *Survey of the Works of Herbert Quain*. He has his implied author say: "From the third story [in *Quain's Statements*] titled 'The Rose of Yesterday,' I was ingenuous enough to extract 'The Circular Ruins,' which is one of the stories in my book *The Garden of Forking Paths*."

The narrator of *The Garden* begins to quote from a statement written by a Dr. Yu Tsun, a former English professor at the *Hochschule* at Tsingtao – but the first two pages of the "statement," we are told, are missing. The statement begins with an ellipsis: "...and I hung up the receiver." The ellipsis (NB its usage in *La Princesse de Clèves* and *Les Liaisons dangereuses*) signifies something that is lacking. It is a syntactical or stylistic omission of one or several words, and the reader is invited, thereby, to supply what is not there. It is similar to Borges's iron ladder that Al-Mu'tasim climbs, some rungs of which are missing. Needless to say, rungs could not be "missing" were the ladder not present. An incomplete structure implies the existence of *some* structure – in order for that structure to be signalled as incomplete.

In addition to Narcissus and to the *Alice* books, one could easily take *The Garden of Forking Paths* as a metaphor for *Sightings*. One particular sentence Borges (or his double, his implied author) uses is one that I have used in the conclusions of the texts chosen for examination in *Sightings*. The man Albert (his first name is Stephen, whose name brings to mind Stephen Dedalus in James Joyce's *Portrait of the Artist as a Young Man*) says to the descendant of Ts'ui Pen that he has reached an hypothesis for the plan of that chapter: "*The Garden of Forking Paths* is an incomplete, but not false, image of the universe...Unlike Newton and Schopenhauer, your ancestor did not believe in a uniform and absolute time; he believed in an infinite series of times, a growing, dizzying web of divergent, convergent, and parallel times." [23] Borges also shows how novels display their own artifice even when they exploit the realist novel. Effects are not necessarily related to causes in a straightforward manner. In the nature of his fictional form, in his plots and constructions, they operate as does *April March*, in something of a logical reversal. Borges's writings are affronts to "common sense" reasoning. It is as if he were speaking of mirrors that are juxtaposed, of kaleidoscopic imagery that is both geometric and moving. He is pulling the rug out from under those who believe that structure is static, unmoving, solid and stable. Instead, he had imagined "a labyrinth of labyrinths, a maze of mazes, a twisting, turning, ever-widening labyrinth that contains both past and future and somehow implied the stars" [24]– or one could say Alice's *Land of Wonder*. It is no wonder that Borges has been seen as a precursor of postmodernism, of the novels written by French "New Novelists," or by American writers such as Thomas Pynchon and John De Lillo.

Chiastic and imbricated structures are esthetically satisfying up to a point. They reveal parities and formal convergences that are comparable to each other, that exist in a variety of ways. [25] But asymmetry questions the "satisfying," or, rather, lulling, as in a nap's lulling, qualities of symmetrical art. *Webster's* tells us that "asymmetry" is the want of proportion between parts of a thing; in mathematics, asymmetry is incommensurability, as when there is no common measure between two quantities. The word "asynartetic" applies to this idea. "Literally," says *Webster*, it means "not fitted or adjusted," while "asynchronism" means failure of two things to occur at the same time. Borges tries, not only playfully but seriously, to convince us that there is "an infinite series of times, a growing, dizzying web of divergent, convergent, and parallel times." The texts I have been studying are both "asynartetic" and "asynchronic." While chiastic and imbricated structures are the fundaments of the texts sighted, the lack, want, or incommensurable elements that defy a rhetorically "neat" conclusion are parts of myriad elements that these works have in common. They form a gigantic kaleidoscope that jolts us, that shakes us up profoundly when we "sight" the world in which we live, or the books, The Book, as Borges would have it, that we read and reread. Mirrors are, indeed, mesmerizing....

Notes

[1] See *Bruges-la-morte*, p. 33.

[2] Oxford University Press, New York, 2000.

[3] Lewis Carroll, *Alices's Adventures in Wonderland* and *Through the Looking-Glass and What Alice Found There*, ed. with introduction and notes by Hugh Haughton, Penguin Books, London, 1998, p. 65.

[4] ibid., p. li.

[5] We note that A. Breton saw in T. Corbière the precursor of Surrealism. "Le Crapaud" is found in *Les Amours jaunes*, 1873, and I reproduce it here:
Un chant dans une nuit sans air...
La lune plaque en métal clair
Les découpures du vert sombre.

...Un chant; come un écho, tout vif,
Enterré, là, sous le massif...
-Ça se tait: Viens, c'est là, dans l'ombre...

-Un crapaud! -Pourquoi cette peur,
Près de moi, ton soldat fidèle!
Vois-le, poète tondu, sans aile,
Rossignol de la boue... -Horreur! –

...Il chante. -Horreur!! –Horreur pourquoi?
Vois-tu pas son oeil de lumière...

Non: il s'en va, froid, sous sa pierre.

....

Bonsoir – ce crapaud-là c'est moi.

[6] G. de Maupassant, *Bel-Ami*, Editions Garnier Frères, Paris,1959, notes et relevé de variantes par Gérard Delaisement, pp. 20-21.

[7] ibid., p. 324.

[8] M. Douglas, *Thinking in Circles, An Essay on Ring Composition,* Yale UP, New Haven, 2007, pp. xii-xiii.

[9] J.W. Welch & D.B. McKinlay eds. Research Press, Provo, Utah, 1999.

[10] Douglas, p. x.

[11] ibid., pp. 102-103.

[12] All citations from J.L. Borges come from *Collected Fictions*, trans. A. Hurley, Penguin Books, N.Y., 1998. All page numbers referring to Borges's works are found in this edition. *A Survey*...is found on pp. 107-111.

[13] ibid., pp. 108.

[14] ibid., pp. 109-110.

[15] ibid., p. 70.

[16] ibid., pp. 82-87.

[17] ibid, p.80.

[18] ibid., p.83.

[19] ibid., p. 85.

[20] ibid., p. 84.

[21] ibid.

[22] ibid., p. 87.

[23] ibid., p. 119.

[24] ibid., p. 122.

[25] When it comes to the diverse meanings of mirrors, the final phrase of the *Foreword* to the catalogue of a recent exhibit of mirrors called *Reflections of Splendor,* Philippe Avila's statements seem appropriate: "The superposition of meaning and uses of mirrors has overlapped for centuries. In our increasingly visual culture, mirrors today are regaining the importance they deserve." The full catalogue was written by and put out by Helen Costantino Fioratti, *L'Antiquaire & The Connaisseur Inc.*, N.Y. 2007, p. 6. And the cover of this book is a reproduction of one of the mirrors that was in the exhibit.